The
Eclectic
Gourmet
Guide to
Greater
New York City

Also available from MENASHA RIDGE PRESS

The Eclectic Gourmet Guide to Atlanta,
   by Jane Garvey
The Eclectic Gourmet Guide to Chicago,
   by Camille Stagg
The Eclectic Gourmet Guide to Los Angeles,
   by Colleen Dunn Bates
The Eclectic Gourmet Guide to New Orleans,
   by Tom Fitzmorris
The Eclectic Gourmet Guide to San Francisco & the Bay Area,
   by Richard Sterling
The Eclectic Gourmet Guide to San Diego,
   by Stephen Silverman
The Eclectic Gourmet Guide to Washington, D.C.,
   by Eve Zibart

The
Eclectic
Gourmet
Guide to

Greater
New York City

Jim Leff

MENASHA
RIDGE
PRESS

Every effort has been made to ensure the accuracy of information throughout this book. Bear in mind, however, that prices, schedules, etc., are constantly changing. Readers should always verify information before making final plans.

Menasha Ridge Press, Inc.
P.O. Box 43059
Birmingham, Alabama 35243

Cover and text design by Suzanne Holt

Cover art by Michele Natale

ISBN 0-89732-279-7

Library of Congress Catalog Card Number: 98-41637

Manufactured in the United States of America

10 9 8 7 6 5 4 3 2

First Edition

CONTENTS

acknowledgments

This book might not have been possible without the help and encouragement of Gloria Montesano, Elliot Egan, Fred Monner, Sam Feldman, Brad Schoepach, Sylvia Carter, and Richard Sterling. Many thanks also to Jamie Adams, Jesse Sheidlower, Jonathan Gold, John and Matt Thorne, Cara Desilva, Jim Dorsch, Eve Zibart, and my parents, Florence and Leonard Leff.

I can't account for every single informant whose tip led to a review, but some of the most reliable scouts were Barry Strugatz, Allan Evans, Beatrice Muzi, Earl Howard, Liz Phillips, Ted Panken, Mark Dresser, Greg Wall, Michael Strasser, Mariko Kobayashi, Roy Moscowitz, and Dave Sit.

The following put their arterial flow at great risk by joining me for research meals: Gary Cheong, Todd Selbert, Howard Turkell, Bob Okumura, Alex Melamid, Katya Arnold, Vitaly Komar, Anna Halberstadt, Kian-Lam Kho, Warren Livesley, David Lerner, Alan Drogin, Cecil Lehar, Dave Feldman, Mr. and Mrs. Carlucci, and Doris, Emma, and Molly Strugatz.

Thanks to the gang at Menasha Ridge Press—Bob Sehlinger, Molly Burns, Katie Woychak, Grace Walton, Caroline Carr, and Clay White—and my editors Allison Boylan and Sarah Nawrocki.

Abigail Adams is my reader, fact checker, and all-around lifesaver. Pierre Jelenc is my technical adviser; Tony Signorini and Pasquale Palmieri keep the chowmobile up and running; Tekserve keeps my hard drive from softening, and Dr. Jeffrey Cusack and Dr. Eric Drucker do their best to maintain my corporeal being amid all the wanton (not to mention wonton) digestive and tendinous punishment.

about the author

Jim Leff learned about food while touring as a jazz trombonist, eating and playing his way through 19 countries on 5 continents. Back home in his native New York, Leff has amassed encyclopedic knowledge of the best bites—from pizza to foie gras—all over town while darting to gigs and rehearsals in his chowmobile.

A frequent guest on Arthur Schwartz's "Food Talk" radio show, Leff has also been a columnist for *Newsday, New York Press, Brooklyn Bridge,* and the legendary food 'zine *Down the Hatch*. He's written for *Wine and Spirits, Time Out, NetGuide,* most of the country's beer magazines, and many online publications such as *Cuisinenet* and Disney's *Family.com*. Leff authored the nightlife section—and half of the restaurant reviews—for Macmillan's *Unofficial Guide to New York City,* and his travel essays appear in *Travelers' Tales: Food* and *Travelers' Tales: Japan,* both published by O'Reilly.

Doubleday author Anya Von Bremzen has dubbed Leff "the godfather of the New York underground food scene." The *New York Times'* Eric Asimov calls him "unsurpassed in discovering unusual restaurants in every corner of the city." And author John Thorne praises his work as "must reading for anyone ... wanting to read some of the best food writing on the continent."

Leff's "Chowhound" website (www.chowhound.com) has been called "exactly what you want to see on the Web" by the *New York Times*. It's a haven for an international community of like-minded eaters who eschew hype and passionately devote themselves to sniffing out the hidden deliciousness that lurks all around us.

GETTING IT RIGHT:
A Note from the Publisher

A lot of thought went into this guide. While producing a dining guide may appear to be a straightforward endeavor, I can assure you that it is fraught with peril. I have read dining guides by authors who turn up their noses at anything except four-star French restaurants (of which there are a whole lot fewer than people think). Likewise, I have seen a guide that totally omits Thai and Indian restaurants—among others—because the author did not understand those cuisines. I have read guides absolutely devoid of criticism, written by "experts" unwilling to risk offending the source of their free meals. Finally, I've seen those books that are based on surveys and write-ins from diners whose credentials for evaluating fine dining are mysterious at best and questionable at least.

How, then, do you go about developing a truly excellent dining guide? What is the best way to get it right?

If dining guides are among the most idiosyncratic of reference books, it is primarily because the background, taste, integrity, and personal agenda of each author are problematical. The authors of most dining guides are vocational or avocational restaurant or food critics. Some of these critics are schooled professionals, with palates refined by years of practical experience and culinary study; others are journalists, often with no background in food criticism or cooking, who are arbitrarily assigned the job of reviewing restaurants by their newspaper or magazine publisher (although it *is* occasionally possible to find journalists who are also culinary professionals). The worst cases are the legions of self-proclaimed food critics who mooch their way from restaurant to restaurant, growing fat on free meals in exchange for writing glowing reviews.

1

Ignorance of ethnic cuisine or old assumptions about what makes for haute cuisine particularly plague authors in cities without much ethnic variety in restaurants, or authors who have been writing for years about the same old, white linen, expense-account tourist traps. Many years ago in Lexington, Kentucky, for example, there was only one Chinese restaurant in town and it was wildly successful—in spite of the fact that it was Chinese in name only. Its specialty dishes, which were essentially American vegetable casseroles smothered in corn starch, were happily gobbled up by loyal patrons who had never been exposed to real Chinese cooking. The food was not bad, but it was not Chinese either. Visitors from out of town, inquiring about a good local Chinese restaurant, were invariably directed to this place. As you would expect, they were routinely horrified by the fare.

And, while you might argue that American diners are more sophisticated and knowledgeable nowadays than at the time of the Lexington pavilion, the evidence suggests otherwise. In Las Vegas, for instance, a good restaurant town with a number of excellent Italian eateries, the local Olive Garden (a chain restaurant) is consistently voted the city's best Italian restaurant in a yearly newspaper poll. There is absolutely nothing wrong with the Las Vegas Olive Garden, but to suggest that it is the best Italian restaurant in the city is ludicrous. In point of fact, the annual survey says much more about the relative sophistication of Las Vegas diners than it does about the quality of local Italian restaurants.

But if you pick up a guide that reflects the views of many survey respondents, a *vox populi* or reader's choice compendium, that is exactly the problem. You are dependent on the average restaurant-goer's capacity to make sound, qualitative judgments—judgments almost always impaired by extraneous variables. How many times have you had a wonderful experience at a restaurant, only to be disappointed on a subsequent visit? Trying to reconcile the inconsistency, you recall that on your previous visit, you were in the company of someone particularly stimulating, and that perhaps you had enjoyed a couple of drinks before eating. What I am getting at is that our reflections on restaurant experiences are often colored by variables having little or nothing to do with the restaurant itself. And while I am given to the democratic process in theory, I have my doubts about depending entirely on survey forms that reflect such experiences.

There are more pragmatic arguments to be made about such eaters' guides as well. If you cannot control or properly qualify your survey respondents, you cannot ensure their independence, knowledge, or critical sensitivity. And, since literally anyone can participate in such surveys, the ratings can be easily slanted by those with vested interests. How many bogus responses would it take to dramatically upgrade a restaurant's rating in a survey-based, big-city dining guide? Forty or even fewer. Why? Because the publisher receives patron reports (survey responses, readers' calls) covering more restaurants than can be listed in the book. Thus the "voting" is distributed over such a large number of candidate restaurants that the median number of reports for the vast majority of establishments is 120 or fewer. A cunning restaurant proprietor who is willing to stuff the ballot box, therefore, could easily improve his own rating—or lower that of a competitor.

So my mission in the *Eclectic Gourmet Guides* is to provide you with the most meaningful, useful, and accessible restaurant evaluations possible. Weighing the alternatives, I have elected to work with culinary experts, augmenting their opinions with a carefully qualified survey population of totally independent local diners of demonstrated culinary sophistication. The experts I have sought to author the *Eclectic Gourmet Guides* are knowledgeable, seasoned professionals; they have studied around the world and written cookbooks or columns, and they closely follow the development of restaurants in their cities. They are well versed in ethnic dining, many having studied cuisines in their native lands. And they have no prejudice about high or low cuisine. They are as at home in a Tupelo, Mississippi, catfish shack as in an exclusive French restaurant on New York's Upper East Side. Thus the name *Eclectic Gourmet*.

Equally important, I have sought experts who make every effort to conduct their reviews anonymously, and who always pay full menu prices for their meals. We are credible not only because we are knowledgeable, but also because we are independent.

You, the reader of this *Eclectic Gourmet Guide*, are the inspiration for and, we hope, the beneficiary of our diligence and methodology. Though we cannot evaluate your credentials as a restaurant critic, your opinion as a consumer—of this guide and the restaurants within—is very important to us. Please tell us about your dining experiences and let us know whether you agree with our reviews.

Eat well. Be happy.

Bob Sehlinger

✠ diNiNG iN
NEW YORk CiTY

New York is both the greatest and the worst city in the world. While the negatives are apparent at a glance, the treasure, by contrast, is largely hidden and not easily sniffed out. Many New Yorkers propel themselves into a quest for the Great Secret Treasure by a primal need for self-preservation. They instinctively sense that Fun City—with its callousness, intolerance, and greed—can erode the spirit of even the most wide-eyed idealist, but that there is another New York that can provide a powerful antidote—a New York where a shack in an abandoned lot near the airport may be home to cosmically delicious ribs, a New York where an otherwise soulless Midtown block might hide a sumptuous basement sashimi oasis. A New York that feeds you so well that you'll feel like screaming, where you can take a subway ride to ethnic dining experiences so authentic and transportive that you'll return home feeling as if you've just come back from vacation.

We've all eaten meals so unexpectedly wonderful that we realize we've been settling for less way too long. The great thing about Gotham is that one need *never* settle for less. Invest some time and energy and you'll always find something extraordinary squirreled away somewhere for whatever grail you seek.

This guide is a collection of just such edible treasures, the *good* places, ranging from full-service meals to quick bites. Much of this choice chow is served in out-of-the-way locales; these are kitchens cooking for a circle of appreciative, discerning regulars, kitchens that build business through word-of-mouth rather than fat advertising budgets and fancy publicists. None of the establishments in this book were discovered via press releases; they've all been ferreted out through dedicated chow-hounding. Some are worlds above the competition while others simply do a thing or two a few notches better. Though most offer outstanding value, not all are inexpensive; different sorts of pleasures are available at different price ranges. But each place—in its own way—is a hot ticket to the secret deliciousness that lurks all around us.

Overcoming Boroughphobia

Manhattanites, in their haughty sophistication, have long blanched at the idea of traveling to other boroughs. "Archie Bunker lives in Queens," a Manhattan-centric friend once sniffed to me. Well, Archie eats a lot better than she does. And the secret is out; even the most bouroughphobic snobs are beginning to acknowledge that Queens and Brooklyn are foodie wonderlands.

While the city's showcase haute joints are, as always, clustered in central Manhattan, kitchens seeking simply to feed people really well rather than make a splash are more easily found away from the spotlight (and high rent) of Midtown. Though there are finds to be found in Manhattan, the prime real estate from Soho to the Upper East and West Sides will never compete in sheer lushness of alternative food choices with, say, Jackson Heights, Queens (perhaps the world's most diverse neighborhood), or Williamsburg, Brooklyn (where Puerto Rican, Jewish, Italian, Mexican, and vegetarian styles are hybridizing into a glorious hodgepodge).

Those holdouts who'd sooner walk over shards of glass than endure a thirty-minute train trip for a Moroccan meal in Brooklyn can indeed stay home and enjoy the cuisine in Manhattan—if they don't mind eating alongside fellow infidels in what might as well be the Epcot Morocco Pavilion. For those who crave the Real Thing, the subway is a magic carpet ride.

As word spreads about the satisfactions of interborough culinary adventuring, the handful of outerborough places touted by the mainstream media are starting to find themselves filled with a reverse "bridge-and-tunnel" crowd of hungry Manhattanites. As one might expect, such spots are hardly cutting-edge. Much better are the undiscovered, less self-conscious locales. This book presents the cream of the crop, each worth a special trip.

Ordering

The vast majority of diners want to order what they feel like eating rather than what the kitchen does best. Restaurateurs understand this and sometimes load their menus with every possible dish customers might crave, though these items may be far from the kitchens' fortes. So even though Tindo (see review) offers chow mein, don't fall for it. It's a tourist choice and will taste mediocre or worse. You wouldn't request steak in a diner even if it was on the menu; it's likewise useful to acquire ordering savvy for other less familiar sorts of restaurants.

The trick is to consider menus as puzzles with the goal being discovery of the Best Stuff. Waiters may or may not prove helpful (some may not know food, others may steer you toward expensive items or ones they mistakenly think outsiders might like), but with practice you can learn to detect the gleam in the eye that indicates a person is earnestly passionate about eating well. If the waiter is not helpful, look out for more enthusiastic staffers you might be able to question on the sly. Don't be afraid to point at plates that look promising or to take a walk toward the kitchen to see whether anything is on open display. Take notes (takeout menus are handy for this) so that you can remember what you've tried. Most crucial of all, take in stride dishes that fail to please; this is about exploration, and short-term pleasure often must be set aside for the greater good of menu mastery. When visiting the following reviewed spots, let the recommended house specialties guide you until you've honed your skills.

Language and Other Cross-Cultural Obstacles

Many ethnic restaurants take incredible pains to guide outsiders and put them at ease, but some of the most authentic are less service oriented, more no-nonsense. They cook serious, undiluted fare for freshly arrived compatriots at prices new immigrants can afford, and they forgo the niceties. While such places don't go out of their way to attract nonnative business, they don't mind serving self-sufficient outsiders, so long as they don't expect the restaurant to act as tour guide to the cuisine. There's work to be done and mouths to feed; taking time to extract orders from confused strangers breaks up the rhythm, especially when—as is often the case—the staff is insecure about speaking English.

Seasoned chowhounds learn to fit smoothly into the groove and relish the chameleonic pleasures of cross-cultural consumption, but novices are advised to start out with more user-friendly places (as reflected by the Friendliness ratings). If you do find yourself warily received in unfamiliar eateries, bear in mind that the frosty reception probably stems not from hostility but from the reluctance of overworked waiters to endure those linguistic and cultural struggles from which their restaurants otherwise stand as refuge.

Ugly American Tourists

The most common mistake in ethnic dining is failure to suspend expectations. There are those who indignantly demand faster service in Caribbean, Latin American, and African establishments (tropical cultures are more relaxed, and pace matches), plead for unsweetened mint tea in Moroccan cafes (not unbelievably sweet Moroccan tea is simply not Moroccan tea), fume at Italian busboys who won't bring the coffee with dessert (coffee is *always* served last and alone in southern Europe), and send back Szechuan dishes because they're too oily (oiliness is integral to the cuisine). Such diners have got it all wrong, and they miss so much. They forget that the mission of expat eateries is to zealously preserve traditions from back home—that's what we *like* about them! To demand that these proud bastions tone down the spice, hurry up with the soup, and *speak English for God's sake* is deeply insulting, and many would rather struggle along with a small clientele than fill to the rafters with imperious gringos.

Only in New York can you enjoy the pure, undiluted, headily transporting tastes of such a myriad of foreign lands. Open yourself to the experience, adopting the same respectful mind-set you would while traveling abroad . . . because, for all intents and purposes, you *are* abroad!

But Is It Clean There?

A few people are skittish about patronizing small, lesser known venues, fearing that hygiene standards might not be up to par. Quite the contrary; a kindly Taiwanese restaurateur serving her own community, a Dominican short-order cook who greets the same customers day after day, an Egyptian grandmother in business not just to pay the bills but because she genuinely cares that families get a delicious healthy meal . . . these are not places that give pause.

That said, dining out is never without risk. Food-handling mishaps can occur anywhere; neither price nor fame are factors, so you can't buy your way out of risk. To improve the odds, look for sincere people whose cooking makes you feel good. The care that goes into serving such food will likely be reflected in everything they do.

BUT IS IT SAFE THERE?

Nowhere in New York City—in any big city—is totally safe. And neither is any neighborhood totally dangerous, either. Contrary to some expectations, you needn't shield yourself from hails of bullets when outside the falsely perceived safety zone of mid-Manhattan. The standard urban cautions apply: be on guard always, look like you know where you're going, and don't go alone if you can help it. The good news, though, is that restaurants—wherever they may be located—are among the safest of havens. Unless you're a Mafia don and thus have an inordinately greater chance of getting snuffed over your stracciatella, you've got nothing to worry about when you bear fork in hand.

GUARANTEE of DISSATISFACTION

It took much passionate investigation to track down the Big Apple's rarest, tastiest, and most evocative restaurants and to determine the best things to order in them all. Herculean efforts were expended in checking and rechecking to ensure timely, fresh observations. Nonetheless, if you faithfully visit every establishment reviewed in these pages, you'll have some mediocre—even bad—meals. Each passing day since research was completed has introduced uncertainty; chef changes, general decline, and plain old off days are all part of the deal with dining out. So rather than curse me and chuck this book down the nearest storm drain after a disappointing dinner, just remember that a restaurant is an ever-changing, organic thing, and the only judgment that's guaranteed timely is the one you have of your own meal as you eat it. If you'll allow me to be your guide, though, you'll make out far, far better than you would on your own in this town of a jillion bites. That's a promise.

Those with Internet access can maximize their odds of supping success by heading to **www.chowhound.com/egnyc** for up-to-the-minute information and a chance to offer feedback to the author and compare notes with other readers.

Special Recommendations

Try our recommendations below for special interest groups. An address is listed if the restaurant is *not* profiled later in the guide.

◆ Best Bagels

The Bagelry
1228 Lexington Avenue, Manhattan   (212) 717-2080
1324 Lexington Avenue, Manhattan   (212) 996-0567
200 West 14th Street, Manhattan   (212) 352-2604
1380 Madison Avenue, Manhattan   (212) 423-9590

◆ Best Barbecue

Alex BAR-B.Q.
Churrasqueira Bairrada
Ihawan
Little Portugal
Mississippi Barbecue (takeout only)
172-14 Brisely Boulevard, Jamaica, Queens   (718) 776-3446
Pearson's Texas Barbecue
Seamorhen II

◆ Best Beer List

85 Down
85 Avenue A, Manhattan   (212) 673-8073
Café de Bruxelles
118 Greenwich Avenue, Manhattan   (212) 206-1830
Grange Hall
Hallo Berlin
Killmeyer's Old Bavaria Inn
North Star Pub
Pearson's Texas Barbecue
Teddy's Bar and Grill
Virgil's
152 West 44th Street, Manhattan   (212) 921-9494
Waterfront Ale House
540 2nd Avenue, Manhattan   (212) 696-4104

- Best Breakfast

  Bissaleh Classic
  City Bakery
  Cupcake Cafe
  Jean's
  The Pink Teacup
  Seamorhen II
  Teresa's
  Tom's Luncheonette
  Wee Kee

- Best Dim Sum

  Do I Tru
  Hop Lee
  Jade Palace
  The Nice Restaurant

- Best Desserts

  Cantina Brazil
  Casablanca
  Chowpatty
  City Bakery
  Cupcake Cafe
  Fortune Gourmet
  Karam Restaurant
  Kervan
  Krystal's Cafe
  69-02 Roosevelt Avenue, Woodside, Queens   (718) 898-1900
  Metropolitan AME Church
  Mocca Hungarian
  Penang Cuisine Malaysia
  Pepe Rosso To Go
  Picholine
  Soul Fixins'
  Sripraphai Thai Bakery
  Sweet-n-Tart Cafe

- Best Family Dining

  Bissaleh Classic
  Chick Chack Chicken
  Chowpatty
  Churrascaria Plataforma
  Churrasqueira Bairrada
  Cono & Son O'Pescatore Restaurant
  The Crab Shanty
  Iammo Bello
  Johnny's Famous Reef
  Pearson's Texas Barbecue
  Ratners
  138 Delancey Street, Manhattan   (212) 677-5588
  Rocco's
  Saigon Grill
  Sweet-n-Tart Cafe
  Virgil's
  152 West 44th Street, Manhattan   (212) 921-9494
  Almost any pizza place would be suitable

- Best Hamburgers

  Corner Bistro
  331 West 4th Street, Manhattan   (212) 242-9502
  Cozy Soup and Burger
  739 Broadway, Manhattan   (212) 477-5566
  Donovan's
  Molly's
  Teddy's Bar and Grill
  Union Square Cafe
  21 East 16th Street, Manhattan   (212) 243-4020

- Best Happening Bars

  Grange Hall
  North Star Pub
  Saka Gura
  Teddy's Bar and Grill
  Zlata Praha

♦ Best Hot and Spicy

Cambodian Cuisine
Famous Pita
The Indonesian Consulate Cafeteria
Jean's
Tiemann Oasis
Wangah Hut
**Any reviewed Indian, Pakistani, Mexican, Korean, or Thai
    restaurant**

♦ Best Kosher

Bissaleh Classic
Chick Chack Chicken
Famous Pita
Hall Street Kosher Cafe
Mabat
Mr. Broadway Kosher Deli
Tadjikstan
Uzbekistan Restaurant

♦ Best Large Groups

Churrascaria Plataforma
Patsy's Pizza
Tadjikstan
Uzbekistan Restaurant

♦ Best Late Night

Bissaleh Classic
Blue Ribbon
Brennan and Carr
Bukhara Restaurant
Cuchifritos
Cuchifritos/Fritura
Donovan's
Famous Pita
Fried World
Hole in One

Hop Lee
Kam Chueh
Kang Suh
Karam Restaurant
Mabat
The Pink Teacup
Punjab
Saka Gura
Teddy's Bar and Grill
Tindo
Woo Chon
Yakitori Taisho

◆ Best Live Music

Churrascaria Plataforma
Gaither's
Killmeyer's Old Bavaria Inn
La Hacienda
Sahara East
Teddy's Bar and Grill
Tiemann Oasis
Xunta

◆ Best Romantic

Grange Hall
Il Buco
Picholine
Tre Pomodori

◆ Best Seafood

The Crab Shanty
Johnny's Famous Reef
Kam Chueh
Pa Do Whae House
Rocco's
Seamorhen
Tindo
Tokyo

- Best Smoker-Friendly

  Donovan's
  El Unico
  Hall Street Kosher Cafe
  Johnny's Famous Reef (outdoors only)
  Kabab Cafe
  Killmeyer's Old Bavaria Inn (outdoors only)
  Little Portugal (bar only)
  Molly's
  North Star Pub
  Pearson's Texas Barbecue (outdoors only)
  Pepe Rosso To Go (outdoors only)
  Sahara East (outdoors only)
  Saka Gura
  Teddy's Bar and Grill
  Tiemann Oasis
  Xunta
  Yakitori Taisho
  Zlata Praha (bar and outdoors only)

- Best Unbelievably Cheap

  Alex BAR-B.Q.
  Bukhara Restaurant
  Cabana Carioca (bar only)
  Cantina Brazil
  Charles Southern Kitchen All You Can Eat Buffet
  Chick Chack Chicken
  Cuchifritos
  Cuchifritos/Fritura
  Cuisine of Pakistan (a.k.a. Kashmir 9)
  Cupcake Cafe
  El Unico
  Excellent Dumpling House
  111 Lafayette Street, Manhattan   (212) 219-0212
  Famous Pita
  5 Stars Punjabi
  Hall Street Kosher Cafe
  Hop Lee (lunch only)

The Indonesian Consulate Cafeteria
Karam Restaurant
La Espiga
La Xelaju
Little Portugal (bar only)
Metropolitan AME Church
Milan's Restaurant
Noodle 88
Pa Do Whae House (lunch only)
Punjab
Rosario's
Ruben Lunch
Sapporo
Seamorhen II
Soul Fixins'
Soul Food Kitchen
Sucelt Coffee Shop
Tadjikstan
Uzbekistan Restaurant
Wangah Hut
White Bear Ice Cream and Wonton Shop Cuisine
Any reviewed pizza place

◆ Best Vegetarian

Angelica Kitchen
300 East 12th Street, Manhattan   (212) 228-2909
Bissaleh Classic
5 Star Punjabi
Grange Hall
Happy Buddha
Jackson Diner
Kate's Joint
Mavalli Palace
Punjab
Any reviewed Chinese, Japanese, or Korean restaurant

UNDERSTANDING THE RATINGS

We have developed detailed profiles for what we consider the best restaurants in town. Each profile features an easy-to-scan heading that allows you to check out the restaurant's name, cuisine, star rating, cost, quality rating, and value rating quickly.

Star Rating. The star rating is an overall rating that encompasses the entire dining experience, including style, service, and ambiance in addition to the taste, presentation, and quality of the food. Five stars is the highest rating possible and connotes the best of everything. Four-star restaurants are exceptional, and three-star restaurants are well above average. Two-star restaurants are good. One star is used to connote a restaurant that may be useful in some way (a decent meal in an otherwise barren neighborhood, an especially rare cuisine, etc).

Cost. Beneath the star rating is an expense description that provides a comparative sense of how much a complete meal will cost. A complete meal for our purposes consists of an entree with vegetable or side dish, and choice of soup or salad. Appetizers, desserts, drinks, and tips are excluded.

Inexpensive	$16 and less per person
Moderate	$17–29 per person
Expensive	$30–40 per person
Very Expensive	$40 or more per person

Quality Rating. Below the cost rating appear a number and a letter. The number is a quality rating based on a scale of 0–100, with 100 being the highest (best) rating attainable. The quality rating is based expressly on the taste, freshness of ingredients, preparation, presentation, and creativity of food served. There is no consideration of price. If you are a person who wants the best food available and cost is not an issue, you need look no further than the quality ratings.

Value Rating. If, on the other hand, you are looking for both quality and value, then you should check the value rating, expressed in letters. The value ratings are defined as follows:

A   Exceptional value, a real bargain
B   Good value
C   Fair value, you get exactly what you pay for
D   Somewhat overpriced
F   Significantly overpriced

Inconsistency. No restaurant is completely consistent, but those marked with this icon tend to vary in quality more than most, so do try again if a meal fails to thrill. Over the course of several visits, sublime cooking will more than offset any occasional duds.

Caution. Be careful ordering in these restaurants; you've got to know what to ask for, and perhaps, even how to go about asking for it. Read the reviews carefully and stick with recommended dishes . . . because not everything's good. Ratings apply only if the suggested strategies are followed.

locating the restaurant

Just below the restaurant name is a designation for geographic zone. This zone description will give you a general idea of where the restaurant described is located. For ease of use, we divide the greater New York City area into 21 geographic zones.

Zone 1   Lower Manhattan (south of Chambers Street on the west side, south of Brooklyn Bridge on the east side)

Zone 2   Soho and Tribeca (Soho: south of Houston Street and
             north of Grand Street. Tribeca is, of course, the
             triangle beneath Canal)

Zone 3   Chinatown, Little Italy, and Lower East Side (east of
             Broadway, south of Grand Street, and north of the
             Brooklyn Bridge)

Zone 4   Greenwich Village (between Houston and 14th
             Streets, west of Broadway)

Zone 5   East Village (between Houston and 14th Streets, east
             of Broadway)

Zone 6   Chelsea West (between 15th and 33rd Streets, west of
             5th Avenue)

Zone 7   Chelsea East and Gramercy (between 15th and 33rd
             Streets, east of 5th Avenue)

Zone 8   Midtown West and Theater District (between 34th
             and 59th Streets, west of Fifth Avenue)

Zone 9   Midtown East (between 34th and 59th Streets, east of
             Fifth Avenue)

Zone 10   Upper West Side (between 60th and 110th Streets,
             west of the Park)

Zone 11   Upper East Side (between 60th and 110th Streets, east
             of the Park)

Zone 12   Harlem, Morningside Heights, and Washington
             Heights (north of 110th Street)

Zone 13   Northern Brooklyn (Park Slope and above): Park
             Slope, Greenpoint, Williamsburg, Bedford
             Stuyvesant, Brooklyn Heights, Carroll Gardens,
             Red Hook, Fort Greene, Crown Heights, Cobble
             Hill

Zone 14   Southern Brooklyn (below Park Slope): Sunset Park,
             Bay Ridge, Borough Park, Flatbush, Canarsie,
             Sheepshead Bay, Bensonhurst

Zone 15   Northwestern Queens (north of the Long Island
             Expressway and west of the Van Wyck Expressway):
             Astoria, Long Island City, Jackson Heights, Wood-
             side, Sunnyside, Corona, Elmhurst

Zone 16	Northeastern Queens (north of the Long Island Expressway and east of the Van Wyck Expressway): Flushing, Whitestone, Bayside
Zone 17	Southern Queens (south of the Long Island Expressway and east of the Van Wyck Expressway): Rego Park, Forest Hills, Jamaica, Queens Village
Zone 18	The Bronx
Zone 19	Staten Island
Zone 20	Nearby in New Jersey
Zone 21	Nassau County, Long Island

If you're on West Broadway and intend to walk or take a cab to dinner, you may want to choose a restaurant from among those located in Zone 2. If you have a car, you might include restaurants from contiguous zones in your consideration.

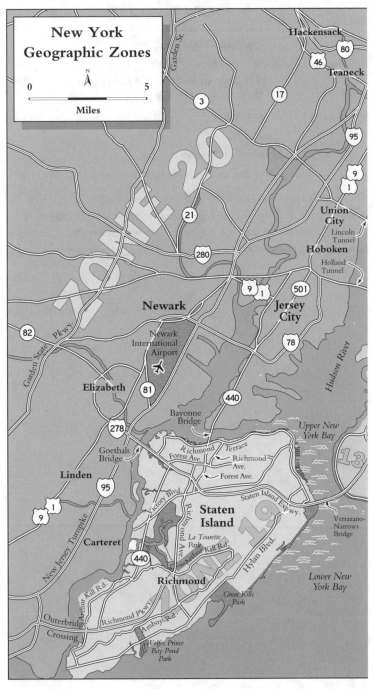

New York
Geographic Zones

N

0 ——————— 5
Miles

Hackensack
80
46
Teaneck
95
Garden St.
3
17
9
1
21
Union City
Lincoln Tunnel
280
Hoboken
Holland Tunnel
9 1
501
Newark
Jersey City
82
Garden State Pkwy.
78
Newark International Airport
Hudson River
Elizabeth
81
440
Bayonne Bridge
Upper New York Bay
278
Richmond Terrace
Goethals Bridge
Forest Ave.
Richmond Ave.
Forest Ave.
Linden
95
Staten Island Expwy.
Verrazano-Narrows Bridge
New Jersey Turnpike
Victory Blvd.
Staten Island
Richmond Ave.
La Tourette Park
Carteret
440
Arthur Kill Rd.
Hylan Blvd.
Lower New York Bay
Richmond
Arthur Kill Rd.
Richmond Pkwy.
Amboy Rd.
Great Kills Park
Outerbridge Crossing
Wolfes Prince Bay Pond Park

20

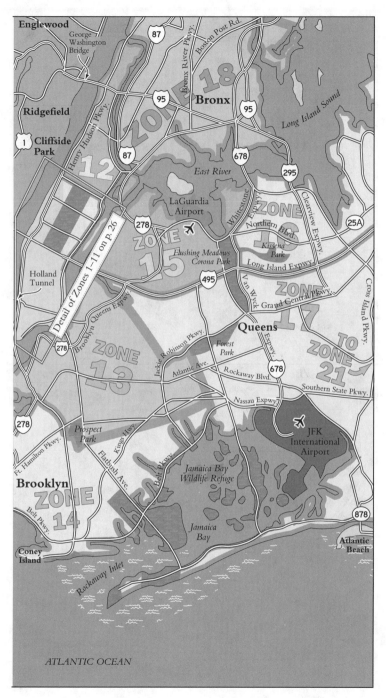

Englewood

George
Washington
Bridge

87

Bronx River Pkwy.

Boston Post Rd.

ZONE 18

Ridgefield

95

Bronx

95

Long Island Sound

1

Cliffside
Park

Henry Hudson Pkwy.

ZONE 12

87

678

East River

678

295

Whitestone Expwy.

ZONE 16

25A

Clearview Expwy.

LaGuardia
Airport

278

ZONE 15

Northern Blvd.

Kissena
Park

Flushing Meadows
Corona Park

Long Island Expwy.

Detail of Zones 1–11 on p. 26

Holland
Tunnel

495

Van Wyck Expwy.

Grand Central Pkwy.

ZONE 17

Cross Island Pkwy.

Brooklyn Queens Expwy.

278

Jackie Robinson Pkwy.

Queens

Forest
Park

TO
ZONE
21

ZONE 13

Atlantic Ave.

Rockaway Blvd.

678

Southern State Pkwy.

Nassau Expwy.

278

Ft. Hamilton Pkwy.

Prospect
Park

Kings Hwy.

Belt Pkwy.

Jamaica Bay
Wildlife Refuge

JFK
International
Airport

Flatbush Ave.

Brooklyn

ZONE 14

Belt Pkwy.

Jamaica
Bay

878

Atlantic
Beach

Coney
Island

Rockaway Inlet

ATLANTIC OCEAN

21

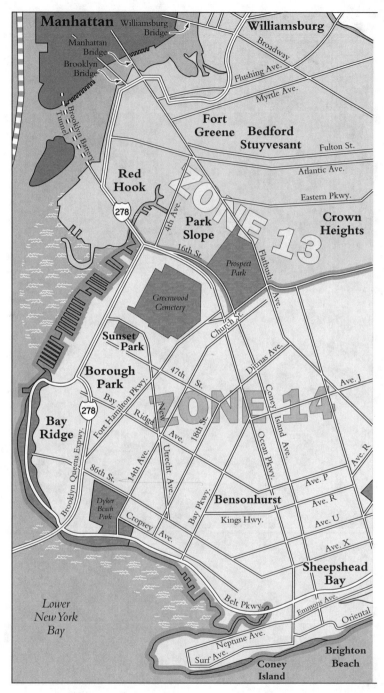

Manhattan

Williamsburg Bridge

Williamsburg

Manhattan Bridge

Brooklyn Bridge

Broadway

Flushing Ave.

Myrtle Ave.

Brooklyn Battery Tunnel

Fort Greene

Bedford Stuyvesant

Fulton St.

Red Hook

Atlantic Ave.

Eastern Pkwy.

278

4th Ave.

Park Slope

16th St.

Prospect Park

Flatbush Ave.

ZONE 13

Crown Heights

Greenwood Cemetery

Church St.

Sunset Park

Ditmas Ave.

Ave. J

Borough Park

47th St.

Coney Island Ave.

Bay Ridge

Bay Ridge Ave.

Fort Hamilton Pkwy.

New Ave.

18th St.

Ocean Pkwy.

ZONE 14

278

Brooklyn Queens Expwy.

86th St.

14th Ave.

Utrecht Ave.

Bay Pkwy.

Bensonhurst

Ave. P

Ave. R

Dyker Beach Park

Cropsey Ave.

Kings Hwy.

Ave. U

Ave. X

Ave. R

Sheepshead Bay

Lower New York Bay

Belt Pkwy.

Emmons Ave.

Oriental

Neptune Ave.

Surf Ave.

Coney Island

Brighton Beach

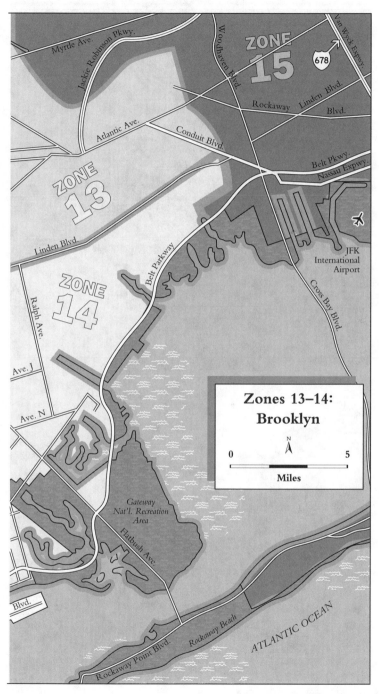

Myrtle Ave.

Jackie Robinson Pkwy.

Woodhaven Blvd.

ZONE 15

Van Wyck Expwy.

678

Rockaway   Linden   Blvd.

Blvd.

Atlantic Ave.

Conduit Blvd.

Belt Pkwy.
Nassau Expwy.

ZONE 13

Linden Blvd.

Belt Parkway

JFK
International
Airport

Cross Bay Blvd.

ZONE 14

Ralph Ave.

Ave. J

Ave. N

Gateway
Nat'l. Recreation
Area

Flatbush Ave.

Blvd.

**Zones 13–14:
Brooklyn**

N

0 ————————————— 5

Miles

Rockaway Point Blvd.

Rockaway Beach

ATLANTIC OCEAN

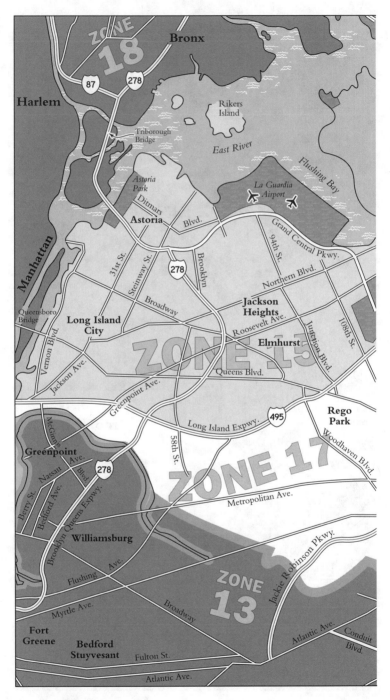

ZONE 18

Bronx

87 278

Harlem

Triborough
Bridge

Rikers
Island

East River

Flushing Bay

Astoria
Park

Ditmars

La Guardia
Airport

Astoria

Blvd.

Grand Central Pkwy.

Manhattan

31st St.

Steinway St.

278

Brooklyn

94th St.

Northern Blvd.

Broadway

Jackson
Heights

Queensboro
Bridge

Long Island
City

Vernon Blvd.

Jackson Ave.

Roosevelt Ave.

Elmhurst

ZONE 15

Junction Blvd.

108th St.

Queens Blvd.

Greenpoint Ave.

Long Island Expwy.

495

Rego
Park

Greenpoint

McGuinness Ave.

278

Nassau

Blvd.

58th St.

ZONE 17

Woodhaven Blvd.

Berry St.

Bedford Ave.

Brooklyn Queens Expwy.

Williamsburg

Flushing   Ave.

Metropolitan Ave.

Myrtle Ave.

Broadway

ZONE 13

Jackie Robinson Pkwy.

Fort
Greene

Bedford
Stuyvesant

Fulton St.

Atlantic Ave.

Conduit
Blvd.

Atlantic Ave.

24

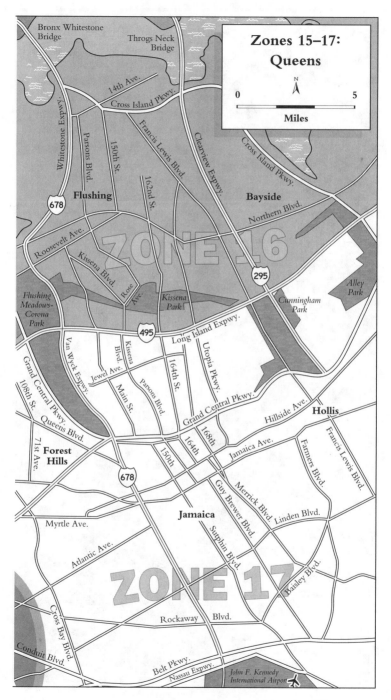

Zones 15–17: Queens

N

0   5

Miles

Bronx Whitestone Bridge

Throgs Neck Bridge

14th Ave.

Cross Island Pkwy.

Francis Lewis Blvd.

Clearview Expwy.

Cross Island Pkwy.

Whitestone Expwy.

Parsons Blvd.

150th St.

162nd St.

678

Flushing

Bayside

Northern Blvd.

Roosevelt Ave.

Kissena Blvd.

Rose Ave.

ZONE 16

295

Alley Park

Flushing Meadows-Corona Park

Kissena Park

Cunningham Park

495

Long Island Expwy.

Van Wyck Expwy.

Jewel Ave.

Kissena Blvd.

Main St.

Parsons Blvd.

164th St.

Utopia Pkwy.

Grand Central Pkwy.

Grand Central Pkwy.

108th St.

Queens Blvd.

71st Ave.

Forest Hills

150th

164th

168th

Hillside Ave.

Hollis

Jamaica Ave.

Farmers Blvd.

Francis Lewis Blvd.

678

Jamaica

Merrick Blvd.

Guy Brewer Blvd.

Linden Blvd.

Myrtle Ave.

Atlantic Ave.

Sutphin Blvd.

ZONE 17

Baisley Blvd.

Cross Bay Blvd.

Rockaway Blvd.

Conduit Blvd.

Belt Pkwy.

Nassau Expwy.

John F. Kennedy International Airport

25

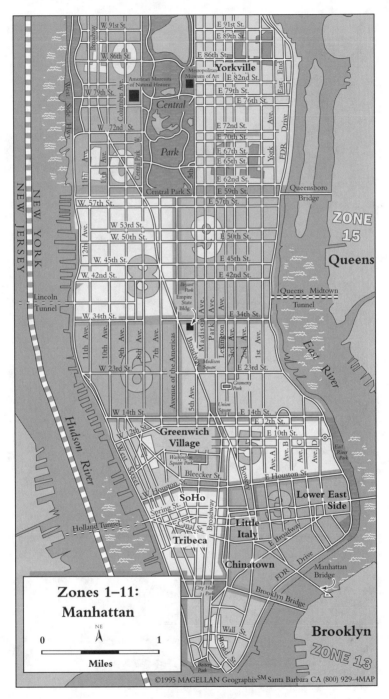

Zones 1–11:
Manhattan

0   1

Miles

©1995 MAGELLAN GeographixSM Santa Barbara CA (800) 929-4MAP

26

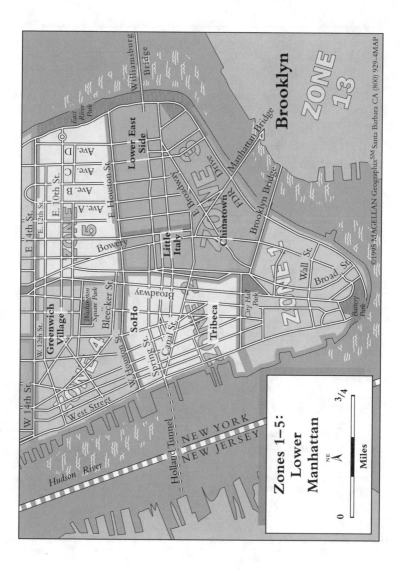

Zones 1–5:
Lower
Manhattan

NE

Miles

0   3/4

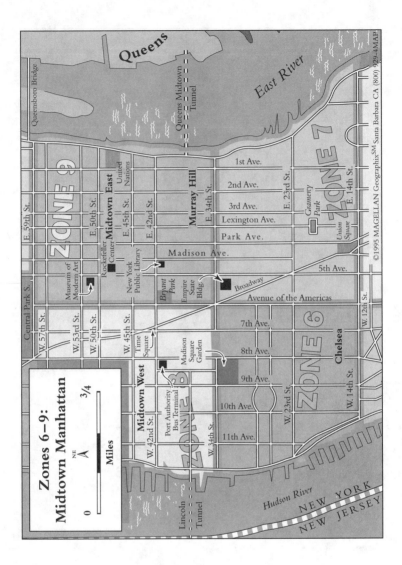

Zones 6–9:
Midtown Manhattan

NE
Miles
0   3/4

©1995 MAGELLAN Geographix℠ Santa Barbara CA (800) 929-4MAP

Queens

East River

Queensboro Bridge

Queens Midtown Tunnel

ZONE 9

ZONE 7

United Nations

1st Ave.

2nd Ave.

3rd Ave.

Lexington Ave.

Park Ave.

Madison Ave.

5th Ave.

Avenue of the Americas

Murray Hill

E. 34th St.

E. 23rd St.

E. 14th St.

Gramercy Park

Union Square

Midtown East

E. 59th St.

E. 50th St.

E. 45th St.

E. 42nd St.

Museum of Modern Art

Rockefeller Center

New York Public Library

Bryant Park

Empire State Bldg.

Broadway

Central Park S.

W. 57th St.

W. 53rd St.

W. 50th St.

W. 45th St.

W. 42nd St.

W. 34th St.

Time Square

Madison Square Garden

Port Authority Bus Terminal

Midtown West

ZONE 8

7th Ave.

8th Ave.

9th Ave.

10th Ave.

11th Ave.

ZONE 6

Chelsea

W. 14th St.

W. 23rd St.

W. 12th St.

Lincoln Tunnel

Hudson River

NEW YORK

NEW JERSEY

28

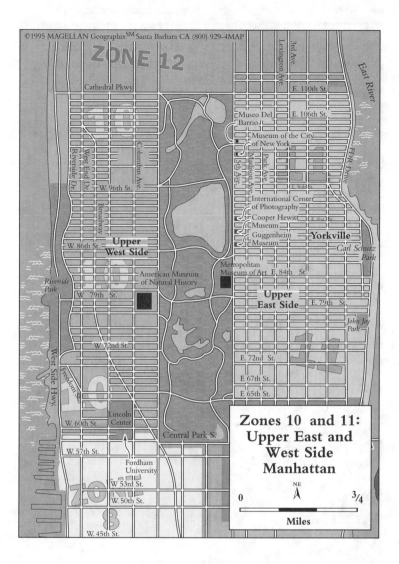

©1995 MAGELLAN Geographix^{SM} Santa Barbara CA (800) 929-4MAP

ZONE 12

Cathedral Pkwy.

Lexington Ave.
3rd Ave.
East River

E. 110th St.

Museo Del Barrio
E. 106th St.

Museum of the City of New York

Columbus Ave.
West End Dr.
Riverside Dr.

5th Ave.
Madison Ave.
Park Ave.

W. 96th St.

E. 96th St.

Broadway

International Center of Photography

Cooper Hewitt Museum
E. 91st St.

Guggenheim Museum
Yorkville

W. 86th St.

Upper West Side

Carl Schurz Park

Riverside Park

American Museum of Natural History

Metropolitan Museum of Art
E. 84th St.

FDR Drive

W. 79th St.

Upper East Side
E. 79th St.

John Jay Park

West Freedom St.

W. 72nd St.

E. 72nd St.

E. 67th St.

E. 65th St.

West Side Hwy.

Lincoln Center

W. 60th St.

Central Park S.

W. 57th St.

Fordham University

W. 53rd St.

ZONE 8

W. 50th St.

W. 45th St.

**Zones 10 and 11:
Upper East and
West Side
Manhattan**

NE

0   3/4

Miles

29

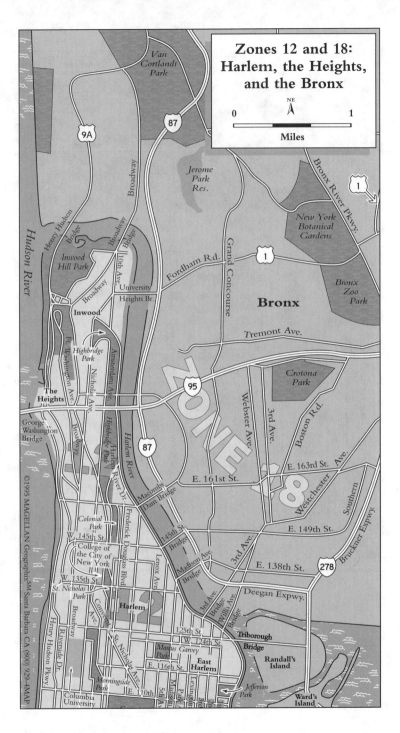

Zones 12 and 18:
Harlem, the Heights,
and the Bronx

NE

0   1

Miles

Van
Cortlandt
Park

9A

87

Jerome
Park
Res.

Bronx River Pkwy.

1

New York
Botanical
Gardens

Broadway

Fordham Rd.

University
Heights Br.

Grand Concourse

1

Bronx

Bronx
Zoo
Park

Henry Hudson
Bridge

10th Ave. Bridge

Broadway

Inwood
Hill Park

Hudson River

Inwood

Ft. Washington Ave.

Highbridge
Park

Amsterdam Ave.

Nicholas Ave.

The
Heights

Harlem River

Tremont Ave.

95

Crotona
Park

Highbridge Park

George
Washington
Bridge

87

Webster Ave.

3rd Ave.

Boston Rd.

©1995 MAGELLAN Geographix℠ Santa Barbara CA (800) 929-4MAP

Broadway

Harlem River Dr.

Frederick Douglass Blvd.

Macombs
Dam Bridge

E. 161st St.

Westchester Ave.

E. 163rd St. Ave.

Southern

Colonial
Park

W. 145th St.

College of
the City of
New York

W. 135th St.

St. Nicholas
Park

145th St.
Bridge

Lenox Ave.

Madison Ave.

E. 149th St.

3rd Ave.

E. 138th St.

ZONE 18

Bruckner Expwy.

278

Henry Hudson Pkwy.

Riverside Dr.

Broadway

St. Nicholas Ave.

Convent Ave.

Harlem

Madison Ave. Bridge

3rd Ave. Bridge

Willis Ave. Bridge

Deegan Expwy.

ZONE 12

125th St.

W. 124th St.

Marcus Garvey
Park

E. 116th St.

East
Harlem

Lexington Ave.

Park Ave.

Madison

Triborough
Bridge

Randall's
Island

Morningside
Park

E. 110th

5th Ave.

Jefferson
Park

Ward's
Island

Columbia
University

30

my pick of the best new york city
RESTAURANTS

Because restaurants open and close all the time in New York, we have confined our list to establishments with a proven track record over a fairly long period of time. Newer restaurants (and older restaurants under new management) are listed but not profiled. Those newer or changed establishments that demonstrate staying power and consistency will be profiled in subsequent editions.

The list is highly selective. Noninclusion of a particular place does not necessarily indicate that the restaurant is not good, but only that it was not ranked among the best in its genre. Note that some restaurants appear in more than one category. Detailed profiles of each restaurant follow in alphabetical order at the end of this chapter. Also, we've listed the types of payment accepted at each restaurant using the following codes:

AMEX	American Express
CB	Carte Blanche
D	Discover
DC	Diners Club
MC	MasterCard
VISA	VISA

A NOTE ABOUT SPELLING

Most diners who enjoy ethnic restaurants have noticed subtle variations in the spelling of certain dishes and preparations from one menu to the next. A noodle dish found on almost all Thai menus, for example, appears in one restaurant as *pad thai,* in another as *Phat Thai,* and in a third as *Phad Thai.*

This and similar inconsistencies arise from attempts to derive a phonetic English spelling from the name of a dish as pronounced in its country of origin. While one particular English spelling might be more frequently used than others, there is usually no definitive correct spelling for the names of many dishes. In this guide, we have elected to use the spelling most commonly found in authoritative ethnic cookbooks and other reference works.

We call this to your attention because the spelling we use in this guide could be different from that which you encounter on the menu in a certain restaurant. We might say, for instance, that the *tabbouleh* is good at the Pillars of Lebanon, while at the restaurant itself the dish is listed on the menu as *tabouli.*

Restaurants by Cuisine

Name	Star Rating	Price Rating	Quality Rating	Value Rating	Zone
Afghan					
Speengar Shish Kebab House	★★★½	Inexp	90	A	15
Albanian					
Tony and Tina's Pizzeria	★★★	Inexp	86	A	18
American					
Grange Hall	★★★★	Exp	91	B	4
La Porteña	★★★★	Mod	91	A	15
The Crab Shanty	★★★	Mod	86	A	18
Tom's Luncheonette	★★★	Inexp	85	B	13
Brennan and Carr	★★	Inexp	83	B	14
Cupcake Cafe	★★	Inexp	80	A−	8
Barbecue					
Alex BAR-B.Q.	★★★★	Inexp	92	A	13
Pearson's Texas Barbecue	★★★	Inexp	88	C	15
Belgian					
Petite Abeille	★★½	Inexp	86	A	6
Brazilian					
Cantina Brazil	★★★	Inexp	91	A	15
Churrascaria Plataforma	★★½	Exp	85	C	8
Cabana Carioca	★★½	Inexp	84	A	8
Cambodian					
Cambodian Cuisine	★★★½	Inexp	90	A	13
Central Asian					
Tadjikstan	★★★★	Inexp	93	A	17
Uzbekistan Restaurant	★★★	Inexp	88	A	17
Chinese					
Do I Tru	★★★★	Inexp	92	A	16
Tindo	★★★★	Mod	92	A	3
Jade Palace	★★★★	Inexp	91	A−	16
Kam Chueh	★★★½	Mod	91	B+	3
The Nice Restaurant	★★★½	Mod	91	B	3

Name	Star Rating	Price Rating	Quality Rating	Value Rating	Zone
Chinese *(continued)*					
Hop Lee	★★★½	Inexp	90	A	3
Joe's Shanghai	★★★½	Mod	90	A	3, 16
Sweet-n-Tart Cafe	★★★	Inexp	91	B−	16
Happy Buddha	★★★	Inexp	86	A−	16
White Bear Ice Cream and Wonton Shop	★★½	Inexp	85	A	16
Fortune Gourmet	★★½	Inexp	84	A	16
New Siu Sam Yuen	★★	Inexp	85	A	3
Noodle 88	★★	Inexp	83	A	8
Chinese/Norwegian/American					
Wee Kee	★★★	Inexp	86	A	14
Czech/Slovak					
Milan's Restaurant	★★★★	Inexp	92	A	14
Zlata Praha	★★	Mod	82	B−	15
Deli					
David's Brisket House	★★★½	Inexp	93	A	13
Mr. Broadway Kosher Deli	★★★½	Mod	87	A	8
Pastrami King	★½	Inexp	88	B+	17
Diner					
Ruben Lunch	★★½	Inexp	90	A	13
Eclectic					
Blue Ribbon	★★★★	Exp	92	C	2
Il Buco	★★★½	Exp	90	C	5
Tiemann Oasis	★★★	Inexp	88	A	12
City Bakery	★★★	Mod	87	D	7
Ecuadoran					
Eva's	★★★	Inexp	87	A	13
Filipino					
Ihawan	★★★	Inexp	87	A−	15
BJ's	★★½	Inexp	84	B	15

Name	Star Rating	Price Rating	Quality Rating	Value Rating	Zone
French/Eclectic					
Picholine	★★★★	Exp	91	C+	10
Fried					
Fried World	★★	Inexp	86	A	6
German					
Killmeyer's Old Bavaria Inn	★★★★	Mod	91	B	19
Hallo Berlin	★½	Inexp	76	B	8
Greek					
Stamatis	★★★	Mod	89	B+	15
Guatemalan					
La Xelaju	★★★★	Inexp	91	A	17
Hungarian					
Mocca Hungarian	★★½	Mod	85	B−	11
Indian/Pakistani					
Bukhara Restaurant	★★★★	Inexp	92	A	14
5 Stars Punjabi	★★★★	Inexp	91	A	15
Jackson Diner	★★★★	Inexp	91	A	15
Mavalli Palace	★★★½	Mod	89	A	7
Cuisine of Pakistan (a.k.a. Kashmir 9)	★★★	Inexp	87	A	8
Chowpatty	★★½	Inexp	85	A	20
Punjab	★★	Inexp	81	A	5
Kasturi	★★	Inexp	75	A−	7
Indonesian					
The Indonesian Consulate Cafeteria	★★★★	Inexp	92	A	11
Italian					
DiFara Pizzeria	★★★★½	Mod	94	A	14
La Pizza Fresca	★★★★	Mod	93	A	7
Piccola Venezia	★★★★	Exp	93	D+	15
Denino's	★★★½	Inexp	92	A	19

Name	Star Rating	Price Rating	Quality Rating	Value Rating	Zone
Italian *(continued)*					
Dominick's	★★★½	Mod	91	B+	18
Pepe Rosso To Go	★★★½	Inexp	91	A	2
Umberto's	★★★½	Mod	91	A	21
Cono & Son O'Pescatore Restaurant	★★★½	Exp	90	B–	13
Ferdinando's	★★★½	Mod	90	A	13
Lento's	★★★	Mod	91	B	13
Rosario's	★★★	Inexp	86	A	1
Tre Pomodori	★★½	Mod	85	A	9
Iammo Bello	★★½	Inexp	84	A	11
Rocco's	★★½	Inexp	83	A	14
Joe's Bar and Grill	★★	Inexp	85	A	14
Jamaican					
Wangah Hut	★★★½	Inexp	91	A	17
Jean's	★★½	Inexp	85	A	17
Japanese					
Hole in One	★★★★½	Very Exp	96	C	9
Saka Gura	★★★★	Mod	91	B+	9
Tokyo	★★★½	Exp	92	C	9
Menchanko-Tei	★★★	Mod	86	B	8, 9
Yakitori Taisho	★★★	Inexp	83	B+	5
Sapporo East	★★½	Mod	83	A–	5
Sapporo	★★	Inexp	78	A	8
Korean					
Healthy Tofu	★★★★	Inexp	93	A	16
Bo	★★★★	Inexp	92	A	16
Pa Do Whae House	★★★½	Mod	90	A	16
Woo Chon	★★★	Exp	88	C	8
Kang Suh	★★½	Mod	84	B	6
Kosher					
Mabat	★★★★	Mod	92	B	14
Chick Chack Chicken	★★★	Inexp	89	A	4

Name	Star Rating	Price Rating	Quality Rating	Value Rating	Zone
Hall Street Kosher Cafe	★★★	Inexp	89	A	13
Bissaleh Classic	★★★	Mod	87	B	11
Famous Pita	★★★	Inexp	87	A	14
Latin Caribbean					
Alex BAR-B.Q.	★★★★	Inexp	92	A	13
Cuchifritos/Fritura	★★★½	Inexp	90	A	12
El Papasito	★★★½	Inexp	90	A	8
El Unico	★★★½	Inexp	90	A	20
Casa Adela	★★★	Inexp	90	A	5
Cuchifritos	★★★	Inexp	88	A	13
Cafe Con Leche	★★½	Inexp	86	B–	10
Margon Restaurant	★★	Inexp	84	A	8
Sucelt Coffee Shop	★★	Inexp	82	A	4
Malaysian					
Penang Cuisine Malaysia	★★★½	Mod	91	A–	16
Nyonya Malaysian Cuisine	★★½	Mod	83	B+	3
Mexican					
Castro's Coffee Shop	★★★½	Inexp	91	A	13
La Espiga	★★★½	Inexp	90	A	15
Gabriela's	★★★	Mod	86	A	10
Antojitos Mexicanos	★★½	Inexp	86	A	13
Bean	★★½	Inexp	86	A	13
La Hacienda	★★½	Inexp	85	A	12
Middle Eastern					
Karam Restaurant	★★★★	Inexp	92	A	14
Kabab Cafe	★★★½	Inexp	90	A	15
Yemen Cafe	★★★½	Inexp	90	A–	13
Moustache Pitza	★★★½	Inexp	87	A–	4, 5
Sahara East	★★½	Mod	83	B	5
Moroccan					
Casablanca	★★★★	Inexp	93	A	14
Peruvian					
Rinconcito Peruano	★★★½	Inexp	92	A	8

Name	Star Rating	Price Rating	Quality Rating	Value Rating	Zone
Peruvian (continued)					
Pio Pio	★★★	Mod	88	B	15
Pizza					
DiFara Pizzeria	★★★★½	Mod	94	A	14
La Pizza Fresca	★★★★	Mod	93	A	7
Denino's	★★★½	Inexp	92	A	19
Nick's Pizza	★★★½	Mod	92	B	17
Patsy's Pizza	★★★½	Inexp	92	A	12
Umberto's	★★★½	Mod	91	A	21
Grimaldi's Pizza	★★★½	Mod	90	B	13
Lento's	★★★	Mod	91	B	13
Sal and Carmine's Pizza	★★★	Inexp	90	A	10
Polish					
Teresa's	★★	Inexp	83	A	5
Portuguese					
Little Portugal	★★★½	Inexp	91	A	21
Churrasqueira Bairrada	★★★	Mod	89	B	21
Pub					
Donovan's	★★★½	Inexp	91	A−	15, 16
Molly's	★★★	Mod	87	B	7
Teddy's Bar and Grill	★★½	Mod	86	A−	13
North Star Pub	★★	Mod	82	C	1
Romanian					
Cornel's Place Restaurant	★★★½	Inexp	93	A	15
Russian					
Uncle Vanya Cafe	★★½	Mod	85	B	8
Emerald Spa & Restaurant	★★½	Mod	81	C	15
Seafood					
Seamorhen II	★★★½	Inexp	91	A	17
The Crab Shanty	★★★	Mod	86	A	18
Rocco's	★★½	Inexp	83	A	14
Johnny's Famous Reef	★★	Mod	84	A	18

Restaurants by Cuisine (continued)

Name	Star Rating	Price Rating	Quality Rating	Value Rating	Zone
Soup					
Soup Kitchen International	★★★½	Inexp	91	A	8
Southern					
Charles Southern Kitchen All You Can Eat Buffet	★★★★½	Inexp	97	A	12
Gaither's	★★★★	Inexp	92	A	14
Seamorhen II	★★★½	Inexp	91	A	17
Metropolitan AME Church	★★★½	Inexp	89	A	12
Soul Food Kitchen	★★★	Inexp	90	A	13
Soul Fixins'	★★★	Inexp	88	A	8
The Pink Teacup	★★★	Mod	86	C	4
Spanish / Tapas					
Xunta	★★★	Inexp	88	B	5
Thai					
Sripraphai Thai Bakery	★★★½	Inexp	90	A	15
Thai Cafe	★★½	Mod	84	B–	13
Chelsea Thai Wholesale	★★	Inexp	87	B	6
Turkish					
Kervan	★★★★	Mod	94	B	20
Cafe Istanbul	★★★★	Inexp	92	A	14
Vegetarian					
Kate's Joint	★★	Mod	83	B	5
Vietnamese					
Pho Bac	★★★★	Inexp	93	A	15
New Pasteur	★★★½	Inexp	87	A	3
Saigon Grill	★★★	Mod	87	B	10
Pho Cong Ly	★★½	Inexp	86	A	3

Restaurants by Food Quality Rating

Name	Quality Rating	Cuisine	Star Rating	Price	Value Rating	Zone
Charles Southern Kitchen All You Can Eat Buffet	97	Southern	★★★★½	Inexp	A	12
Hole in One	96	Japanese	★★★★½	Very Exp	C	9
DiFara Pizzeria	94	Italian/Pizza	★★★★½	Mod	A	14
Kervan	94	Turkish	★★★★	Mod	B	20
Casablanca	93	Moroccan	★★★★	Inexp	A	14
Healthy Tofu	93	Korean	★★★★	Inexp	A	16
La Pizza Fresca	93	Italian/Pizza	★★★★	Mod	A	7
Pho Bac	93	Vietnamese	★★★★	Inexp	A	15
Piccola Venezia	93	Italian	★★★★	Exp	D+	15
Tadjikstan	93	Central Asian	★★★★	Inexp	A	17
Cornel's Place Restaurant	93	Romanian	★★★½	Inexp	A	15
David's Brisket House	93	Deli	★★★½	Inexp	A	13
Alex BAR-B.Q.	92	Barbecue/ Puerto Rican	★★★★	Inexp	A	13
Blue Ribbon	92	Eclectic	★★★★	Exp	C	2
Bo	92	Korean	★★★★	Inexp	A	16
Bukhara Restaurant	92	Pakistani	★★★★	Inexp	A	14
Cafe Istanbul	92	Turkish	★★★★	Inexp	A	14
Do I Tru	92	Chinese	★★★★	Inexp	A	16
Gaither's	92	Southern	★★★★	Inexp	A	14
The Indonesian Consulate Cafeteria	92	Indonesian	★★★★	Inexp	A	11
Karam Restaurant	92	Lebanese	★★★★	Inexp	A	14
Mabat	92	Kosher/Israeli	★★★★	Mod	B	14
Milan's Restaurant	92	Slovakian	★★★★	Inexp	A	14
Tindo	92	Chinese	★★★★	Mod	A	3
Denino's	92	Italian/Pizza	★★★½	Inexp	A	19
Nick's Pizza	92	Pizza	★★★½	Mod	B	17
Patsy's Pizza	92	Pizza	★★★½	Inexp	A	12
Rinconcito Peruano	92	Peruvian	★★★½	Inexp	A	8
Tokyo	92	Japanese	★★★½	Exp	C	9
5 Stars Punjabi	91	Indian	★★★★	Inexp	A	15
Grange Hall	91	American	★★★★	Exp	B	4
Jackson Diner	91	Indian	★★★★	Inexp	A	15
Jade Palace	91	Chinese	★★★★	Inexp	A−	16

Name	Quality Rating	Cuisine	Star Rating	Price	Value Rating	Zone
Killmeyer's Old Bavaria Inn	91	German	★★★★	Mod	B	19
La Porteña	91	Argentinian	★★★★	Mod	A	15
La Xelaju	91	Guatemalan	★★★★	Inexp	A	17
Picholine	91	French/ Eclectic	★★★★	Exp	C+	10
Saka Gura	91	Japanese	★★★★	Mod	B+	9
Castro's Coffee Shop	91	Mexican	★★★½	Inexp	A	13
Dominick's	91	Italian	★★★½	Mod	B+	18
Donovan's	91	Pub	★★★½	Inexp	A–	15, 16
Kam Chueh	91	Chinese	★★★½	Mod	B+	3
Little Portugal	91	Portuguese	★★★½	Inexp	A	21
The Nice Restaurant	91	Chinese	★★★½	Mod	B	3
Penang Cuisine Malaysia	91	Malaysian	★★★½	Mod	A–	16
Pepe Rosso To Go	91	Italian	★★★½	Inexp	A	2
Seamorhen II	91	Seafood/ Southern	★★★½	Inexp	A	17
Soup Kitchen International	91	Soup	★★★½	Inexp	A	8
Umberto's	91	Italian/Pizza	★★★½	Mod	A	21
Wangah Hut	91	Jamaican	★★★½	Inexp	A	17
Cantina Brazil	91	Brazilian	★★★	Inexp	A	15
Lento's	91	Italian/Pizza	★★★	Mod	B	13
Sweet-n-Tart Cafe	91	Chinese	★★★	Inexp	B–	16
Cambodian Cuisine	90	Cambodian	★★★½	Inexp	A	13
Cono & Son O'Pescatore Restaurant	90	Italian	★★★½	Exp	B–	13
Cuchifritos/Fritura	90	Puerto Rican	★★★½	Inexp	A	12
El Papasito	90	Dominican	★★★½	Inexp	A	8
El Unico	90	Cuban	★★★½	Inexp	A	20
Ferdinando's	90	Italian	★★★½	Mod	A	13
Grimaldi's Pizza	90	Pizza	★★★½	Mod	B	13
Hop Lee	90	Chinese	★★★½	Inexp	A	3
Il Buco	90	Eclectic	★★★½	Exp	C	5
Joe's Shanghai	90	Chinese	★★★½	Mod	A	3, 16
Kabab Cafe	90	Egyptian	★★★½	Inexp	A	15

Name	Quality Rating	Cuisine	Star Rating	Price	Value Rating	Zone
La Espiga	90	Mexican	★★★½	Inexp	A	15
Pa Do Whae House	90	Korean	★★★½	Mod	A	16
Speengar Shish Kebab House	90	Afghan	★★★½	Inexp	A	15
Sripraphai Thai Bakery	90	Thai	★★★½	Inexp	A	15
Yemen Cafe	90	Yemeni	★★★½	Inexp	A–	13
Casa Adela	90	Puerto Rican	★★★	Inexp	A	5
Sal and Carmine's Pizza	90	Pizza	★★★	Inexp	A	10
Soul Food Kitchen	90	Southern	★★★	Inexp	A	13
Ruben Lunch	90	Diner	★★½	Inexp	A	13
Mavalli Palace	89	Indian	★★★½	Mod	A	7
Metropolitan AME Church	89	Southern	★★★½	Inexp	A	12
Chick Chack Chicken	89	Kosher	★★★	Inexp	A	4
Churrasqueira Bairrada	89	Portuguese	★★★	Mod	B	21
Hall Street Kosher Cafe	89	Kosher	★★★	Inexp	A	13
Stamatis	89	Greek	★★★	Mod	B+	15
Cuchifritos	88	Puerto Rican	★★★	Inexp	A	13
Pearson's Texas Barbecue	88	Barbecue	★★★	Inexp	C	15
Pio Pio	88	Peruvian	★★★	Mod	B	15
Soul Fixins'	88	Southern	★★★	Inexp	A	8
Tiemann Oasis	88	Eclectic	★★★	Inexp	A	12
Uzbekistan Restaurant	88	Central Asian	★★★	Inexp	A	17
Woo Chon	88	Korean	★★★	Exp	C	8
Xunta	88	Spanish/Tapas	★★★	Inexp	B	5
Pastrami King	88	Deli	★½	Inexp	B+	17
Moustache Pitza	87	Middle Eastern	★★★½	Inexp	A–	4, 5
Mr. Broadway Kosher Deli	87	Deli	★★★½	Mod	A	8
New Pasteur	87	Vietnamese	★★★½	Inexp	A	3
Bissaleh Classic	87	Kosher/ Israeli	★★★	Mod	B	11
City Bakery	87	Eclectic	★★★	Mod	D	7
Cuisine of Pakistan (a.k.a. Kashmir 9)	87	Pakistani	★★★	Inexp	A	8
Eva's	87	Ecuadorian	★★★	Inexp	A	13

Name	Quality Rating	Cuisine	Star Rating	Price	Value Rating	Zone
Famous Pita	87	Kosher/ Israeli	★★★	Inexp	A	14
Ihawan	87	Filipino	★★★	Inexp	A–	15
Molly's	87	Pub	★★★	Mod	B	7
Saigon Grill	87	Vietnamese	★★★	Mod	B	10
Chelsea Thai Wholesale	87	Thai	★★	Inexp	B	6
The Crab Shanty	86	American/ Seafood	★★★	Mod	A	18
Gabriela's	86	Mexican	★★★	Mod	A	10
Happy Buddha	86	Chinese	★★★	Inexp	A–	16
Menchanko-Tei	86	Japanese	★★★	Mod	B	8, 9
The Pink Teacup	86	Southern	★★★	Mod	C	4
Rosario's	86	Italian	★★★	Inexp	A	1
Tony and Tina's Pizzeria	86	Albanian	★★★	Inexp	A	18
Wee Kee	86	Chin/Amer/ Norwegian	★★★	Inexp	A	14
Antojitos Mexicanos	86	Mexican	★★½	Inexp	A	13
Bean	86	Mexican	★★½	Inexp	A	13
Cafe Con Leche	86	Dominican	★★½	Inexp	B–	10
Petite Abeille	86	Belgian	★★½	Inexp	A	6
Pho Cong Ly	86	Vietnamese	★★½	Inexp	A	3
Teddy's Bar and Grill	86	Pub	★★½	Mod	A–	13
Fried World	86	Fried	★★	Inexp	A	6
Tom's Luncheonette	85	American	★★★	Inexp	B	13
Chowpatty	85	Indian	★★½	Inexp	A	20
Churrascaria Plataforma	85	Brazilian	★★½	Exp	C	8
Jean's	85	Jamaican	★★½	Inexp	A	17
La Hacienda	85	Mexican	★★½	Inexp	A	12
Mocca Hungarian	85	Hungarian	★★½	Mod	B–	11
Tre Pomodori	85	Italian	★★½	Mod	A	9
Uncle Vanya Cafe	85	Russian	★★½	Mod	B	8
White Bear Ice Cream and Wonton Shop	85	Chinese	★★½	Inexp	A	16
Joe's Bar and Grill	85	Italian	★★	Inexp	A	14
New Siu Sam Yuen	85	Chinese	★★	Inexp	A	3

Name	Quality Rating	Cuisine	Star Rating	Price	Value Rating	Zone
BJ's	84	Filipino	★★½	Inexp	B	15
Cabana Carioca	84	Brazilian	★★½	Inexp	A	8
Fortune Gourmet	84	Chinese	★★½	Inexp	A	16
Iammo Bello	84	Italian	★★½	Inexp	A	11
Kang Suh	84	Korean	★★½	Mod	B	6
Thai Cafe	84	Thai	★★½	Mod	B–	13
Johnny's Famous Reef	84	Seafood	★★	Mod	A	18
Margon Restaurant	84	Latin American	★★	Inexp	A	8
Yakitori Taisho	83	Japanese	★★★	Inexp	B+	5
Nyonya Malaysian Cuisine	83	Malaysian	★★½	Mod	B+	3
Rocco's	83	Italian/ Seafood	★★½	Inexp	A	14
Sahara East	83	Middle Eastern	★★½	Mod	B	5
Sapporo East	83	Japanese	★★½	Mod	A–	5
Brennan and Carr	83	American	★★	Inexp	B	14
Kate's Joint	83	Vegetarian	★★	Mod	B	5
Noodle 88	83	Chinese	★★	Inexp	A	8
Teresa's	83	Polish	★★	Inexp	A	5
North Star Pub	82	Pub	★★	Mod	C	1
Sucelt Coffee Shop	82	Puerto Rican/ Cuban	★★	Inexp	A	4
Zlata Praha	82	Czech/Slovak	★★	Mod	B–	15
Emerald Spa & Restaurant	81	Russian	★★½	Mod	C	15
Punjab	81	Indian	★★	Inexp	A	5
Cupcake Cafe	80	American	★★	Inexp	A–	8
Sapporo	78	Japanese	★★	Inexp	A	8
Hallo Berlin	76	German	★½	Inexp	B	8
Kasturi	75	Indian	★★	Inexp	A–	7

Restaurants by Star Rating

Name	Cuisine	Price Rating	Quality Rating	Value Rating	Zone
Four-and-a-Half-Star Restaurants					
Charles Southern Kitchen	Southern	Inexp	97	A	12
Hole in One	Japanese	Very Exp	96	C	9
DiFara Pizzeria	Italian/Pizza	Mod	94	A	14
Four-Star Restaurants					
Kervan	Turkish	Mod	94	B	20
Casablanca	Moroccan	Inexp	93	A	14
Healthy Tofu	Korean	Inexp	93	A	16
La Pizza Fresca	Italian/Pizza	Mod	93	A	7
Pho Bac	Vietnamese	Inexp	93	A	15
Piccola Venezia	Italian	Exp	93	D+	15
Tadjikstan	Central Asian	Inexp	93	A	17
Alex BAR-B.Q.	Barbecue/ Puerto Rican	Inexp	92	A	13
Blue Ribbon	Eclectic	Exp	92	C	2
Bo	Korean	Inexp	92	A	16
Bukhara Restaurant	Pakistani	Inexp	92	A	14
Cafe Istanbul	Turkish	Inexp	92	A	14
Do I Tru	Chinese	Inexp	92	A	16
Gaither's	Southern	Inexp	92	A	14
The Indonesian Consulate Cafeteria	Indonesian	Inexp	92	A	11
Karam Restaurant	Lebanese	Inexp	92	A	14
Mabat	Kosher/Israeli	Mod	92	B	14
Milan's Restaurant	Slovakian	Inexp	92	A	14
Tindo	Chinese	Mod	92	A	3
5 Stars Punjabi	Indian	Inexp	91	A	15
Grange Hall	American	Exp	91	B	4
Jackson Diner	Indian	Inexp	91	A	15
Jade Palace	Chinese	Inexp	91	A−	16
Killmeyer's Old Bavaria Inn	German	Mod	91	B	19
La Porteña	Argentinian	Mod	91	A	15

Name	Cuisine	Price Rating	Quality Rating	Value Rating	Zone
Four-Star Restaurants *(continued)*					
La Xelaju	Guatemalan	Inexp	91	A	17
Picholine	French/Eclectic	Exp	91	C+	10
Saka Gura	Japanese	Mod	91	B+	9
Three-and-a-Half-Star Restaurants					
Cornel's Place Restaurant	Romanian	Inexp	93	A	15
David's Brisket House	Deli	Inexp	93	A	13
Denino's	Italian/Pizza	Inexp	92	A	19
Nick's Pizza	Pizza	Mod	92	B	17
Patsy's Pizza	Pizza	Inexp	92	A	12
Rinconcito Peruano	Peruvian	Inexp	92	A	8
Tokyo	Japanese	Exp	92	C	9
Castro's Coffee Shop	Mexican	Inexp	91	A	13
Dominick's	Italian	Mod	91	B+	18
Donovan's	Pub	Inexp	91	A–	15, 16
Kam Chueh	Chinese	Mod	91	B+	3
Little Portugal	Portuguese	Inexp	91	A	21
The Nice Restaurant	Chinese	Mod	91	B	3
Penang Cuisine Malaysia	Malaysian	Mod	91	A–	16
Pepe Rosso To Go	Italian	Inexp	91	A	2
Seamorhen II	Seafood/Southern	Inexp	91	A	17
Soup Kitchen International	Soup	Inexp	91	A	8
Umberto's	Italian/Pizza	Mod	91	A	21
Wangah Hut	Jamaican	Inexp	91	A	17
Cambodian Cuisine	Cambodian	Inexp	90	A	13
Cono & Son O'Pescatore Rest.	Italian	Exp	90	B–	13
Cuchifritos/Fritura	Puerto Rican	Inexp	90	A	12
El Papasito	Dominican	Inexp	90	A	8
El Unico	Cuban	Inexp	90	A	20
Ferdinando's	Italian	Mod	90	A	13

Name	Cuisine	Price Rating	Quality Rating	Value Rating	Zone
Grimaldi's Pizza	Pizza	Mod	90	B	13
Hop Lee	Chinese	Inexp	90	A	3
Il Buco	Eclectic	Exp	90	C	5
Joe's Shanghai	Chinese	Mod	90	A	3, 16
Kabab Cafe	Egyptian	Inexp	90	A	15
La Espiga	Mexican	Inexp	90	A	15
Pa Do Whae House	Korean	Mod	90	A	16
Speengar Shish Kebab House	Afghan	Inexp	90	A	15
Sripraphai Thai Bakery	Thai	Inexp	90	A	15
Yemen Cafe	Yemeni	Inexp	90	A–	13
Mavalli Palace	Indian	Mod	89	A	7
Metropolitan AME Church	Southern	Inexp	89	A	12
Moustache Pitza	Middle Eastern	Inexp	87	A–	4, 5
Mr. Broadway Kosher Deli	Deli	Mod	87	A	8
New Pasteur	Vietnamese	Inexp	87	A	3

Three-Star Restaurants

Name	Cuisine	Price Rating	Quality Rating	Value Rating	Zone
Cantina Brazil	Brazilian	Inexp	91	A	15
Lento's	Italian/Pizza	Mod	91	B	13
Sweet-n-Tart Cafe	Chinese	Inexp	91	B–	16
Casa Adela	Puerto Rican	Inexp	90	A	5
Sal and Carmine's Pizza	Pizza	Inexp	90	A	10
Soul Food Kitchen	Southern	Inexp	90	A	13
Chick Chack Chicken	Kosher	Inexp	89	A	4
Churrasqueira Bairrada	Portuguese	Mod	89	B	21
Hall Street Kosher Cafe	Kosher	Inexp	89	A	13
Stamatis	Greek	Mod	89	B+	15
Cuchifritos	Puerto Rican	Inexp	88	A	13
Pearson's Texas Barbecue	Barbecue	Inexp	88	C	15
Pio Pio	Peruvian	Mod	88	B	15
Soul Fixins'	Southern	Inexp	88	A	8
Tiemann Oasis	Eclectic	Inexp	88	A	12

Name	Cuisine	Price Rating	Quality Rating	Value Rating	Zone
Three-Star Restaurants *(continued)*					
Uzbekistan Restaurant	Central Asian	Inexp	88	A	17
Woo Chon	Korean	Exp	88	C	8
Xunta	Spanish/Tapas	Inexp	88	B	5
Bissaleh Classic	Kosher/Israeli	Mod	87	B	11
City Bakery	Eclectic	Mod	87	D	7
Cuisine of Pakistan (a.k.a. Kashmir 9)	Pakistani	Inexp	87	A	8
Eva's	Ecuadoran	Inexp	87	A	13
Famous Pita	Kosher/Israeli	Inexp	87	A	14
Ihawan	Filipino	Inexp	87	A–	15
Molly's	Pub	Mod	87	B	7
Saigon Grill	Vietnamese	Mod	87	B	10
The Crab Shanty	American/ Seafood	Mod	86	A	18
Gabriela's	Mexican	Mod	86	A	10
Happy Buddha	Chinese	Inexp	86	A–	16
Menchanko-Tei	Japanese	Mod	86	B	8, 9
The Pink Teacup	Southern	Mod	86	C	4
Rosario's	Italian	Inexp	86	A	1
Tony and Tina's Pizzeria	Albanian	Inexp	86	A	18
Wee Kee	Chinese/Amer/ Norwegian	Inexp	86	A	14
Tom's Luncheonette	American	Inexp	85	B	13
Yakitori Taisho	Japanese	Inexp	83	B+	5
Two-and-a-Half-Star Restaurants					
Ruben Lunch	Diner	Inexp	90	A	13
Antojitos Mexicanos	Mexican	Inexp	86	A	13
Bean	Mexican	Inexp	86	A	13
Cafe Con Leche	Dominican	Inexp	86	B–	10
Petite Abeille	Belgian	Inexp	86	A	6
Pho Cong Ly	Vietnamese	Inexp	86	A	3
Teddy's Bar and Grill	Pub	Mod	86	A–	13

Name	Cuisine	Price Rating	Quality Rating	Value Rating	Zone
Chowpatty	Indian	Inexp	85	A	20
Churrascaria Plataforma	Brazilian	Exp	85	C	8
Jean's	Jamaican	Inexp	85	A	17
La Hacienda	Mexican	Inexp	85	A	12
Mocca Hungarian	Hungarian	Mod	85	B–	11
Tre Pomodori	Italian	Mod	85	A	9
Uncle Vanya Cafe	Russian	Mod	85	B	8
White Bear Ice Cream and Wonton Shop	Chinese	Inexp	85	A	16
BJ's	Filipino	Inexp	84	B	15
Cabana Carioca	Brazilian	Inexp	84	A	8
Fortune Gourmet	Chinese	Inexp	84	A	16
Iammo Bello	Italian	Inexp	84	A	11
Kang Suh	Korean	Mod	84	B	6
Thai Cafe	Thai	Mod	84	B–	13
Nyonya Malaysian Cuisine	Malaysian	Mod	83	B+	3
Rocco's	Italian/Seafood	Inexp	83	A	14
Sahara East	Middle Eastern	Mod	83	B	5
Sapporo East	Japanese	Mod	83	A–	5
Emerald Spa & Restaurant	Russian	Mod	81	C	15

Two-Star Restaurants

Name	Cuisine	Price Rating	Quality Rating	Value Rating	Zone
Chelsea Thai Wholesale	Thai	Inexp	87	B	6
Fried World	Fried	Inexp	86	A	6
Joe's Bar and Grill	Italian	Inexp	85	A	14
New Siu Sam Yuen	Chinese	Inexp	85	A	3
Johnny's Famous Reef	Seafood	Mod	84	A	18
Margon Restaurant	Latin American	Inexp	84	A	8
Brennan and Carr	American	Inexp	83	B	14
Kate's Joint	Vegetarian	Mod	83	B	5
Noodle 88	Chinese	Inexp	83	A	8
Teresa's	Polish	Inexp	83	A	5

Name	Cuisine	Price Rating	Quality Rating	Value Rating	Zone
Two-Star Restaurants *(continued)*					
North Star Pub	Pub	Mod	82	C	1
Sucelt Coffee Shop	Puerto Rican/ Cuban	Inexp	82	A	4
Zlata Praha	Czech/Slovak	Mod	82	B–	15
Punjab	Indian	Inexp	81	A	5
Cupcake Cafe	American	Inexp	80	A–	8
Sapporo	Japanese	Inexp	78	A	8
Kasturi	Indian	Inexp	75	A–	7
One-and-a-Half-Star Restaurants					
Pastrami King	Deli	Inexp	88	B+	17
Hallo Berlin	German	Inexp	76	B	8

Restaurants by Zone

Name	Star Rating	Price Rating	Quality Rating	Value Rating
Zone 1—Lower Manhattan				
◆ *Italian*				
Rosario's	★★★	Inexp	86	A
◆ *Pub*				
North Star Pub	★★	Mod	82	C
Zone 2—Soho and TriBeCa				
◆ *Eclectic*				
Blue Ribbon	★★★★	Exp	92	C
◆ *Italian*				
Pepe Rosso To Go	★★★½	Inexp	91	A
Zone 3—Chinatown, Little Italy, and Lower East Side				
◆ *Chinese*				
Tindo	★★★★	Mod	92	A
Hop Lee	★★★½	Inexp	90	A
Joe's Shanghai	★★★½	Mod	90	A
Kam Chueh	★★★½	Mod	91	B+
The Nice Restaurant	★★★½	Mod	91	B
New Siu Sam Yuen	★★	Inexp	85	A
◆ *Malaysian*				
Nyonya Malaysian Cuisine	★★½	Mod	83	B+
◆ *Vietnamese*				
New Pasteur	★★★½	Inexp	87	A
Pho Cong Ly	★★½	Inexp	86	A
Zone 4—Greenwich Village				
◆ *American*				
Grange Hall	★★★★	Exp	91	B
◆ *Kosher*				
Chick Chack Chicken	★★★	Inexp	89	A
◆ *Middle Eastern*				
Moustache Pitza	★★★½	Inexp	87	A–

Name	Star Rating	Price Rating	Quality Rating	Value Rating
Zone 4—Greenwich Village *(continued)*				
◆ *Puerto Rican/Cuban*				
Sucelt Coffee Shop	★★	Inexp	82	A
◆ *Southern*				
The Pink Teacup	★★★	Mod	86	C
Zone 5—East Village				
◆ *Eclectic*				
Il Buco	★★★½	Exp	90	C
◆ *Indian*				
Punjab	★★	Inexp	81	A
◆ *Japanese*				
Yakitori Taisho	★★★	Inexp	83	B+
Sapporo East	★★½	Mod	83	A–
◆ *Middle Eastern*				
Moustache Pitza	★★★½	Inexp	87	A–
Sahara East	★★½	Mod	83	B
◆ *Polish*				
Teresa's	★★	Inexp	83	A
◆ *Puerto Rican*				
Casa Adela	★★★	Inexp	90	A
◆ *Spanish/Tapas*				
Xunta	★★★	Inexp	88	B
◆ *Vegetarian*				
Kate's Joint	★★	Mod	83	B
Zone 6—Chelsea West				
◆ *Belgian*				
Petite Abeille	★★½	Inexp	86	A
◆ *Fried*				
Fried World	★★	Inexp	86	A

Restaurants by Zone (continued)

Name	Star Rating	Price Rating	Quality Rating	Value Rating
◆ *Korean*				
Kang Suh	★★½	Mod	84	B
◆ *Thai*				
Chelsea Thai Wholesale	★★	Inexp	87	B
Zone 7—Chelsea East and Gramercy				
◆ *Eclectic*				
City Bakery	★★★	Mod	87	D
◆ *Indian*				
Mavalli Palace	★★★½	Mod	89	A
Kasturi	★★	Inexp	75	A–
◆ *Italian/Pizza*				
La Pizza Fresca	★★★★	Mod	93	A
◆ *Pub*				
Molly's	★★★	Mod	87	B
Zone 8—Midtown West and Theater District				
◆ *American*				
Cupcake Cafe	★★	Inexp	80	A–
◆ *Brazilian*				
Churrascaria Plataforma	★★½	Exp	85	C
Cabana Carioca	★★½	Inexp	84	A
◆ *Chinese*				
Noodle 88	★★	Inexp	83	A
◆ *Deli*				
Mr. Broadway Kosher Deli	★★★½	Mod	87	A
◆ *Dominican*				
El Papasito	★★★½	Inexp	90	A
◆ *German*				
Hallo Berlin	★½	Inexp	76	B

Restaurants by Zone (continued)

Name	Star Rating	Price Rating	Quality Rating	Value Rating
Zone 8—Midtown West and Theater District (continued)				
◆ *Japanese*				
Menchanko-Tei	★★★	Mod	86	B
Sapporo	★★	Inexp	78	A
◆ *Korean*				
Woo Chon	★★★	Exp	88	C
◆ *Latin American*				
Margon Restaurant	★★	Inexp	84	A
◆ *Pakistani*				
Cuisine of Pakistan (a.k.a. Kashmir 9)	★★★	Inexp	87	A
◆ *Peruvian*				
Rinconcito Peruano	★★★½	Inexp	92	A
◆ *Russian*				
Uncle Vanya Cafe	★★½	Mod	85	B
◆ *Soup*				
Soup Kitchen International	★★★½	Inexp	91	A
◆ *Southern*				
Soul Fixins'	★★★	Inexp	88	A
Zone 9—Midtown East				
◆ *Italian*				
Tre Pomodori	★★½	Mod	85	A
◆ *Japanese*				
Hole in One	★★★★½	Very Exp	96	C
Saka Gura	★★★★	Mod	91	B+
Tokyo	★★★½	Exp	92	C
Menchanko-Tei	★★★	Mod	86	B
Zone 10—Upper West Side				
◆ *Dominican*				
Cafe Con Leche	★★½	Inexp	86	B–

Restaurants by Zone (continued)

Name	Star Rating	Price Rating	Quality Rating	Value Rating
◆ Pub				
Teddy's Bar and Grill	★★½	Mod	86	A–
◆ Puerto Rican				
Cuchifritos	★★★	Inexp	88	A
◆ Southern				
Soul Food Kitchen	★★★	Inexp	90	A
◆ Thai				
Thai Cafe	★★½	Mod	84	B–
◆ Yemeni				
Yemen Cafe	★★★½	Inexp	90	A–
Zone 14—Southern Brooklyn				
◆ American				
Brennan and Carr	★★	Inexp	83	B
◆ Chinese/Norwegian/American				
Wee Kee	★★★	Inexp	86	A
◆ Italian/Pizza				
DiFara Pizzeria	★★★★½	Mod	94	A
Joe's Bar and Grill	★★	Inexp	85	A
◆ Italian/Seafood				
Rocco's	★★½	Inexp	83	A
◆ Kosher/Israeli				
Mabat	★★★★	Mod	92	B
Famous Pita	★★★	Inexp	87	A
◆ Lebanese				
Karam Restaurant	★★★★	Inexp	92	A
◆ Moroccan				
Casablanca	★★★★	Inexp	93	A
◆ Pakistani				
Bukhara Restaurant	★★★★	Inexp	92	A

Name	Star Rating	Price Rating	Quality Rating	Value Rating
Zone 14—Southern Brooklyn *(continued)*				
◆ *Slovakian*				
Milan's Restaurant	★★★★	Inexp	92	A
◆ *Southern*				
Gaither's	★★★★	Inexp	92	A
◆ *Turkish*				
Cafe Istanbul	★★★★	Inexp	92	A
Zone 15—Northwestern Queens				
◆ *Afghan*				
Speengar Shish Kebab House	★★★½	Inexp	90	A
◆ *Argentinian*				
La Porteña	★★★★	Mod	91	A
◆ *Barbecue*				
Pearson's Texas Barbecue	★★★	Inexp	88	C
◆ *Brazilian*				
Cantina Brazil	★★★	Inexp	91	A
◆ *Czech/Slovak*				
Zlata Praha	★★	Mod	82	B–
◆ *Egyptian*				
Kabab Cafe	★★★½	Inexp	90	A
◆ *Filipino*				
Ihawan	★★★	Inexp	87	A–
BJ's	★★½	Inexp	84	B
◆ *Greek*				
Stamatis	★★★	Mod	89	B+
◆ *Indian*				
5 Stars Punjabi	★★★★	Inexp	91	A
Jackson Diner	★★★★	Inexp	91	A

Name	Star Rating	Price Rating	Quality Rating	Value Rating
◆ *Italian*				
Piccola Venezia	★★★★	Exp	93	D+
◆ *Mexican*				
La Espiga	★★★½	Inexp	90	A
◆ *Peruvian*				
Pio Pio	★★★	Mod	88	B
◆ *Pub*				
Donovan's	★★★½	Inexp	91	A–
◆ *Romanian*				
Cornel's Place Restaurant	★★★½	Inexp	93	A
◆ *Russian*				
Emerald Spa & Restaurant	★★½	Mod	81	C
◆ *Thai*				
Sripraphai Thai Bakery	★★★½	Inexp	90	A
◆ *Vietnamese*				
Pho Bac	★★★★	Inexp	93	A
Zone 16—Northeastern Queens				
◆ *Chinese*				
Do I Tru	★★★★	Inexp	92	A
Jade Palace	★★★★	Inexp	91	A–
Joe's Shanghai	★★★½	Mod	90	A
Sweet-n-Tart Cafe	★★★	Inexp	91	B–
Happy Buddha	★★★	Inexp	86	A–
White Bear Ice Cream and Wonton Shop	★★½	Inexp	85	A
Fortune Gourmet	★★½	Inexp	84	A
◆ *Korean*				
Healthy Tofu	★★★★	Inexp	93	A
Bo	★★★★	Inexp	92	A
Pa Do Whae House	★★★½	Mod	90	A

Name	Star Rating	Price Rating	Quality Rating	Value Rating
Zone 16—Northeastern Queens *(continued)*				
◆ *Malaysian*				
Penang Cuisine Malaysia	★★★½	Mod	91	A–
◆ *Pub*				
Donovan's	★★★½	Inexp	91	A–
Zone 17 - Southern Queens				
◆ *Central Asian*				
Tadjikstan	★★★★	Inexp	93	A
Uzbekistan Restaurant	★★★	Inexp	88	A
◆ *Deli*				
Pastrami King	★½	Inexp	88	B+
◆ *Guatemalan*				
La Xelaju	★★★★	Inexp	91	A
◆ *Jamaican*				
Wangah Hut	★★★½	Inexp	91	A
Jean's	★★½	Inexp	85	A
◆ *Pizza*				
Nick's Pizza	★★★½	Mod	92	B
◆ *Seafood / Southern*				
Seamorhen II	★★★½	Inexp	91	A
Zone 18—The Bronx				
◆ *Albanian*				
Tony and Tina's Pizzeria	★★★	Inexp	86	A
◆ *American / Seafood*				
The Crab Shanty	★★★	Mod	86	A
◆ *Italian*				
Dominick's	★★★½	Mod	91	B+
◆ *Seafood*				
Johnny's Famous Reef	★★	Mod	84	A

Restaurants by Zone (continued)

Name	Star Rating	Price Rating	Quality Rating	Value Rating
Zone 19—Staten Island				
◆ *German*				
Killmeyer's Old Bavaria Inn	★★★★	Mod	91	B
◆ *Italian/Pizza*				
Denino's	★★★½	Inexp	92	A
Zone 20—Nearby in New Jersey				
◆ *Cuban*				
El Unico	★★★½	Inexp	90	A
◆ *Indian*				
Chowpatty	★★½	Inexp	85	A
◆ *Turkish*				
Kervan	★★★★	Mod	94	B
Zone 21—Nassau County, Long Island				
◆ *Italian/Pizza*				
Umberto's	★★★½	Mod	91	A
◆ *Portuguese*				
Little Portugal	★★★½	Inexp	91	A
Churrasqueira Bairrada	★★★	Mod	89	B

Alex BAR-B.Q.

Barbecue/Puerto Rican	
★★★★	
Inexpensive	
Quality 92	Value A

Zone 13   Northern Brooklyn
56 Broadway, Williamsburg, Brooklyn
(No phone)

Reservations:	Not accepted
When to go:	Weekend early afternoons (the lechon runs out early!)
Kind of service:	Stand at counter or takeout
Entree range:	Sandwiches, $3.25; lechon, $5.50/lb.
Payment:	Cash only
Service rating:	★★
Friendliness rating:	★★
Transit:	J/M to Hewes Street
Bar:	None
Wine selection:	None
Dress:	Casual
Disabled access:	Step up, no rest rooms
Clientele:	Locals, workers
Open:	Everyday, 8 A.M.–11 P.M.

Atmosphere/setting: Alex BAR-B.Q. looks like an anonymous *bodega* (Latin grocery store), but you step inside to Puerto Rican barbecue heaven. Unspeakably cool guys with dangling cigarettes wield their cleavers with the blasé expertise that comes from decades of experience.

House specialties: Pernil (roast pork) sandwiches, lechon (suckling pig) on weekends only, costillas (pork ribs), and cuajo (tripe, best ordered over maduros—sweet plantains—with hot sauce). This is starter tripe with the power to seduce even entrailophobes.

Other recommendations: Despite the red-meat ambience, the barbecued chicken is surprisingly good here . . . but skip rice and beans and other side dishes. As with Texas barbecue, the meat's the thing.

Summary & comments: Dominicans and other recently immigrated Latinos have almost completely replaced Puerto Ricans in the restaurant biz, but Alex BAR-B.Q. is a proud P. R. holdout. The macho chopper/servers are no-nonsense about their important work; don't mistake their terseness for unfriendliness. A pilgrimage to Alex BAR-B.Q. is an awesome experience; pork enthusiasts will shed tears of joy, and even committed vegetarians will be sorely tempted.

Antojitos Mexicanos ⩜⩘

Zone 13   N Brooklyn
105 Graham Avenue,
   Williamsburg, Brooklyn
(718) 384-9076

Mexican	
★★½	
Inexpensive	
Quality 86 Value A	

Reservations:	Not accepted
When to go:	Weekend afternoons
Kind of service:	Waiter service at tables
Entree range:	$3–6
Payment:	Cash only
Service rating:	★★★★
Friendliness rating:	★★½
Transit:	L to Montrose Avenue or J/M to Flushing Avenue
Bar:	None
Wine selection:	None
Dress:	Casual
Disabled access:	Poor; big step up, bathrooms not accessible
Clientele:	Locals, ethnic
Open:	Every day, 8 A.M.–7 P.M.

Atmosphere/setting: Nothing to look at, just a tiny room with a few tables and walls covered with hand-written signs announcing specials. Clientele is mostly Hispanic kids and workers from this interior Williamsburg neighborhood.

House specialties: Goat tacos (tacos de barbacoa de chivo) from heaven, wonderful tostadas and quesadillas, and hard-to-find pambazos. All three kinds of tamales (mole—red, stuffed with pork; verde—green, stuffed with chicken; and rajas—stuffed with cactus) are plump, fresh, and excellent.

Other recommendations: Good beveraging. Try a creamy, not-too-sweet oatmeal drink called avena; it's like a milk shake with just a touch of cinnamon (homemade and so fresh that a thick sediment of creamy oatmeal accumulates on the bottom of the cup). A cereal drink made from rice—horchata—is milky and sweet, a very drinkable rice pudding in a glass. Jamaica, tangy and scarlet-colored from hibiscus, would be refreshing if it were a bit less sweet.

Summary & comments: The goat tacos (weekends only) could inspire poetry; lots of deep goat flavor sings through these brown-edged, toothsome, stewy chunks, and the taco as a whole is so unified in juicy tenderness that it's hard to tell where tortilla ends and goat begins. (Don't forget to doctor all tacos by squeezing lime and spooning excellent green sauce.) When done right, tostadas are more than fried tortillas with stuff piled on, and here they're done right; even the simplest, denoted as *sin carne* and made with only beans, cheese, and cream, have uncommon depths of flavor. Another deceptively simple dish this kitchen makes great: tender, plain quesadillas (pour on hot sauce to catalyze the flavor). Pambazos are a holy grail (see La Espiga review for more info); this is one of only a handful of restaurants that make them. Posole (a hearty soup of pork and large kernels of hominy corn) requires the customary shakes of Mexican oregano and red pepper powder (also add chopped onion and a squirt of lime). Antojitos Mexicanos has another branch with similar menu and ambience at 28 Throop Avenue (phone (718) 384-9812).

Note: Antojitos Mexicanos reserves its best dishes—and best cooking—for Saturdays and Sundays. Culinary catharsis is *not* guaranteed on weekdays.

BEAN

Zone 13   Northern Brooklyn
167 Bedford Avenue (enter around
    corner on North 8th Street),
    Williamsburg, Brooklyn
(718) 387-8222

Mexican
★★½
Inexpensive
Quality 86   Value A

Reservations:	Not accepted
When to go:	Anytime
Kind of service:	Waiter service at tables
Entree range:	$5.95–10.95
Payment:	Cash only
Service rating:	★★
Friendliness rating:	★★★½
Transit:	L to Bedford Avenue
Bar:	None
Wine selection:	None
Dress:	Casual
Disabled access:	Fair; step up, rest rooms not accessible
Clientele:	Local artsy bohemian kids and a surprising number of out-of-neighborhood adults
Open:	Every day, 2–11 P.M.

Atmosphere/setting: Situated on a residential block just around the corner from the thriving Bedford Avenue restaurant row, this colorful little joint looks like a mildly psychedelic roadhouse with mismatched tablecloths and chairs and cheesy hanging lamps that look like they're straight out of an amateur sci-fi film. Music helps set the roadhouse atmosphere; tapes range from Ella Fitzgerald to Patsy Cline.

House specialties: Food is prepared and presented with far more flair than you'd expect from the homespun decor. The sole fancy-sounding concoction—lavishly priced at $10.95—is grilled shrimp and Prince Edward Island mussels in tomatillo chipotle sauce; incongruous with the rest of the snacky menu, it screams "don't order me!" but is actually quite well cooked, with a savory reduced sauce, flawless grilled vegetables, and top-notch creamy mashed potatoes. Quesadillas with spinach and shitakes, served with zesty pico de gallo, are light and very tasty; there are also dairyless yucadillas, moistened with a yucca mash in place of cheese. Baked plantain, filled with moist chunks of chicken and smothered in slightly sharp cheese, is very likeable (and not nearly as gloppy as it sounds), as is the impeccably fresh Caesar salad, which comes nicely dressed but sans anchovies (Williamsburg hippy restaurant Caesar salads *never* have anchovies); it's not at all clear, however, that tortilla chips are an improvement over more traditional croutons. Free-range turkey mole is a perpetual special, and first-rate chunky guacamole is made to order.

Other recommendations: Don't miss terrific juices and lemonades (the latter dosed with lime or blueberry). Dessert fruit cobblers are on tempting display, but they look better than they taste.

Summary & comments: If it's real Mexican you seek, hit Antojitos Mexicanos (see review). Bean is a whole other story: this is hippy-dippy-trippy bohemian café fare disguised as Mexican food. There are other places of this genre around town (though we don't hear much about, say, Benny's Burritos since a decade of heavy immigration has brought more authentic Mexican to Gotham), but few prepare the food so skillfully. This is hardly health food, but Bean uses less meat, less grease, less salt (and, regrettably, less spice . . . apply hot sauce liberally) than real Mexican recipes. Try it if you're in the mood for a relatively healthful meal that's totally delicious in its gringo way.

Bissaleh Classic

Zone 11 Upper East Side	Kosher/Israeli
1435 2nd Avenue, Manhattan	★★★
(212) 717-2333	Moderate
	Quality 87 Value B

Reservations:	Only for groups of 6 or more
When to go:	Anytime
Kind of service:	Waiter service at tables
Entree range:	$6.50–18
Payment:	VISA, MC
Service rating:	★★★
Friendliness rating:	★★★
Transit:	6 to 77th Street
Bar:	Full service
Wine selection:	Extensive kosher
Dress:	Casual, but shorts and short dresses out of place
Disabled access:	Good
Clientele:	Families, Israeli immigrants
Open:	Sunday–Thursday, 10 A.M.–1 A.M.; Saturday, a half-hour past sundown until 2 A.M.; Monday, closed

Atmosphere/setting: High ceilings, wood floors, and walls painted in desert/earth colors with framed pictures of Middle Eastern scenes; in all, a much nicer ambience than you'd expect from the fast food–style à la carte menu and low prices. Long tables make this place great for families.

House specialties: Eggplant or Turkish salads, hummus (chickpea spread), borekas (savory pies in flaky pastry), bissaleh (long pastry pies, like calzones) with potato, malawahs (dense, buttery, multilayered flatbreads), cheese blintzes, fish dishes, smoothies (unsweetened, milkless mixed fruit shakes), mint tea.

Other recommendations: Middle Eastern breakfasts are served all day and include foul madamas ("full madamas" on menu), a garlicky fava bean stew; various blintzes; and omelets—including "Israeli Breakfast," which is an omelet with chopped cucumbers, tomatoes, and sour cream. The freebie rolls (with garlic butter on the side) are almost worth the trip, as is the excellent tomato puree condiment dosed with shrug, a fiery, green spice blend.

Summary & comments: When most people think of Jewish food, they think of Ashkenazi staples like knishes, bagels, and chicken soup. Bissaleh serves the *other* Jewish cuisine, the Yemenite recipes found in Israeli cafes; this kosher cooking recalls Lebanon and Morocco more than Poland or Germany. You'll find, for example, lots of Mediterranean ingredients (lemon, olives, fava beans, eggplant, honey). The menu features delicious flaky pastries (bissaleh, malawah, boreka, and ftut) stuffed or topped with things such as feta cheese, spinach, potato, and mushrooms. "Pizza" is the topping/filling to avoid, but most everything else will please . . . and this meatless dairy kitchen is a dream come true for vegetarians.

BJ's

Zone 15   NW Queens
40-07 69th Street,
   Woodside, Queens
(718) 639-8706

Filipino	
★★½	
Inexpensive	
Quality 84 Value B	

Reservations: Not accepted
When to go: Anytime
Kind of service: Waiter service at tables
Entree range: $4.50–6.50
Payment: Cash only
Service rating: ★★
Friendliness rating: ★★★
Transit: 7 to 69th Street
Bar: None
Wine selection: None
Dress: Casual
Disabled access: Good; rest rooms not accessible
Clientele: Locals
Open: Every day, 10 A.M.–8 P.M.

Atmosphere/setting: A closet-sized space with blasting television and a sparse clientele of Filipinos who look well settled-in. At first you may fear you've intruded upon someone's private kitchen, but the mom-and-pop owners kindly beckon from their alcove stovetop and invite you to be seated at one of a scatter of tables.

House specialties: Pancit (noodles) of great delicacy and richness with strips of tender chicken, chunks of pork, slivers of Chinese sausage, bits of vegetables and—if you ask emphatically—hot peppers. Lumpiang sariwa, kind of like Vietnamese summer rolls, are vegetable crêpes doused with peanut sauce (skip the fried lumpiang, here reminiscent of La Choy frozen spring rolls). Caldo arroz, a hearty rice porridge, is likeable, but best of all is a specialty from the chef's hometown: shrimp in coconut milk with squash, scallions, and green beans. He cooks it on request only, and request you must (and beg him to make it spicy!).

Other recommendations: Avoid beef dishes.

Summary & comments: New Yorkers are growing more and more familiar with Asian cuisines, but Filipino food (a hodgepodge of Chinese, Spanish, Malaysian, Indonesian, Mexican, American, and Indian influences) remains unfamiliar and daunting to most. The chef here has been worn down by outsiders spurning the heat, the sourness, and the fishiness of authentic Filipino cooking, and he will—unless you plead with him not to—tone everything down into bland oblivion. Smile knowingly and beseech him to make it the serious way. Ask for hot peppers in your pancit, and don't stray too far from the suggestions here.

BLUE RibboN

Zone 2   Soho and Tribeca
97 Sullivan Street (between Prince and
    Spring Streets), Manhattan
(212) 274-0404

Eclectic	
★★★★	
Expensive	
Quality 92	Value C

Reservations:	Groups of 5 to 8 only
When to go:	The later the better to miss crowds
Kind of service:	Table and counter seating/service (lots of action at the latter)
Entree range:	$14.50–27 ($75 for paella royale)
Payment:	VISA, MC, AMEX, D, DC, JCB
Service rating:	★★★
Friendliness rating:	★★★
Transit:	C/E to Spring Street
Bar:	Full service
Wine selection:	300–400 selections (featured in *Wine Spectator*)
Dress:	Casual chic
Disabled access:	Fair; one step up, bathrooms OK
Clientele:	Trendy early, hipper later
Open:	Tuesday–Sunday, 4 P.M.–4 A.M.; Monday, closed

Atmosphere/setting: Appearancewise, this is a typical slick-but-boxy Soho bar/restaurant space. The people provide the decoration, and the place is jammed with them until the wee hours of the morning. The nonstop party consists of equal parts restaurant insiders (chefs come here after work), don't-talk-to-me-don't-look-at-me Beautiful People, and late-night hungry hipsters. The combination of interesting clientele, superb food, and smart servers, and the collective conspiratorial glee of everyone's having sniffed out such a great bite at 1 A.M., (good luck getting in much earlier) make the room practically hum with excitement.

House specialties: Fried chicken is second best in the city (after Charles Southern Kitchen All You Can Eat Buffet; see review), with ambrosial collard greens and honest (but perfect) mashed potatoes—real soul food cooked with the nuances and subtleties of a classically trained chef. The menu is a treasure chest of iconoclastic miscellany, from matzo ball soup to beef marrow (with oxtail marmalade), from sweet and spicy catfish to tofu ravioli (even—Lord help us—something called Vegetable K-Bob Pita). Little things impress . . . french fries, for example, are awesome. The raw bar is uniformly excellent, and it mirrors the unpretentious kitchen (the oysters aren't Kumamotos or some other rare, coveted type; they're just Blue Points . . . but some of the best Blue Points ever). Memorable crème brûlée comes with an impeccably crisp glaze capping luscious, ultracomforting custard. Chocolate Bruno, adorned with ice cream from Ciao Bello, is a mousse on a white chocolate crust, the whole drizzled in a great bitter fudge sauce.

Other recommendations: A few menu duds to avoid: paella, whole steamed flounder, and the pupu platter.

Summary & comments: Although reviewed almost to death, this will always be a renegade restaurant. In a town where big-time chefs chase trends and up-and-comers stream out of culinary schools cooking like mindless automatons, it's refreshing to find a chef who doesn't try to plug into the machine, a maverick confident enough to go his own way—and skillful enough to back it up. Chef-owner Eric Bromberg's cooking is effortless; nothing tastes show-offy or preciously clever. He's an iconclast, with the resumé to back it up; so if someone considers a dish like fried chicken and collard greens—prepared with no arch-revisionist nuances, just a supremely deft touch—unfit for the kitchen of a Cordon Bleu instructor (he was the first American to teach there), screw 'em. And the same goes for anyone who'd balk at paying $18.50 for the plate. If quality counts and you're not down to your last nickel, pay the price; it's not often that a $40 meal tastes four times more delicious than the best $10 meal, but Bromberg's touch can't be bought for less.

Note: Nearby Blue Ribbon Sushi (119 Sullivan Street, (212) 343-0404) is just as good, but Blue Ribbon Bakery (33 Bedford Street, (212) 337-0404) is only dependably good for baked stuff.

Bo

Zone 16   Northeastern Queens
59-16 Kissena Boulevard (just north of
    the Long Island Expressway),
    Flushing, Queens
(718) 661-3775

Korean
★★★★
Inexpensive
Quality 92   Value A

Reservations:	Accepted
When to go:	Anytime
Kind of service:	Waiter service at tables
Entree range:	$6.95–10.95
Payment:	Cash only
Service rating:	★★★★★
Friendliness rating:	★★★★★
Transit:	7 to Flushing/Main Street, walk to Kissena, take the 17 or 25/34 bus
Bar:	None
Wine selection:	None
Dress:	Casual
Disabled access:	Good; rest rooms not accessible
Clientele:	Local, ethnic
Lunch:	Monday–Saturday, 11:30 A.M.–3 P.M.; Sunday, closed
Dinner:	Monday–Saturday, 3–10 P.M.

Atmosphere/setting: Chef-owner Maria Cho has made the most of her small space; it's chic and sedate, and the well-spaced tables lend a feeling of roominess. The elegantly minimalist decor is sleek in shades of white and beige.

House specialties: Beef ribs slow-potted for an eternity until meat is meltingly tender and the sauce richly concentrated; delicate potato or mung-bean pancakes. Specials are ace, as are the panchan (appetizer plates of pickles, vegetables, and such).

Summary & comments: Ms. Cho was once the pastry chef at Sign of the Dove but returned to her Korean roots with this small, magical restaurant in a most unlikely neighborhood. This is the only place in New York for real Korean comfort food, the kind of home cooking usually unavailable in restaurants. It's a well-schooled hominess, however; everything's cooked with delicacy, subtlety, and great care. The kitchen is so honest, so genuine and loving, that homesick Koreans journey from far and wide to eat here, and equal numbers of occidentals (many from nearby Queens College) are also fiercely loyal.

BRENNAN AND CARR

Zone 14 Southern Brooklyn	American
34-32 Nostrand Avenue (at Avenue U),	★★
Sheepshead Bay, Brooklyn	Inexpensive
(718) 769-1254	Quality 83 Value B

Reservations:	Not accepted
When to go:	Anytime
Kind of service:	Waiter service at tables
Entree range:	$2.95–9.25
Payment:	Cash only
Service rating:	★★½
Friendliness rating:	★★½
Transit:	D to Avenue U
Bar:	Beer only
Wine selection:	None
Dress:	Casual
Disabled access:	Good; narrow rest-room door
Clientele:	Local
Lunch/Dinner:	Sunday–Thursday, 11 A.M.–1 A.M.; Friday and Saturday, 11 A.M.–2 A.M.

Atmosphere/setting: Outside: a cross between an alpine ski lodge and a log cabin; be on the lookout for grizzly bears heading up Nostrand Avenue. Inside: a woody hunter's cabin with fireplace and mounted elk horns. Frank Sinatra is singing on the jukebox, and all three beer taps pour Bud.

House specialties: Hot beef, either as a platter (with french fries and a vegetable, e.g., a huge mound of bright orange carrots) or as a sandwich, accompanied by a large helping of broth for pouring and/or dunking.

Other recommendations: All other offerings (burgers, franks) are mere decoration.

Summary & comments: This quirky Brooklyn landmark, in operation since 1938, figured out long ago what it does best and doesn't fool around much with lesser stuff. It's tough to say whether Brennan and Carr's "hot beef" (a.k.a. roast beef) is of such an entirely different class from all others as to deserve its own sobriquet, but there's no denying that it's damned good: extra thin slices of perfectly cooked, utterly unfatty meat that offers nothing for even the pickiest eater to discard.

Bukhara Restaurant

Zone 14 Southern Brooklyn	Pakistani
1095 Coney Island Avenue (between	★★★★
Glenwood and Avenue H),	Inexpensive
Midwood, Brooklyn	Quality 92 Value A
(718) 859-8033	

Reservations:	Not accepted
When to go:	Anytime
Kind of service:	Order at counter, waiter brings dishes
Entree range:	$3–10
Payment:	Cash only
Service rating:	★★½
Friendliness rating:	★★★½
Transit:	D to Avenue H
Bar:	None
Wine selection:	None
Dress:	Casual
Disabled access:	With assistance
Clientele:	White-collar Pakistanis
Open:	Every day, 11:30 A.M.–1 A.M.

Atmosphere/setting: It feels as if this stark, noisy restaurant sprung up here overnight. Third World decor notwithstanding, the affable clientele is middle class (lots of suits and cell phones) and savvy enough to skip the zillions of inferior restaurants nearby. With its utter lack of decoration, its easy to miss Bukhara's scrupulous cleanliness; servers apologize and immediately wash their hands if they so much as cough.

House specialties: The sign in the window pledges "the best chicken tikka in town," and they aren't kidding; these kebabs, marinated to a bright yellow hue and charcoal broiled, are positively heavenly with brown, smoky-crunchy edges and assertively spicy, juicy interiors (be sure to squeeze lemon over them). The lentil dal is so cannily seasoned that it's impossible to pick out individual flavors. Eggplant pakora (batter fried), though starkly unseasoned, captures the very soul of eggplant. Kofta kebab, made from very spicy ground meat, is recommended, as are the creamy pickle curries. Aloo paratha, a potato bread made in the tandoori oven, is spicier and coarser than that made in Indian restaurants; it bursts with concentrated earthy potato flavor. Even plain old nan bread—studded with sesame seeds—is extra tasty (rice is available but everyone opts for bread). Daily specials may include gorgeous, juicy, roasted chicken legs; pilaf-like mounds of meat-studded rice; or several curries, such as goat (slow cooked for hours, very simple, very elemental, and very, very delicious) or potato (also long stewed, with blistering orange peppers, until the perfect texture is attained).

Other recommendations: A full range of sweets, brightly colored, exotically flavored, and amply perfumed, as per tradition.

Summary & comments: Many Indo-Pak restaurants line this strip of Coney Island Avenue, but Bukhara—serving Punjabi Pakistani cuisine—stands way above the competition (a nearby sweet shop also called Bukhara is not recommended, so be careful not to confuse them). There are menus floating around the restaurant, but they're barely legible copies-of-copies-of-copies and don't mention specials. The best way to order is to bring your companions en masse to the counter to view dishes and order from harried—but ever-polite—countermen (their English is good and everything is clearly displayed) who will send the meal to your table. Prices are shockingly low and food is without exception fresh and transporting, so any trepidations about this intimidating locale should be overcome in the interest of great food.

Unsolvable Restaurant Mystery: Why does this neighborhood have not one but two Pakistani restaurants bearing the name of a city hundreds of miles from Pakistan?

Cabana Carioca

Zone 8   Midtown
    West and Theater District
123 West 45th Street (between 6th and
    7th Avenues), Manhattan
(212) 581-8088

Brazilian
★★½
Inexpensive

Quality 84   Value A

Reservations:	Not accepted for lunch; dinner for 4 or more
When to go:	Lunch for buffet, dinner for bar specials
Kind of service:	Table and bar service
Entree range:	$4.99–18.95
Payment:	VISA, MC, AMEX, D, DC, JCB; cash only at bar
Service rating:	★★★
Friendliness rating:	★★
Transit:	B/D/F/Q to 47–50 Streets/Rockefeller Center or N/R/S/1/2/3/7/9 to 42nd Street/Times Square
Bar:	Full service
Wine selection:	Small
Dress:	Casual
Disabled access:	Fair
Clientele:	Businesspeople at lunch; tourists, theater workers, ethnic at dinner.
Lunch:	Every day, 11:30 A.M.–3 P.M. (first floor); Monday–Friday, 11:30 A.M.–2:30 P.M. (third floor)
Dinner:	Monday–Thursday, 3–11 P.M.; Friday and Saturday, 3 P.M.–midnight; Sunday, 3–10 P.M.

Atmosphere/setting: Service is offered on three floors connected by steep steps painted in garish Happy Colors. With tables close together and sound levels high, this is not the place for lingering or romance. Management tries for a fun, colorful, tropical look, but it's been a while since the last makeover and things are starting to get just a tad seedy at the edges. Don't look too closely, just enjoy.

House specialties: The best bar special is roast chicken, broiled crunchy with tons of garlic. Like all of Carioca's bar specials, it's ringed by fried potatoes and served with excellent black beans and rice, all for about $5 or $6 (for good measure, the price includes unlimited salad bar). At lunch there's an amazing all-you-can-eat buffet where less than $10 (price varies by floor) buys you unlimited access to a large array of meat, salad, and vegetable dishes, as well as desserts; come early—the steam tables are less frequently replenished later on. The Brazilian national dish of feijoada is not recommended here; for a good one, check out Cantina Brasil (see review).

Other recommendations: Other good bar specials include caldo verdhe, a potato and kale soup with a slice of intense chorizo sausage; a huge mound of garlicky-spicy baby shrimp gumbo (not really gumbo, but tasty); and an equally garlicky marinated shell steak (tenderized, but, at $8, clearly not a superior cut). The homemade hot sauce is vinegary and terrific (shake the bottle), and don't forget to spoon farofa (toasted yucca flour) over the beans.

Summary & comments: Cabana Carioca is like 1980s Frank Sinatra: a pale shadow of its former self but still more than getting by on personality. I only eat at the bar counters (or the nearby bar area tables) for good, flavorful, fast, and ultracheap meals that will keep me going for hours, if not days. The bar-only specials are immense, sturdy eats, none costing more than $8, but bargain hunters should beware of drinks: ordering beer or cocktails will almost double your tab (although they do make good caipirinhas—Brazilian cocktails of distilled sugar cane and tons of limes). Dining in the main rooms costs twice as much, and while choices are wider there, quality can be spotty. In either case, come before 7 P.M. to miss the crowds; weekday lunches are mobbed but turnover is fast.

Numerological oddity: One of the world's most mnemonic addresses: 1-2-3 West 4-5 Street between 6-7 Avenues . . . and you ate (8) there.

CAfE CON LEche

Zone 10   Upper West Side
424 Amsterdam Avenue (between 80th
    and 81st Streets), Manhattan
(212) 595-7000

Dominican	
★★½	
Inexpensive	
Quality 86	Value B–

Reservations:	Accepted Monday–Wednesday only
When to go:	Anytime (especially bargain weekday lunch specials)
Kind of service:	Waiter service at tables
Entree range:	$4.95–25.95
Payment:	AMEX, VISA, MC
Service rating:	★★
Friendliness rating:	★★
Transit:	1/9 to 79th Street
Bar:	Full service
Wine selection:	Limited
Dress:	Casual
Disabled access:	Fair; small step up; rest rooms not accessible
Clientele:	Locals
Breakfast:	Every day, 8–11 A.M.
Lunch:	Every day, 11 A.M.–4 P.M.
Dinner:	Monday–Thursday, 4–11 P.M.; Friday–Sunday, 4 P.M.–midnight

Atmosphere/setting: This sunny café looks like any old joint from outside, but the interior is a pleasant surprise: pizazzy updated coffee shop with a colorful, tropical look (carnival masks, silver trim on bright yellow walls).

House specialties: The pernil asado (roast pork) is intense, amazingly rich stuff; delicious, revisionist chicharrones de pollo (chunks of on-the-bone chicken) are herbacious and expertly deep fried with a batter that's more St. Louis than San Juan. Black bean soup is awesome with good crunchy onions, and sancocho (a ubiquitous thick Dominican soup), often a special, is even better—an intense, golden-brown broth, clearly the product of long, careful cooking, with lovingly cooked root vegetables and a few chunks of pork. Beans and rice served in appealing decorative bowls are quite good (the rice is *never* dry here), and both tostones (starchy green plantains) and maduros (sweet ripe plantains) are skillfully fried.

Other recommendations: The condiments almost steal the show; there's a sensational hot sauce with incendiary flecks of black, green, and red and an innocent-looking, thick white dressing that looks like sour cream but is actually potent garlic sauce . . . great on bread toasts. Not all the clever touches work: surprisingly light and greaseless mofungo (fried mash of plantains, pork, and garlic) comes with a fatally overwrought gravy, and the Cuban sandwiches taste too cleaned up—not compressed-greasy-garlicky enough for the flavors to come together.

Summary & comments: Cafe con Leche is the diametrical opposite of those trendy new pan-Latino fusion places. The latter tend to start with four million dollars and a publicist and try to graft Latino flavors onto the kitchen's carefully designed Product. Cafe con Leche has solid Dominican coffee-shop credentials: the salsa music is what the staff wants to hear, not "Latin atmosphere"; the roast pork is rich and garlicky, and they shmoosh the bread slices when they toast them. Their innovative touches—that frothy puree of a garlic sauce replacing the standard emulsion of garlic chunks and oil—have grown organically from serious tradition.

There's a second Cafe con Leche further up Amsterdam Avenue (at 726 Amsterdam), but it's nowhere near as good.

Cafe Istanbul

Zone 14 Southern Brooklyn	Turkish
1715 Emmons Avenue (between	★★★★
Sheepshead Bay Road and East 16th	Inexpensive
Street), Sheepshead Bay, Brooklyn	Quality 92 Value A
(718) 368-3587	

Reservations:	On weekends or for large groups
When to go:	Anytime
Kind of service:	Waiter service at tables
Entree range:	$4–9.50
Payment:	Cash only
Service rating:	★★★★
Friendliness rating:	★★★★½
Transit:	D/Q to Sheepshead Bay
Bar:	None
Wine selection:	None
Dress:	Nice casual
Disabled access:	Good; rest rooms not accessible
Clientele:	Locals and Turkish families
Open:	Every day, 11 A.M.–11 P.M.

Atmosphere/setting: A tiny cafe with an ocean view, beautiful tiled floors, several comfortable tables, and one intimate, lavishly carpeted, Turkish-style booth.

House specialties: Much of the menu consists of small bread and pastry concoctions baked in the brick oven, such as boreks (unbelievably delicious flaky pastry pies stuffed with herby spinach, black-peppery ground meat, or challengingly funky feta cheese), lahmacun (pies baked with a topping of spiced minced meat—lamb, not beef as the menu incorrectly states), and chicken cacik (a puffier, shinier bread topped with aromatic, spicy chopped chicken). Pide, a pizzalike dough, comes with toppings such as pastirma (also known as basturma), a paper-thin dried beef that melts in your mouth; it embraces the accompanying kashar cheese in a way that pepperoni can only dream of bonding with mozzarella. Non-bread items include terrific patlican salatasi (chunky eggplant salad with plenty of garlic, onion, tomato . . . and no tahini), hummus (chickpea spread dusted with sumac and dosed with yogurt for extra creaminess), and stuffed grape leaves. There's a great off-menu dessert of caramelized pastry fingers filled with milk custard and sprinkled with ground pistachios, as well as excellent baklava (best ordered with some luxurious kunefe—brick oven–baked cheese). Everything's good here; order without fear.

Other recommendations: One thing, however, needs to be ordered with just a bit of fear: salgam suyu, a most bizarre red, slightly salty, very tart woody drink, tastes like sour cherries. It's actually carrot juice doctored with special spices.

Summary & comments: While some dishes here are very traditional, many are original and unique creations. The tricky recipes fool you by masking and morphing flavors: chicken cacik is most un-chickeny, lamb on the lahmacun has been mellowed through deft spicing, and the carrot juice doesn't taste anything like carrots. The recipes are also extremely well honed; the kitchen really knows how to use their brick oven (many places have one, but very few have thoroughly mastered its use); and the friendly management and servers love to guide newcomers through the unique (and consistently tasty) menu. This is a must-eat.

Cambodian Cuisine

Zone 13   Northern Brooklyn
87 South Elliot Place (between Lafayette
   Avenue and Fulton Street),
   Fort Greene, Brooklyn
(718) 858-3262

Cambodian	
★★★½	
Inexpensive	
Quality 90 Value A	

Reservations:	Not accepted
When to go:	Anytime
Kind of service:	Waiter service at tables
Entree range:	$6–14
Payment:	MC, VISA
Service rating:	★★★
Friendliness rating:	★★★½
Transit:	G to Fulton Street or 4 to Atlantic Avenue
Bar:	None
Wine selection:	None
Dress:	Casual
Disabled access:	Good
Clientele:	Locals, occasional questing chowhounds
Lunch/Dinner:	Sunday–Tuesday, 11 A.M.–10:30 P.M.;
	Wednesday–Saturday, 11 A.M.–11 P.M.

Atmosphere/setting: Located on one side of a triangular plaza, this modest space exudes a sweet peacefulness that originates with the family that runs it. Tidy tables are neatly topped with blue and green tablecloths, and a scatter of Cambodian travel posters decorate the pastel-colored walls.

House specialties: Everyone uses "you sunk my battleship"–style numbers in lieu of hard-to-pronounce dish names. R16: a beautifully fried fish doused in luxurious, pungent sauce with sweet basil, galangal, and lemon grass (order extra rice to absorb every drop of sauce). N9: an exotic sweet-and-sour mélange of nine ingredients with crispy rice noodles. N19: Cambodian curry over vermicelli with seafood, a delicious elemental preparation heavy on coconut, turmeric, and basil, with french fries a surprising addition to the tangle of fresh seafood. C27: S.E.A. ground chicken with lemon sauce is zestfully spiced with lemon and tangy lemon grass, piled high with coriander sprigs and sprouts, and studded with small, smoky microchunks of chicken. It's so light that the mouth hardly realizes it's ingesting. S8, S10, and S12: various presentations of fried whole tilapia fish cooked to flaky perfection. S14: a very spicy, limey shrimp soup with mushrooms and fish balls. C17: chicken ahmok, an otherworldly diśk of chopped chicken floating in a memorable sauce of lemon grass, coconut, chili, and Thai lime leaves. SP6m and SP7: wonderfully satisfying bawbaws—rice broths like Chinese congee only sharper.

Other recommendations: The chef makes some Chinese dishes, but he doesn't quite play straight. Check out N4—very spicy, meltingly tender rice noodles with Chinese vegetables and more of those smoky, ground chicken chunks; this is his souped-up version of chicken chow fun.

Summary & comments: This place started out as a cheap neighborhood Chinese/Cambodian noodle shop. Management has added more and more purely Cambodian dishes, but budget-minded regulars won't support the price increases necessary for use of top ingredients. So don't expect prime meat or free-range chicken; this place squeezes every drop of goodness out of supermarket provisions. Nonetheless, the appealing and rare Cambodian touch (the cuisine is light like Vietnamese but as fiery and flavorful—if not quite as complex—as Thai) is tonic for jaded palates. Servers vary in their mastery of English, but they'll do their best to guide you through the extensive (but well-translated) menu.

Cantina Brazil

CAUTION

Zone 15   NW Queens
31-90 30th Street
  (near Broadway), Astoria, Queens
(718) 204-0303

Brazilian	
★★★	
Inexpensive	
Quality 91	Value A

Reservations:	Not accepted
When to go:	Saturdays; come early for feijoada (or phone ahead to reserve your order)
Kind of service:	Self-service (mostly takeout)
Entree range:	$7–13
Payment:	Cash only
Service rating:	★★★
Friendliness rating:	★★★★
Transit:	N to Broadway
Bar:	None
Wine selection:	None
Dress:	Casual
Disabled access:	Poor; no steps, but tiny and cramped
Clientele:	Local Brazilians
Lunch/Dinner:	Wednesday–Sunday, 11 A.M.–6:30 P.M.; Monday and Tuesday, closed

Atmosphere/setting: This microscopic kitchen can barely be called a restaurant; there are two tables with two chairs each, all crammed between take-out counter and door. Good Brazilian background music, extremely sweet mom-and-pop management, and stellar feijoada more than make up for an utter lack of standard restaurant niceties.

House specialties: Feijoada (Saturdays only).

Other recommendations: Great desserts such as yucca cake, various puddings, and incredible caramel banana coffee cake.

Entertainment & amenities: The lilting Portuguese cadences of the many Brazilians stopping by for takeout.

Summary & comments: During the week, Cantina Brazil serves utilitarian lunches (beef stew, white beans and tripe, chicken with okra) for the increasing number of Brazilian immigrants living in Astoria. Nothing's particularly Brazilian or particularly tasty, though a $7 lunch of sturdy, home-cooked food certainly has its attractions. But every Saturday this place turns into a luminous star on the New York food scene. Only on this traditional day for cooking Brazil's national dish can you enjoy the best feijoada in town. Feijoada is a black bean stew with all manner of meats and sausages thrown in, much of which dissolves into the tarry black murk, yielding a supremely flavorful, frightfully heavy dish requiring months of hibernation to digest. Feijoada is served with farofa (toasted yucca flour that absorbs liquid), rice, shredded collard greens, and orange segments. The version at Cantina Brazil can be quibbled with: they use no carne seca (dried meat, a customary ingredient), and the black beans are the larger American kind rather than the smaller Brazilian variety. But grandmotherly chef Lina Santanna is the only NYC feijoada chef who manages to coax the stew's myriad ingredients into utterly seamless marriage. Get it to go if you must (you're only a block from the N train, and feijoada travels well), but use any means necessary to experience this masterful—it would rate respectably even in Rio—rendition.

Casa Adela

Zone 5   East Village
66 Avenue C (between 4th and
    5th Streets), Manhattan
(212) 473-1882

Puerto Rican	
★★★	
Inexpensive	
Quality 90 Value A	

Reservations:	Not accepted
When to go:	Anytime (rough neighborhood after dark)
Kind of service:	Table and counter seating/service
Entree range:	$6.50–8
Payment:	Cash only
Service rating:	★★
Friendliness rating:	★½
Transit:	F to 2nd Avenue
Bar:	None
Wine selection:	None
Dress:	Casual
Disabled access:	Good; rest rooms not accessible
Clientele:	Artsy/political locals
Open:	Every day, 7 A.M.–8 P.M.

Atmosphere/setting: A tidy kitchen in a proud neighborhood. One avenue east of quickly gentrifying Avenue B, this block is still solidly Puerto Rican with few yuppie intrusions. Adela, well-respected here in Loisaida (Latino slang for "Lower East Side"), displays the work of local artists on her walls, and the Puerto Rican flag hangs proudly against the back wall.

House specialties: Amazing mofungo (a fried ball of mashed plantains, pork, and garlic), pernil (roast pork), yucca (stewed with tons of mojo, a garlic sauce), rice and beans, tostones (fried starchy plantains with garlic sauce), and bacalao (cod stew). Adela's mondongo (tripe soup) has inspired songs. As in many Latin restaurants, the most and best stuff is served weekends.

Summary & comments: Everything here is cooked *abuelita* (grandma) style, and those whose experience with the cuisine comes from harsh rice-'n'-bean slinging luncheonettes or watered-down, fusion chic-aterias will be amazed at the softness of the cooking, the nourishing wholesomeness of the beans, the rich garlickiness of the yucca. Adela Fargas is an activist who does a lot of good for the neighborhood, and her restaurant is a local landmark. Newcomers may be received a bit frostily, but after a couple of visits you're one of the family.

Casablanca

Zone 14 Southern Brooklyn	**Moroccan**
6744 5th Avenue (near 68th Street),	★★★★
Bay Ridge, Brooklyn	Inexpensive
(718) 491-0105	Quality 93 Value A

Reservations:	Accepted but usually not necessary
When to go:	Anytime
Kind of service:	Waiter service at tables
Entree range:	$7–10
Payment:	MC, VISA, DC
Service rating:	★★½
Friendliness rating:	★★★★½
Transit:	R to Bay Ridge Avenue
Bar:	None (and BYO is not permitted)
Wine selection:	None
Dress:	Casual
Disabled access:	Good; step up to rest room
Clientele:	Moroccan immigrants, locals
Open:	Every day, 11:30 A.M.–11 P.M.

Atmosphere/setting: Samovars, scabbards, and Islamic-green walls festooned with knicknacks and ceramics in this mirage of Morocco lend a colorfully Moorish flavor to an otherwise drab block. Owner Nacer El Makhloufi is a sincere, friendly man who makes visitors feel welcome whether they are seated in the comfortable indoor dining room or outdoors in the small garden. The clientele is a good mix of Moroccans and Westerners.

House specialties: Bastilla is a famous Moroccan delicacy unable to decide whether it's entree or dessert: chopped chicken well-marinated in yellow aromatic spices along with nuts and herbs is stuffed into flaky pastry, baked, and served with a dusting of powdered sugar and cinnamon. Casablanca gets this difficult dish precisely right (skip the seafood version, though). Couscous is tasty and comforting, if not terribly exciting (zing it up with hot sauce); more intriguing are the tagines—ultracomplex and refined stews such as rich, broad-flavored chicken and olives or sweetish lamb with okra and prunes. The best appetizer is Moroccan salad, a platter of good marinated carrots, pickled beets, potato chunks, and a dash of green salad. Kebab-wise, the inexpensive brochettes are fine but best ordered to accompany more enticing dishes. Cow foot may fail to entice skittish diners, but this is a great version. Some of the best items are sweets, so don't pass on dessert (best: macaroons and chobbakia, a sweet, sesame-studded fried dough confection with a caramelized nutty glaze). Close with mint tea served in the traditional samovar and made aromatic by orange blossoms.

Other recommendations: Call a day ahead to order beghrir and rghif— buttery crêpes drizzled with delicate orange blossom–scented honey . . . they're stupendous.

Entertainment & amenities: Management plays excellent folk recordings from back home (ask to hear the Berber tapes) rather than the pan-Arabic pop played in other Middle Eastern spots.

Summary & comments: Casablanca is staunchly traditional (don't even think of bringing in alcohol or of asking for unsweetened tea) yet warmly welcomes outsiders. No other area Moroccan restaurant comes close for authenticity, deliciousness, or value; despite the remote location, it's a must-visit.

Castro's Coffee Shop

Zone 13   Northern Brooklyn
511 Myrtle Avenue (between Grand and
    Ryerson Streets), Fort Greene,
    Brooklyn
(718) 398-1459

Mexican	
★★★½	
Inexpensive	
Quality 91 Value A	

Reservations:	Not accepted
When to go:	Anytime
Kind of service:	Table and counter seating/service
Entree range:	$5–10.95
Payment:	Cash only
Service rating:	★★½
Friendliness rating:	★★★
Transit:	G to Washington Avenue
Bar:	Beer only
Wine selection:	None
Dress:	Casual
Disabled access:	Good, rest rooms not accessible
Clientele:	Locals
Breakfast:	Every day, 7–11 A.M.
Lunch/Dinner:	Every day, 11 A.M.–10 P.M.

Atmosphere/setting: The most generic-looking taqueria imaginable; appearances betray nary a clue to the culinary brilliance that awaits you.

House specialties: The mole poblano is among New York's best. Its extremely complex sauce (tasting more of chocolate than most) miraculously doesn't obscure the roast chicken flavor. Burritos are tenderly wrapped and filled with impeccably moist meat and good sharp cheese; the roast pork is tender; the guacamole unbelievably fresh and delicate. Barbecued goat tacos contain good-gamey goat meat (be sure to squirt limes). The refried beans manage creamy, silken richness without the use of lard; most platters come with the beans as well as plump tasty rice. Even the pico de gallo offered gratis with chips is unusually sprightly and perfectly balanced.

Other recommendations: While fancier platter dishes (like steak ranchero, pipian con pollo, pepper steak, and mole poblano) are uncommonly well-prepared, you will also want to try street-food items like chiles rellenos, sopes (oblong thick tortillas spread with beans and topped with cheese, cream, and—optionally—meat), and gorditas (fat, stuffed tortillas).

Summary & comments: Castro's is undistinguishable from ten thousand similar Mexican joints; both ambience and menu are totally deja food. The difference is all in the chef, whose deft touch and big heart transcend the formulaic, culminating in food so above the norm that you'll be plotting your return visit before the check arrives. The key is balance; time and care are taken to ensure that flavors blend harmoniously. One result of the glorious balance pervading all cooking here: the spiciness never obtrudes.

Charles Southern Kitchen All You Can Eat Buffet

	Southern
	★★★★½
Zone 12 Harlem, Morningside	Inexpensive
Heights, and Washington Heights	Quality 97 Value A
2837 8th Avenue (between 151st and	
152nd Streets), Manhattan	
(212) 926-4313	

Reservations:	Not accepted
When to go:	Anytime
Kind of service:	Self-service
Entree range:	$10, fixed price; $11, includes drink with refill
Payment:	Cash only
Service rating:	★★★
Friendliness rating:	★★★★
Transit:	3 to Harlem/148th Street or C/D to 155th Street
Bar:	None
Wine selection:	None
Dress:	Casual
Disabled access:	Good; small step for takeout
Clientele:	Local
Buffet:	Monday, closed; Tuesday–Thursday, 1–11 P.M.; Friday, 1 P.M.–midnight; Saturday, 4 P.M.–midnight; Sunday, 1–8 P.M.
Take-Out Window:	Monday, 6 P.M.–midnight; Tuesday–Friday, 1 P.M.–3 A.M.; Saturday, 4 P.M.–3 A.M.; Sunday, 1–8 P.M.

Atmosphere/setting: This block is becoming a fiefdom, dominated by various Charles-related ventures. The northernmost store, not yet open, has uncertain destiny in the Charles empire. Immediately to the south lies the takeout stand, with a queue of hungry customers constantly crowding its small vestibule. Southernmost (appropriately enough) is the buffet restaurant, boxy and simple/institutional but very well run. Friendly servers carefully maintain an impeccably spotless buffet full of whatever's cooking next door. Seating is not particularly comfortable, music is Smooth Jazz from a boombox, but you won't have much time to settle in, anyway, since management asks that diners restrict their stay to thirty minutes at peak hours.

House specialties: Salmon cakes so light they float; crusty, juicy fried chicken that would turn any southern grandmother green with envy; tender oxtail in a sauce of unfathomable depth; earthy black-eyed peas; melt-in-your-mouth collard greens; and fish fried with wise, deft simplicity.

Other recommendations: If Charles cooks it, I recommend it. The buffet isn't quite as fresh as the takeout (truth be told, Charles' stratospheric quality rating is most deserved by the latter), and the overstuffed $7 dinners amount to all you can eat anyhow, so you may want to opt for a meal to go (Charles' food travels very well).

Summary & comments: Charles Gambriel, New York's greatest soul food chef, spent years motoring around Harlem in his Mobile Soul Food Kitchen, an ice cream truck retrofitted for pork chops and corn bread. He sold many hundreds of lunches a day, saving up to open this stationary location. Those of us who remember him from his truck period have been gratified to see Charles hit the big time, with crowds (mostly local) thronging his restaurant and the press writing glowing reviews (although reporting has unfortunately focused on his astonishingly good fried chicken to the exclusion of other similarly brilliant offerings). This is a rough neighborhood, but Charles' place is an oasis; staff and customers alike are warm and friendly. Nobody nasty eats at Charles'; and if they did, they wouldn't stay nasty for long.

Chelsea Thai Wholesale

◆ CAUTION

Zone 6   Chelsea West
75 West 15th Street (between
    9th and 10th Avenues), Manhattan
(212) 924-2999

	Thai
	★★
	Inexpensive
	Quality 87 Value B

Reservations:	Not accepted
When to go:	When shopping in Chelsea Market
Kind of service:	Self-service
Entree range:	$6.75–8.25
Payment:	Cash only
Service rating:	★½
Friendliness rating:	★★
Transit:	1/2/3/9/A/C/E to 14th Street
Bar:	None
Wine selection:	None
Dress:	Casual
Disabled access:	Good; rest rooms not accessible
Clientele:	Hungry shoppers
Lunch/Dinner:	Monday–Saturday, 11 A.M.–8 P.M.; Sunday, till 6

Atmosphere/setting: There's an open kitchen in front and a small Thai grocery toward the rear of this minimalist spot inside wholesale-chic Chelsea Market. The cooks are cool young Thai kids in bandanas, and the surroundings are equally hip: wood floors, saffron walls, gleaming metallic light fixtures hung from high ceilings with ductwork painted in primary colors. There are a few informal tables and chairs but most opt for takeout or delivery.

House specialties: One thing and one thing only: chicken lemongrass. Perhaps some rice as well.

Other recommendations: Nope!

Entertainment & amenities: If you buy Thai provisions here, the cooks will demonstrate their use.

Summary & comments: Chelsea Thai seems at first to have the makings for the perfect get-away-from-it-all lunch; informal market dining is a pleasure greatly lacking in New York, and this scene has great potential. But the chow, for the most part, is nowhere near as cool as the ambience. Noodle dishes are poorly balanced, salads are prepackaged, and the menu is a minefield of clunkers. Spare yourself pain and go for the sole toothsome offering: lemongrass chicken— beautifully grilled juicy meat and well-seasoned crunchy skin strewn with crunchy nubs of seared garlic. Grab dessert at the nearby Ronnybrook Farm ice cream shop.

Chick Chack Chicken

Kosher
★★★
Inexpensive

Quality 89   Value A

Zone 4   Greenwich Village
121 University Place, Manhattan
(212) 228-3100; (212) 228-3102

Reservations:	Not accepted
When to go:	Anytime (chicken freshest at lunchtime)
Kind of service:	Self-service
Entree range:	$3.29–6.99
Payment:	VISA, MC, AMEX
Service rating:	★★★
Friendliness rating:	★★★
Transit:	L/N/R/4/5/6 to 14th Street/Union Square
Bar:	None
Wine selection:	None
Dress:	Casual
Disabled access:	Good
Clientele:	Local workers
Lunch/Dinner:	Sunday–Thursday, 11 A.M.–10 P.M.; Friday, 11 A.M. till 2 hours before sundown; Saturday, closed

Atmosphere/setting: A small, wedge-shaped space containing a few tables and a stand-'n'-scarf counter. The atmosphere—punctuated by crackling hot coals and permeated with the scent of wood smoke and spinning, roasting chickens—easily compensates for the merely functional decor.

House specialties: Rotisserie chicken, mashed potatoes, kasha varnichkes (oniony buckwheat groats with bow-tie pasta), potato pancakes—all glatt kosher.

Entertainment & amenities: They deliver.

Summary & comments: This place turns out some of the best charcoal-fired marinated chicken in town, and their mashed potatoes (Jewish-style, with lots of chicken fat) are tops as well. Kasha varnichkes are properly soulful. Eating in is a pleasant but utilitarian experience; many prefer to get takeout. Either way, this kid-friendly establishment is the only great quick meal in the area (hit nearby City Bakery—see review—for dessert).

Chowpatty

Zone 20   Nearby in New Jersey
809 Newark Avenue (near Kennedy
    Avenue), Jersey City
(201) 222-1818

Reservations:	Not accepted
When to go:	Anytime
Kind of service:	Waiter service at tables
Entree range:	$6–13
Payment:	VISA, MC ($20 minimum)
Service rating:	★★½
Friendliness rating:	★★½
Transit:	PATH Train to Journal Square Station
Bar:	None
Wine selection:	None
Dress:	Casual
Disabled access:	Good
Clientele:	Gujarati families
Lunch/Dinner:	Tuesday–Sunday, 11:15 A.M.–8:30 P.M.;
	Monday, closed

Atmosphere/setting: Large, modern, and brightly lit Chowpatty looks like a bakery as you enter—display cases groaning with all manner of gaily colored Indian desserts and snacks. Lots of takeout is ordered here, but there are plenty of tables in an adjoining room, usually filled with Indian families. The shiny, noisy ambience doesn't lend itself to relaxed lingering; even dinner-hour meals feel like lunch. Bring the kids.

House specialties: A full menu of Gujarati snacks featuring crazy mixtures of unlikely ingredients (see Summary & comments, below), plus thalis (decorative metal pans containing assorted snacks), dosai (lentil crêpes filled with oniony mashed potatoes), iddly (fluffy lentil cakes), and uthappam (a spongy pancake, sort of like Indian pizza). There are also good, creamy ice creams (kulfis), tandoori breads, and multicolored, aromatic sweets.

Other recommendations: All manner of crunchy snacks are sold by the pound up front (kids will go nuts); servers offer samples. Try before you buy, as few things taste like they look!

Summary & comments: The most interesting *chat* (snacks) are outrageous hodgepodges of ingredients you'd never have imagined together; they taste as if an Indian toddler decided to make lunch. The ingredients themselves are familiar enough—like samosas (fried potato and pea or meat turnovers), chutneys, those crunchy fried pea snacks you see in Asian foodstores, and potato croquettes. But when two or more of the above are mixed with gravy, onions, noodles, yogurt, sprouts, beans, and pickles, the result is something else again. It takes getting used to (especially since most of us are accustomed to more austere Indian cuisine), but if approached with an open mind, the intense flavor mélanges can become addictive. Dosai, thalis, uthappam, breads, and sweets are all available elsewhere (though rarely as good), so it's these weird concoctions that make Chowpatty worth the trip. The restaurant is located on an amazing street full of Gujurati and South Indian shops and restaurants that make for a great afternoon shopping/eating excursion.

Churrascaria Plataforma

Zone 8   Midtown West and
   Theater District
316 West 49th Street, Manhattan
(212) 245-0505

Brazilian	
★★½	
Expensive	
Quality 85	Value C

Reservations: Required (preferably a few days in advance)
When to go: Anytime
Kind of service: Waiters and self-service food bar
Entree range: Prix fixe $27.50 for dinner, $25 for lunch; chil-
                       dren under 5 years, free; children 5–10 years,
                       half price
Payment: VISA, MC, AMEX, DC
Service rating: ★½
Friendliness rating: ★½
Transit: C/E to 50th Street
Bar: Full service
Wine selection: Decent
Dress: Casual
Disabled access: Rest rooms not accessible
Clientele: Tourists, rabid carnivores
Lunch: Every day, noon–4 P.M.
Dinner: Every day, 4 P.M.–midnight

Atmosphere/setting: An enormous space, dominated by a monster central
salad bar. The place is brightly lit with refined, understated decor, but amid all the
swirling meat and return trips to the salad bar, there's far too much action to pay
much attention to surroundings. Sound level is high at peak times. Desserts and
cocktails are dispensed by beautiful young waitresses wheeling carts.

House specialties: All-you-can-eat meat with all the trimmings (including
Brazilian salad—and other food—bar and good fried stuff). The best cuts by far
are picanha (top sirloin, always the most prized meat in a proper radizio) and
costelas de boi, beef ribs so gargantuan that they must be wheeled to the table. It's
best to specially request both from one of the skewer guys.

Other recommendations: Caipirinhas are the traditional accompaniment;
they're a cocktail of cachaça (a spirit similar to rum) and lots of fresh lime. As in
Brazil, you can have them made with passion fruit for an extra tropical flavor.

Entertainment & amenities: Live Brazilian music Wednesday through Sunday nights.

Summary & comments: *Rodizio* is a Brazilian tradition that entails a dizzy-
ing array of roast meats brought to your table by skewer-bearing waiters. It's all
very ritualized in Brazil, and this is the only one of a rash of city rodizios that

observes all the rituals (it's also the only one that's Brazilian-owned and operated). You're served the traditional plates of fried yucca, french fries, batter-fried bananas, and particularly good fried polenta. Management hopes you'll fill up on this cheap stuff and at the extensive salad/food bar (vegetarians will be more than sated: tons of salads, vegetables, and even a few entrees like shrimp moqueca, a peppery stew with coconut milk), but savvy diners hold out for the meat. Pace yourself carefully as more than a dozen cuts come around; as with dim sum, you must learn to just say no. The best thing of all doesn't come unless you ask for it, though: unbelievably delicious black beans made with specially imported small, silky beans (spoon farofa—garlicky toasted yucca flour—over them). If all the meat doesn't give you a coronary, the service will: confused and incompetent waiters take their cue from the managers, who pompously stroll through in their suits, scanning the room for trouble spots and summarily ignoring your desperate pleas for service, dessert, or the check. Bad service also extends to the reservations line . . . call three times for three different answers regarding table availability.

Churrasqueira
Bairrada

CAUTION

	Portuguese
	★★★
	Moderate
	Quality 89 Value B

Zone 21   Nassau County,
Long Island
144 Jericho Turnpike (at Willis Avenue),
Mineola, Long Island
(516) 877-1857

Reservations:	Not accepted
When to go:	Weekends, for leitao
Kind of service:	Waiters and self-service food bar
Entree range:	$12–20 (for rodizio)
Payment:	AMEX, MC, VISA, DC
Service rating:	★★★
Friendliness rating:	★★★
Transit:	Taxi from Long Island Railroad Mineola Station
Bar:	Full service
Wine selection:	Portuguese
Dress:	Casual
Disabled access:	Good
Clientele:	Locals
Lunch/Dinner:	Tuesday–Sunday, 11:30 A.M.–10:30 P.M.; Monday, closed

Atmosphere/setting: It's so crowded here—there's almost always a wait—that you'll hardly notice the decor in this corner location, right on the main thoroughfare in Portuguese Mineola. That's OK—there's not that much to see. This is neither posh nor a hole-in-the-wall; it's a dead medium, decoratively neutral spot for serious eating. It's warmly lit and great for families.

House specialties: Leitao (roast suckling pig, weekends only) and frango assado (roast chicken) are the things to get (see details, below).

Other recommendations: If you can't resist the rodizio deal (complete with massive salad bar), you'll dine pleasantly if not memorably.

Summary & comments: Though the two are very different, many people confuse Portuguese and Brazilian cultures. Shrugging their shoulders, the management of Churrasqueira Bairrada, formerly a traditional Portuguese barbecue place, smelled a business opportunity and decided to ride the trendy wave of Brazilian rodizio. Their $20 all-the-meat-you-can-eat rodizio's pretty good (though Manhattan's Churrascaria Plataforma—see review—does it better), but the really great things are still the traditional Portuguese barbecue items hidden on a menu most customers overlook. The leitao (roast suckling pig) is the best item offered here. Bairrada—the city in Portugal—has more leitao restaurants than Brooklyn has pizzerias. These places make world-famous baby oinkers crunchy of skin and succulently moist of meat with tons of black pepper and a wham of garlic. The owners of Churrasqueira Bairrada are from there, and their leitao is very much in this tradition. Also, the Portuguese have a rare touch with roast chicken, and frango assado is magnificently marinated and full of spicy, smoky flavor from the wood fire.

City Bakery

Zone 7 Chelsea East and
    Gramercy
22 East 17th Street (between Union
    Square and 5th Avenue), Manhattan
(212) 366-1414

	Eclectic
	★★★
	Moderate
	Quality 87 Value D

Reservations:	Not accepted
When to go:	Anytime (lunches half price after 5 P.M.)
Kind of service:	Self-service
Entree range:	$3.25–7.50; salad bar, $8.50/lb.
Payment:	AMEX, VISA, MC
Service rating:	★★½
Friendliness rating:	★
Transit:	L/N/R/4/5/6 to 14th Street/Union Square
Bar:	None
Wine selection:	None
Dress:	Casual
Disabled access:	Good; rest room not accessible
Clientele:	Local workers, chocoholics
Breakfast/Lunch:	Monday–Saturday, 7:30 A.M.–6 P.M.; Sunday, closed

Atmosphere/setting: Quite modern, expensively minimalist design, with rather dramatic lighting for a bakery. There's seating at chic little tables.

House specialties: City Bakery's homemade granola in vanilla milk (great all-natural Ronnybrook Farm milk that's been permeated with vanilla beans) is one of the most delicious quick breakfasts ever. Other than that, stray to non-baked items only if you're one of those disciplined types who needs to suffer through a meal (here, decent but overpriced soups and shmancy salads that rarely live up to their mouth-watering names are the fare in this category) in order to earn dessert. But, oh, what dessert. This is the place to try those fancy little tarts that elsewhere are pretentious frilly nothings; here, it's all more rewarding to eat than to look at. Don't be afraid to try goofy-sounding offerings like Milkyway tart—nothing clunks. Wintertimes, there's a revolving assortment of flavored hot chocolates made with the finest chocolate, including a mind-bendingly luscious version dosed with hot pepper.

Summary & comments: City Bakery is expensive, yes, but for pastries this wonderful the price is a bargain (the food itself becomes a much better deal after 5 P.M. when remainders are marked down to half price). If you go, stop afterward at the great farmer's market in nearby Union Square Park where some of the city's top chefs shop. There you can buy bottles of Ronnybrook Farm milk (their chocolate and coffee milks are particularly good), as well as all sorts of produce.

CONO & SON O'PESCATORE RESTAURANT

Zone 13   N Brooklyn
301 Graham Avenue (near Ainslie Street),
   Williamsburg, Brooklyn
(718) 388-0168

Italian	
★★★½	
Expensive	
Quality 90 Value B−	

Reservations:	Parties of 6 or more
When to go:	Family friendly early, more formal later; weekends crowded
Kind of service:	Waiter service at tables
Entree range:	$11.50–22.95
Payment:	AMEX, VISA, MC, DC
Service rating:	★★★★½
Friendliness rating:	★★★
Transit:	L to Graham Avenue
Bar:	Full service
Wine selection:	Good Italian selections
Dress:	Nice casual to dressy
Disabled access:	Good
Clientele:	Pinkie rings, families, couples (later)
Lunch/Dinner:	Sunday–Thursday, 11 A.M.–11 P.M.; Friday and Saturday, 11 A.M.–midnight; Monday, closed

Atmosphere/setting: Old-fashioned classy Brooklyn Italian with nice linens, a "romantic" grotto, career waiters, the works. The open kitchen is a model of spotless efficiency. Weekends bustle, but it's a good kind of bustle.

House specialties: Perfectly grilled portobello mushrooms; zesty, garlicky pasta fagioli; charry-topped stuffed artichokes; linguini à la Cono with a great mild fish sauce; fettucine, cavatelli, or ravioli (all three are homemade) in pomodoro sauce; gnocci with meat sauce; stuffed squid; tornido di pesci (a huge pile of clams, shrimp, squid, mussels, whiting, and sole on a snowy blanket of rice with a mellow tomato sauce); sweet fennel sausage; spaghetti with white clam sauce; seafood oreganata; broccoli rabe; escarole; Italian-style cheesecake.

Other recommendations: Cono's makes some of the best hot heroes in Brooklyn, but you can only order them at a separate takeout window. Especially good: calamari with hot sauce, potato and egg, and chicken, veal, or eggplant parmigiana. Optionally, they'll add in some broccoli rabe or prepare the whole hero on garlic bread.

Summary & comments: This may be the finest Italian restaurant in town, and it's more traditional than many places even in Naples. While the cuisine has changed greatly in the last few decades, this kitchen offers a snapshot of Neapolitan cooking a half-century ago. Olive oil, now ubiquitous, is a fairly new arrival to the region, and this kitchen still uses the more traditional salt pork for a lusty, deep flavor. The many sauces are stunning, with no two alike. Stick with seafood (pristinely fresh), and avoid veal chop preparations (sliced veal's better) and Northern dishes such as fettucine alfredo.

CORNEL'S PLACE
RESTAURANT

CAUTION

Zone 15   NW Queens
41-04 Greenpoint Avenue
  (between 41st and 42nd Streets),
  Long Island City, Queens
(718) 786-7894

Romanian	
★★★½	
Inexpensive	
Quality 93	Value A

Reservations:	Parties of 5 or more
When to go:	Anytime
Kind of service:	Waiter service at tables
Entree range:	$5–10
Payment:	Cash only
Service rating:	★★★½
Friendliness rating:	★★★★
Transit:	7 to 40th Street
Bar:	None
Wine selection:	None
Dress:	Casual
Disabled access:	Good; rest rooms not accessible
Clientele:	Old Romanian guys
Open:	Every day, 11:30 A.M.–10 P.M.

Atmosphere/setting: A cozy little coffee shop/restaurant, tidy and welcoming. Pains have been taken to make the place appear less overtly ethnic, but the fact that nearly all customers are chatting in Romanian quickly gives it away. It's easier to find seating than it looks; lonely older Romanian guys hang out all day drinking coffee and will gladly double up at other tables so new arrivals can eat.

House specialties: Soulful stuffed cabbage (with filling that's light and fresh, wrapped in slightly sour cabbage), mamaliga (a thick corn mush that accompanies most specials—and beats the pants off any pricey Manhattan polenta); pork goulash (featuring smoky, deep-flavored meat in a lusty sauce that soaks happily into the accompanying mamaliga); fat, meaty, and juicy grilled Romanian sausages; simple, charming soups (especially the incredible beetless borscht made from sour fermented rye bread).

Other recommendations: For dessert, try papanasi, freshly made doughnuts bathed in apricot preserves. Another option: grab dessert down the block at Nita's European Bakery (40-10 Greenpoint Avenue, 784-4047), which bakes the best Romanian pastries (choose from the topmost shelf in the center of the display case).

Summary & comments: Romanian food is squarely in the Eastern European mold. It ain't sprightly, spicy cooking; this is sturdy, comforting stuff. And Cornel's, a landmark in this increasingly Romanian neighborhood, cooks the real deal. The menu describes only middle-of-the-road American fare (fried fish, for one thing, is actually quite decent), but opt instead for the off-menu specials (described above) of true home-cooked Romanian soul food.

The Crab Shanty

	American/Seafood
Zone 18 The Bronx	★★★
361 City Island Avenue (near Tier Street), City Island, the Bronx	Moderate
(718) 885-1810	Quality 86 Value A

Reservations:	Accepted
When to go:	Lunch
Kind of service:	Waiter service at tables
Entree range:	Lunches, $6.95–14.95; dinners cost much more
Payment:	VISA, MC, AMEX, D, DC, JCB
Service rating:	★★★
Friendliness rating:	★★★
Transit:	6 to Pelham Bay, then take the 29 bus
Bar:	Full service
Wine selection:	Limited
Dress:	Casual
Disabled access:	Good
Clientele:	Tourists at dinner, locals at lunch
Lunch:	Monday–Saturday, 11:30 A.M.–4 P.M.; Sunday, 11:30 A.M.–3 P.M.
Dinner:	Monday–Thursday, 4 P.M.–1:30 A.M.; Friday and Saturday, 4 P.M.–2:30 A.M.; Sunday, 3 P.M.–1:30 A.M.

Atmosphere/setting: A huge thatched cottage facade occupies one wall, and the over-the-top seaside shanty theme is carried further with white picket fences, ceiling fans, and *Gilligan's Island*–style chairs. Cozy booths are separated by stained glass windows depicting happy swimming fish, and giant philodendrons hang everywhere. By day there's a real New England family fish dive feeling; at night, border lights and colored spotlights create a more grown-up atmosphere. There's a summery dining tent in back with plastic tables and AstroTurf.

House specialties: Sensational lunch specials, each including soup or salad, pasta or potato, garlic bread, coffee, and dessert. The fish is uniformly fresh and—for the most part—expertly cooked; get the excellent fried clams or choose from the special fish-of-the-day menu, which lists choices like bluefish, redfish, tilapia, catfish, and sole available fried, broiled, or "Cajun-style" (the latter—rubbed down with some mild spices—doesn't try to be very authentically Cajun, which is probably just as well). The Fisherman's Lunch presents a combination of either broiled or fried things; broiled is better, with a generous portion of scallops, mussels, clams, shrimp, and sole, all tender and garlicky with moist bread crumbs baked in (one drawback: tenderness may edge slightly toward mushiness on a bite or two since it's hard to time combo plates). Get clam chowder (so-so broth but very nice clams) rather than blah salad, and french fries (frozen but OK) or baked potato rather than linguine (a definite pass, like all preparations bearing the icky commercial tomato sauce). Garlic bread dusted with parmesan cheese is awesome, and even at these prices the kindly servers will bring a second helping. Desserts are not made on the premises, but carrot cake with luscious cream cheese frosting is primo.

Other recommendations: Barbecued chicken and ribs, fried chicken, and various heroes for landlubbers (again, skip anything with red sauce), plus a nice kid's menu.

Summary & comments: While this is a stellar $10 lunch bargain in a touristy area known for mediocre clip-joints, dinner prices are much steeper . . . but still a great value for City Island.

Cuchifritos

Zone 13   Northern Brooklyn
293 Broadway (near Marcy Avenue),
   Williamsburg, Brooklyn
(No phone)

	Puerto Rican
	★★★
	Inexpensive
	Quality 88 Value A

Reservations:	Not accepted
When to go:	Anytime
Kind of service:	Waiter service at counter
Entree range:	$3–6
Payment:	Cash only
Service rating:	★★½
Friendliness rating:	★
Transit:	J/M to Marcy Avenue
Bar:	None
Wine selection:	None
Dress:	Casual
Disabled access:	Good
Clientele:	Local, musicians (late)
Open:	Every day, 24 hours

Atmosphere/setting: A glaringly lit, spotlessly clean lunch counter with myriad meats and fried stuff displayed in the window, and a long, long formica bar with spinning stools. There's lots of commotion with people dashing in and out for bites at all hours of the day and night.

House specialties: Alcapurrias (banana-meat croquettes), bacalaitos (codfish fritters), papas or platanos rellenas (potatoes or plantains stuffed with spicy meat), roast chicken, costillas (ribs), chicharrones (pork rinds), pernil (roast pork), chicken fricassee (with great rice and beans), mofungo (fried mash of plantains, pork, and garlic), chorizo (pork sausage), morcilla (blood sausage), mondongo (tripe soup).

Other recommendations: Myriad fruit drinks slosh away in a bank of fountains. One of the most interesting is ajonjolí, a sweet beverage made from sesame seeds.

Summary & comments: Cuchifritos places offer traditional Puerto Rican fast food—not terribly healthy, mostly fried snacks served quick and cheap. The style's gotten a bad reputation from restaurants serving greasy, ancient-tasting stuff to an undiscerning clientele, but this spot is a noble exception. Humble though it seems, this under-the-subway, nameless, phoneless place is revered by Puerto Rican chowhounds all over the city for spic and span hygiene and delicious, truly homestyle victuals (even more ambitious dishes like roast chicken, rarely advisable in lowlier cuchifritos kitchens, are worthy). Little English is spoken, but the terse counter guys don't want to talk much anyway. Point at things or check out the age-old menu painted on the wall, and get down to some serious eating. Gringos may be charged a slight premium, but no sweat; you'll still have to work very hard to spend more than a ten spot.

Cuchifritos/Fritura

Zone 12   Harlem, Morningside
    Heights, and Washington Heights
168 East 116th Street (between 3rd and
    Lexington Avenues), Manhattan
(No phone)

Puerto Rican
★★★½
Inexpensive

Quality 90   Value A

Reservations:	Not accepted
When to go:	Anytime (the neighborhood's rough at night)
Kind of service:	Waiter service at counter
Entree range:	$3–7
Payment:	Cash only
Service rating:	★★★
Friendliness rating:	★★
Transit:	6 to 116 Street
Bar:	None
Wine selection:	None
Dress:	Casual
Disabled access:	Good; rest rooms not accessible
Clientele:	Locals
Lunch/Dinner:	Sunday–Thursday, 9 A.M.–3 A.M.; Friday and Saturday 9 A.M.–6 A.M.

Atmosphere/setting: While East Harlem—one of the city's last bastions of Puerto Rican culture—has been turning more and more Mexican in recent years, this block of East 116th Street remains more salsa than mariachi. Any old-time Puerto Rican neighborhood has its anonymous late-night, ultracheap cuchifritos joint with bright lighting, no-nonsense servers, formica counter seating, and a window piled high with soul food. But this is one of the city's best. And people know about it; hungry crowds queue up at all hours.

House specialties: Everything's impressive. Here's an overview: rotisserie chicken, fried chicken, barbecued spare ribs, chicharrones (pork rinds), chicharrones de pollo (little bits of sautéed chicken), pasteles (Puerto Rican tamales), mofungo (fried compressed ball of mashed plantains, pork, and garlic bits), fried maduros or tostones (sweet or green plantains, respectively), sublimely smooth, oniony yucca (a rich tuber something like a yam). The ajonjolí (a sesame drink, one of several sloshing in a row of fountains) is sensational, as are small snacky items like bacalaitos (codfish fritters), papas or platanos rellenas (potatoes or plantains stuffed with spicy ground beef), and alcapurrias (green plantain croquettes stuffed with spicy ground beef). Ask for mojo (garlic sauce) or hot sauce for dipping.

Cuchifritos/Fritura *(continued)*

Other recommendations: Real hard-core cuchifritos include things like lengua (tongue), oreja (pig ear), cuajo (stomach), and morcilla (blood sausage), all cut up with scissors and served unadorned.

Summary & comments: Cuchifritos joints used to dot the city; they served immigrant Puerto Rican workers comfort food from back home at prices they could afford. Decades of assimilation later, there's less of a market for this kind of down-home cooking, and there are only a handful of such places left. This is a great one; prices remain shockingly low—four bucks buys a feast—and the cooking is superb, especially the barbecued chicken. This bird is cooked with no overtly Caribbean touches; it's the kind of scrumptious golden brown rotisserie chicken so hard to find nowadays. It comes with yucca, which by contrast is purely Latino—permeated with garlic and sweet onions and cooked to the point where teeth glide effortlessly through rich, moist tuber. As with all cuchifritos places, the most intimidating stuff (fried pork skins the size of bicycle wheels and various unidentified frying objects) is displayed in the window, so skittish eaters are encouraged to show fortitude. The menu's not as varied as at Cuchifritos in Williamsburg (see review), but the countermen here are more egalitarian about serving gringos and the chicken and ajonjolí are better.

Cuisine of Pakistan
(a.k.a. Kashmir 9)

Zone 8   Midtown West/Theater Dist.
478 9th Avenue (between 36th and 37th
   Streets), Manhattan
(212) 736-7745

Pakistani	
★★★	
Inexpensive	
Quality 87	Value A

Reservations:	Not accepted
When to go:	Go for the lunch special
Kind of service:	Self-service
Entree range:	$4–6
Payment:	Cash only
Service rating:	★★½
Friendliness rating:	★★★
Transit:	A/B/C/D/2/3/4 to 34th street
Bar:	None
Wine selection:	None
Dress:	Casual
Disabled access:	Good; rest room not accessible
Clientele:	Indo-Pak cab drivers, local workers
Lunch:	Every day, noon–4 P.M.
Dinner:	Every day, 4 P.M.–5 A.M.

Atmosphere/setting: Fluorescently lit, sparklingly clean self-service cafeteria. As a separate concession, a clerk sells Pakistani music in his glassed-in corner booth.

House specialties: While aloo bhujia (potato stew) and haleem (meat and lentils stewed for eternity) are the two standouts, neither is available every day. But there are myriad other delicious stewy things and an ever-changing assortment of sturdy concoctions like chicken and spinach (with tender chicken retaining a surprising amount of its flavor) and at least two bean dishes (definitely choose the yellow dal, made from tiny yellow lentils; it's blazingly hot, ferociously garlicky, and swooningly scrumptious), and some spicy (beef) sausage or perhaps roast chicken. Rich and spicy, it's satisfying cold weather sustenance.

Summary & comments: Check out this underappreciated Midtown spot for the tastiest, heartiest Pakistani cooking in the borough. It makes for a nice change of pace for those bored with the standard Indo-Pak food; this purebred Pakistani cooking is accessible (for those who can stand the heat) yet noticeably different from the Bangladeshi fare served elsewhere. Don't sweat the lack of menus; a well-mannered waiter presides over point-out-your-order steam tables, and preparations are simple ingredient-wise. Bear in mind, though: This ain't lean cuisine; plenty of oil is used in the cooking.

Cupcake Cafe

	American
	★★
	Inexpensive
	Quality 80 Value A−

Zone 8   Midtown West and
  Theater District
522 9th Avenue (corner of 39th Street),
  Manhattan
(212) 465-1530

Reservations:	Not accepted
When to go:	Breakfast
Kind of service:	Self-service
Entree range:	Soups/salads $2.25–3.50
Payment:	Cash only
Service rating:	★★½
Friendliness rating:	★★
Transit:	A/C/E to 42nd Street/Port Authority
Bar:	None
Wine selection:	None
Dress:	Casual
Disabled access:	Fair; step up
Clientele:	Locals
Breakfast/Lunch:	Monday–Friday, 7 A.M.–7 P.M.; Saturday, 8 A.M.–7 P.M.; Sunday, 9 A.M.–5 P.M.

Atmosphere/setting: Humble Midwestern small town–style bakery/coffee shop located a few short blocks from the bus terminal. Service could be friendlier, but bear in mind you're not *really* in the Midwest.

House specialties: Those namesake cupcakes are very nice; sweetly old-fashioned and decorated to a T. Also, excellent doughnuts and cakes, very good coffeecakes and muffins, and worthy soups (with terrific bread) and salads, plus fresh waffles on weekends only.

Other recommendations: This is the place for custom-ordered birthday and other occasion cakes. They taste as good as they look (especially if you like buttercream).

Summary & comments: Dorothy told Toto "We're not in Kansas anymore," but a bite here will transport you in the opposite direction: step off of Ninth Avenue and enjoy breakfast or lunch in Topeka. No four million dollar designer was hired to evoke this theme, so it feels natural. This is the perfect place to read your newspaper, sip your coffee, and be left pretty much alone.

David's Brisket House

CAUTION

Zone 13   N Brooklyn
533 Nostrand Avenue (between
    Fulton Street and Atlantic Avenue),
    Crown Heights, Brooklyn
(718) 783-6109

Deli
★★★½
Inexpensive
Quality 93   Value A

Reservations:	Not accepted
When to go:	Anytime
Kind of service:	Waiter service at counter
Entree range:	Sandwiches, $6
Payment:	Cash only
Service rating:	★★
Friendliness rating:	★★
Transit:	A/C to Nostrand Avenue
Bar:	None
Wine selection:	None
Dress:	Casual
Disabled access:	Good; rest rooms not accessible
Clientele:	Locals
Breakfast/Lunch:	Monday–Friday, 6 A.M.–5:30 P.M.; Saturday, 6 A.M.–5 P.M.; Sunday, closed

Atmosphere/setting: This reggae sun-splashed West Indian nabe is no place for a Jewish deli, and David's Brisket House couldn't possibly look less like one. To all appearances, it's a no-frills luncheonette with Caribbean staff and clientele, counter seating, and steam tables in the window—exactly like a thousand other such joints. If this was ever actually a Jewish deli, there are no visible traces left.

House specialties: Incredible, mind-blowingly great brisket sandwiches (best ordered on a roll with gravy). Nearly as good: intense, almost challengingly strong and rich pastrami and mild, ultratender corned beef sandwiches. All are masterfully hand-sliced.

Other recommendations: There's coffee shop–style breakfasts and steam table blue plates; none of it even remotely deli-like. Don't even think of ordering anything but sandwiches.

Summary & comments: David's Brisket House is one of New York's biggest food mysteries. Who are these guys, and where did they learn to slice meat like this? My speculation is that the slicers must have worked as kids at some long gone Lower East Side deli where they trained with the old guys. I've never mustered the courage to ask; folks here aren't exactly hostile, but sullenness is the rule.

It must be tough for them to be so sadly unappreciated by the vast majority of their customers—locals who order stuff like french toast or soup, oblivious to the magnificence that lurks just a few lines down the menu. Only the price hints at the worth of this place's secret treasure: while most things cost pennies, the blessed sandwiches fetch (and properly so) a relatively astronomical $6.

DENINO'S

Zone 19   Staten Island
524 Port Richmond Avenue
    (near Hooker Place), Staten Island
(718) 442-9401

Italian/Pizza	
★★★½	
Inexpensive	
Quality 92 Value A	

Reservations:	Not accepted
When to go:	Off hours
Kind of service:	Waiter service at tables
Entree range:	$3.75–15
Payment:	Cash only
Service rating:	★★½
Friendliness rating:	★★½
Transit:	Ferry to 46 or 40 bus
Bar:	Full service
Wine selection:	Very limited
Dress:	Casual
Disabled access:	Good
Clientele:	Pizza pilgrims from all over
Lunch/Dinner:	Sunday–Thursday, 11:30 A.M.–11:15 P.M.; Friday and Saturday, 11:30–12:15 A.M.

Atmosphere/setting: The neighborhood looks like 1950s upstate New York, and Denino's interior seems even more so. The beige-paneled, boxy room has a dismal bar area up front, and a crop of slightly cheerier tables beckon in the dining room to the rear. Things are not nearly as Schenectady as they seem, however; check out the bartender's state-of-the-art touch-screen ordering system.

House specialties: The most lauded rendition of Staten Island–style pizza: pies on the smallish side with delectable cracker-crisp crust and subtly spiced, mellow—that is, not very acidic—sauce. No slices are served, as it would be disrespectful to subdivide such landmark pizzas.

Other recommendations: Perhaps refering to their proximity to gigantic Fresh Kills Landfill, Denino's offers a "garbage pie" festooned with all the meat toppings. Also available are a few standard appetizers (fried calamari, fried shrimp, mozzarella sticks, scungili, buffalo wings) and some heroes (meatball, chicken, shrimp, or sausage parmigiana). For dessert, head across the street to legendary Ralph's Italian Ices.

Entertainment & amenities: There's a pool table.

Summary & comments: Just like the place itself, the pizza here presents a deceptively low-profile appearance. But it's a breed apart from that served in the other four boroughs. The sauce is spiked with a carefully chosen array of

117

seasonings in such subtle quantities that their effect is nearly subliminal. The crust is magnificently crisp without the cheap trick of rubbing oil into the bottom of the dough. And the cheese is neither the gluey standard nor buttery premium mozzarella; it takes a middle road, calling little attention to itself, contributing selflessly to a superbly balanced pie. If the restaurant's mobbed (as is often the case on weekends), you might try nearby Jimmy Mack's (280 Watchouge Road, (718) 983-6715), where a former Denino's chef serves up pizzas of a similar style (unlike Denino's, Jimmy Mack's also offers an extensive non-pizza menu).

DiFara Pizzeria

Zone 14   Southern Brooklyn
1424 Avenue J (near East 15th Street),
  Midwood, Brooklyn
(718) 258-1367

Italian/Pizza
★★★★½
Moderate

Quality 94   Value A

Reservations:	Not accepted
When to go:	Every chance you get
Kind of service:	Self-service
Entree range:	$7–12
Payment:	Cash only
Service rating:	★★½
Friendliness rating:	★★★½
Transit:	D to Avenue J
Bar:	None
Wine selection:	None
Dress:	Casual
Disabled access:	Poor; step up; rest rooms difficult
Clientele:	Locals, all on a first-name basis with the owner
Open:	Every day, 11 A.M.–10 P.M.

Atmosphere/setting: This early 1960s–style Brooklyn neighborhood pizza parlor has seen better days. The beige wall paneling is beginning to curl, fluorescent fixtures throb overhead, and the linoleum floor tiles have grown crooked. You eat at long, industrial, junior high art project–type tables beneath faded posters showing Italy as it looked two generations ago; scratchy Italian opera blasts from the kitchen. Sit here a few minutes and you'll be drawn back in time. And you'll begin to notice that everywhere you look there are crates of impressively ripe tomatoes; the place is practically bursting with them.

House specialties: Pizzas, both round and Sicilian, are made from real sauce, cheese, and crust, sacred artifacts from the days when slices had personality. Pastas—the spaghetti marinara is a great choice—are served in oversized bowls, properly al dente with incredible garlic-studded sauce made from all those fresh tomatoes. Heroes (the usual: sausage and peppers, meatball parmigiana, etc.) are nothing short of ideal, served on crusty, ultrafresh Italian bread with good cheese and that amazing sauce, and by the time you get to the entrees (veal or chicken scaloppini, shrimp marinara, scungili, lasagna, and manicotti) you'll be wondering whether you've just found the restaurant of your dreams.

Other recommendations: Look for specials like slices of fresh artichoke pizza; the artichoke leaves have been carefully sautéed with garlic to precisely the right point; it is to your standard "veggie" artichoke pizza what a Chopin

DiFara Pizzeria *(continued)*

Nocturne is to an advertising jingle. While six bucks may seem a bit high for salad here (Owner Domenico De Marco apologizes to customers for the price), it's a lavish affair, brimming with chunks of fresh mozzarella, various lettuces, hothouse tomatos, and a nice balsamic vinegar dressing.

Summary & comments: Those tomato crates piled up in the narrow passage back to the kitchen . . . and under the counter . . . and over by the window are from the Orchard, a mega-premium produce store at 1367 Coney Island Avenue. They're transformed into one of New York's great tomato sauces: a restrained, low-profile masterpiece of optimal acidity and spicing bolstered by a goodly shake of black pepper. Like everything here, it's delicious in a magically old-fashioned way. Mr. De Marco doesn't like modern shortcuts. "To me," he says, "a drink in a plastic cup doesn't taste as good as one in glass." Since 1963, this humble artisan has quietly practiced his craft (his son now handles kitchen orders). De Marco is a hold-out, Brooklyn's last proud neighborhood pizza baker, and each bite is a small historical event.

Do I Tru

<CAUTION>

Zone 16   NE Queens
41-28 Main Street (entrance
    on 41st Road), Flushing, Queens
(718) 445-1770; (718) 445-1761

Chinese	
★★★★	
Inexpensive	
Quality 92 Value A	

Reservations:	Large groups only
When to go:	Anytime (weekend mornings for Taiwanese breakfast)
Kind of service:	Waiter service at tables
Entree range:	$5.95–14.95
Payment:	Cash only
Service rating:	★★★
Friendliness rating:	★★
Transit:	7 to Flushing/Main Street
Bar:	Beer only
Wine selection:	None
Dress:	Casual
Disabled access:	Not accessible
Clientele:	Local Chinese
Breakfast:	Saturday and Sunday, 9 A.M.–3 P.M.
Lunch/Dinner:	Every day, 11 A.M.–10 P.M.

Atmosphere/setting: Shiny and modern, most of the large round tables are equipped with lazy susans; customers come in big groups to try lots of dishes.

House specialties: Few people realize that Shanghai has a bread-baking tradition; the big round loaves of baked-to-order bread here are multilayered with scallions mixed into the dough and sesame seeds studding the deep golden crust. Dunk this incredible manna in the brown sauce that accompanies succulent pork ribs or in the spicy, rich duck blood and tripe. Also don't miss salt-baked shrimp, jellyfish in sesame oil, and sensational drunken crab (cooked by marination in rice wine).

Other recommendations: Weekend mornings only, a special dumpling chef turns out some of the best fried pork dumplings ever (the meltingly crisp skin is left open on the ends to allow dipping sauce to penetrate), melt-in-your-mouth vegetable dumplings, pastry turnip buns (with lard in the dough for extra flakiness), and fried chive buns (with small chunks of tofu and tangles of noodles mixed in with the chopped greens). Start off with a Taiwanese breakfast bowl of soybean milk, traditionally ordered with long skinny fried crullers and flatbread (wrap folded-together crullers in the bread for a starchy sandwich). There are two soybean milks to choose from: sweet and not sweet (definitely opt for the latter).

DO I TRU *(continued)*

Summary & comments: Chung King (who—for obvious reasons—prefers the nickname Kim), the manager of Do I Tru, has been the driving force behind a number of Flushing's most highly regarded restaurants. He's an affable, savvy fellow who loves to recommend dishes to intrepid outsiders. Since waiters speak scant English and the menu is largely untranslated, you're going to need some assistance (the staff does understand the English names for the above items, however). This is definitely not a place for beginners, but enduring some rigors has its rewards: extremely undiluted cooking, and a toothsome combination of Taiwanese and Shanghai styles. If you come for weekend breakfast, arrive by 11 A.M. to be sure the dumplings haven't run out.

Dominick's

Zone 18   The Bronx
2335 Arthur Avenue (south of East 187th
    Street), the Bronx
(718) 733-2807

Italian
★★★½
Moderate

Quality 91   Value B+

Reservations:	Not accepted
When to go:	Weekday lunches and off hours to avoid hellish waits
Kind of service:	Waiter service at tables
Entree range:	Who can say?
Payment:	Cash only
Service rating:	★★★½
Friendliness rating:	★★★
Transit:	C/D to Fordham Road, BX 12 bus to Arthur Avenue
Bar:	Full service
Wine selection:	Limited
Dress:	Neat casual
Disabled access:	Poor; small step up, rest rooms not accessible
Clientele:	Locals and far-trekking foodie pilgrims
Lunch/Dinner:	Monday, Wednesday, Thursday, and Saturday, noon–10 P.M.; Friday, noon–11 P.M.; Sunday, 1–9 P.M.; Tuesday, closed

Atmosphere/setting: With lots of tan paneling, tiled floors, and shmoozing across long tables, this feels like a suburban family rec room set up for a reunion. The upstairs dining room is sunnier but a bit removed from the action.

House specialties: There are no menus, so pay careful attention to your waiter's spiel. Daily specials include things like stuffed baby squid, mussels, meaty stuffed peppers, baked stuffed breast of veal, spaghetti with squid, fillet of sole francese and various fish grilled and sautéed in various ways. There's almost always pasta fagioli, lemony-peppery chicken scarpariello (perhaps the most loved item here), and pastas such as linguine with shrimp or clam sauce. Dominick's will give you a new respect for chicken and veal parmigiana (veal is very good here in general).

Other recommendations: For a refreshing treat, order salad with lemon rather than vinegar. Small touches count: the Parmesan cheese in the shakers is much better than usual, as is the crusty bread.

Summary & comments: Wear old shoes. Dominick's doesn't divulge its price until after you've eaten, at which time the sum is mentally calculated by

Dominick's *(continued)*

your waiter. As he stands before your table, silently compiling an estimate (through some mysterious formula) for the damage your party incurred, you won't want shiny, expensive shoes nudging his figures upward. Figure around $20 to $25 per person, not including drinks, regardless of how much is eaten (you might as well go berserk when ordering, since quantity rarely seems to affect the tab). Whatever your cost, it will be a small price to pay for such high-powered cooking. It's Italian American—not Italian—style all the way; the fact that Dominick's string beans (with highly roasted garlic chunks) are a lot better than their bland broccoli rabe says it all. This is the kind of place where people shake red pepper flakes over everything and the hearty cooking easily stands up to such treatment. Walk around the neighborhood while you're there; the shopping can't be beat. Unlike Manhattan's Little Italy, this is a real, vibrant Italian community.

DONOVAN'S

Zone 15   NW Queens
57-24 Roosevelt Avenue
   (between 57th and 58th Streets),
   Woodside, Queens
(718) 429-9339

Zone 16   NE Queens
214-16 41st Avenue (near Bell Boulevard), Bayside, Queens
(718) 423-5178

Pub	
★★★½	
Inexpensive	
Quality 91 Value A–	

Reservations:	Large parties only
When to go:	Anytime
Kind of service:	Waiter service at tables and bar
Entree range:	$6.45–13.45 (burgers, $4.75–5.95)
Payment:	Cash only
Service rating:	★★★
Friendliness rating:	★★★
Transit:	7 to Woodside/61st Street (Zone 15); Long Island Railroad (from Penn Station) to Bayside Station (Zone 16)
Bar:	Full service
Wine selection:	Limited (Bayside), decent (Woodside)
Dress:	Casual
Disabled access:	One step up (Bayside); use side door (Woodside); rest rooms not accessible (both locales)
Clientele:	Boisterous Irish of all ages
Lunch:	*Bayside:* Monday–Friday, 10:30 A.M.–3 P.M.; Saturday, 11 A.M.–3 P.M.; Sunday brunch noon–2:45 P.M.
	Woodside: Every day, 11 A.M.–4 P.M.
Dinner:	*Bayside:* Monday–Friday, 3 P.M.–2 A.M.; Saturday, 3 P.M.–3 A.M.; Sunday, 2:45 P.M.–2 A.M.
	Woodside: Sunday–Tuesday, 4 P.M.–midnight; Wednesday and Thursday, 4 P.M.–1 A.M.; Friday and Saturday, 4 P.M.–2 A.M.

Atmosphere / setting: Prototypical cozy Irish pubs; inviting Tudorish façades with stucco, thatched roof, and faux gas lamps. Inside, lots of dark wood and brick, a juke box, tables and booths. Naturally, there's a big handsome bar stocked with Queens characters. It's mostly an oldster crowd, but while this is certainly not anyone's idea of "hip," all ages fit. Avoid at all costs Bayside's very incongruous rear dining room . . . picture a department store lunchroom designed by a leprechaun.

House specialties: New York's best cheeseburgers (sautéed onions a must).

Other recommendations: There's a full menu of items like shell steak, shepherd's pie, and seafood both fried and broiled, but all pale beside the glory that is the Donovan's cheeseburger. Going to Donovan's and not ordering a burger is like going to Joe's Shanghai and not ordering crab buns, like going to Pisa and not leaning. But a pint of Guinness Stout is permissible, even encouraged; they pour the finest in town.

Summary & comments: What makes a burger great? Careful broiling, loose compaction, *never* impatiently mushing the pattie with a spatula, and using fresh—not frozen—inferior meat (good cuts like sirloin aren't fatty enough). What makes a pint of Guinness great? The correct blend of nitrogen and carbon dioxide, clean lines, proper temperature, slow, careful pouring, and daily turnover of kegs. Here all of the above pains are taken religiously and a thousand tiny errors are deftly avoided. The result demands a pilgrimage.

El Papasito

Zone 8   Midtown West and
    Theater District
370 West 52nd Street (near 9th Avenue),
    Manhattan
(212) 265-2225; (212) 265-2227

Reservations:	Not required
When to go:	Anytime
Kind of service:	Waiter service at tables
Entree range:	$6.50–19
Payment:	VISA, MC, AMEX, D, DC, JCB
Service rating:	★★★
Friendliness rating:	★★★
Transit:	C/E to 50th Street
Bar:	Beer and wine only
Wine selection:	Minimal
Dress:	Casual
Disabled access:	Fair; small step up, rest room doors narrow
Clientele:	Local Latinos
Breakfast:	Every day, 7 A.M.–noon
Lunch/Dinner:	Every day, 7 A.M.–10 P.M.

Atmosphere/setting: A colorful, inviting **L**-shaped space with mustard yellow walls, neatly arranged tables with glass-covered green tablecloths, autographed photos of Dominican baseball players, and one bizarre black velvet flock painting with blinking electric lights. There's a bar tucked into a corner that's been built to resemble a thatched Caribbean hut.

House specialties: New York is shockingly bean deprived, quality-wise, but El Papasito is legume heaven; several varieties (possibilities include white/pink/red/black beans, chickpeas, pigeon peas, etc.) are made daily, each according to a separate recipe (silky, intense black beans have a hint of vinegar, pink beans are more starkly elemental, etc.). Mofungo—a fried mash of starchy plantains, garlic, and pork that's one of the heaviest dishes on earth (and easy to miss under the "Side Orders" heading) somehow manages to taste light and greaseless, served with a cup of delicious, intense gravy that's instantly absorbed. Chicharrones are crunchy pieces of on-the-bone pork or chicken, not just fried skin as the dish is often mistranslated; squirt lime over them. Asopado is a thick, intensely garlicky rice soup; one order is easily enough for three. Don't miss stewed goat when it's a special or the off-menu silky yucca (a yam-ish vegetable usually cooked to death in other establishments) served with great marinated onions that enhance the tuber's sweetness. Chicken in any form (ubiquitous on the daily specials menu) is dependably good, and flan (caramel custard) is downright fantastic—just the right balance of eggy richness and lightness with a non-cloying, intense caramel sauce.

Other recommendations: Surprisingly, the café con leche is mediocre.

Summary & comments: This is the class act for Dominican cooking in lower Manhattan. El Papasito serves—in a jazzy, comparatively upscale ambiance—great fresh plates with all the soulful authenticity of a Spanish Harlem hole-in-the-wall. Servers are very friendly but utterly unprofessional; they speak decent English but you'll ask twice for silverware and the check is a major production (also beware of the dreaded pre-dessert Windex tabletop spray-down). Perhaps the waiters figure that with food so good at such low prices, they don't need to do much more than carry plates—and they may be right.

El Unico

Zone 20   Nearby in New Jersey
42-11 Park Avenue, Union City
(201) 864-3931

	Cuban
	★★★½
	Inexpensive
	Quality 90 Value A

Reservations:	Not accepted
When to go:	Food is freshest at lunchtime
Kind of service:	Waiter service at tables and counter
Entree range:	$1.50–4
Payment:	Cash only
Service rating:	★★½
Friendliness rating:	★★★
Transit:	Take the 156 NJ Transit bus from Gate 200 at Port Authority. Get off at Pathmark.
Bar:	None
Wine selection:	None
Dress:	Casual
Disabled access:	Fair
Clientele:	Local Cuban foodie workers and bargain-hunters
Open:	Every day, 4 A.M.–9:30 P.M.

Atmosphere/setting: A bustling, scruffy Cuban cafeteria with friendly waiters who speak little English but try to help nonetheless. It boasts an enormously diverse clientele that includes Anglo chowhounds, workers from the neighborhood, and assimilated white-collar Cubanos darting in from double-parked Saabs for a takeout taste of undiluted tradition.

House specialties: Specials rotate, but there's always moist roast chicken, chicken soup (a huge, wallopingly concentrated bowlful featuring broad mushy noodles), liver steak, chicken fricassee, some sort of pork, and often caldo gallego (a thick Galician cabbage and potato soup). The rice and beans (go for black; everyone makes red beans, but only Cubans and Brazilians can be relied on for black ones) are superb, as is stewed garlicky yucca, and the batidos (milkshakes, best with banana, guanabana, or mamey) are first-rate as well. On weekends they make outstanding moros, the Cuban mish-mash of black beans and rice alongside rich, crunchy/tender pernil (roast pork) and yucca.

Summary & comments: Really good Cuban food is not to be found in the five boroughs, but Union City (full of excellent Cuban restaurants, of which this is a favorite) is closer than Manhattanites realize. El Unico is just three minutes from the Lincoln Tunnel by car (take Local Streets/Hoboken exit, make a **U**-turn and head back up the hill, then follow signs to Park Avenue; for bus directions, see above). This is the cheapest good restaurant in the tri-state area (believe it or not,

129

it's hard to spend more than $5 for even the most sumptuous feast; an entire family can eat for under $10), so the money you'll save on dinner will more than compensate for tunnel toll or bus fare. Resiste the urge to tip 200 percent; the other customers get annoyed when newcomers do this.

Emerald Spa & Restaurant

Zone 15   Northwestern Queens
38-15 Northern Boulevard (near Steinway Street), Long Island City, Queens
(718) 433-1224

Russian	
★★½	
Moderate	
Quality 81	Value C

Reservations:	Not accepted
When to go:	Anytime
Kind of service:	Waiter service at tables
Entree range:	$13–18
Payment:	AMEX, MC, VISA, D
Service rating:	★★
Friendliness rating:	★★½
Transit:	G/R to 36th Street
Bar:	Full service
Wine selection:	Limited
Dress:	Anywhere from bathrobe to business suit
Disabled access:	None
Clientele:	Russian businessmen and their dates
Lunch:	Every day, noon–2:30 P.M.
Dinner:	Every day, 2:30–10:30 P.M.

Atmosphere/setting: From outside, this looks like a warehouse, perched between a car wash and an auto dealership. Head up a rather lavish staircase—and just off the corridor leading back into a very clean, modern, coed steambath, there's a carpeted dining nook where Russians in terry cloth bathrobes lounge around, eating lamb chops and sipping tea. It's very "nice," even upscale, with soft golden lighting, snazzy beige and olive table settings, and comfortable chairs. Clueless but friendly waiters run helter-skelter in a state of perpetual damage control, and while the scent of chlorine soon fades, it may take a few vodkas before you're able to ignore the health club–style bouncy pop music.

House specialties: This is spa cuisine for the coronary bypass set: slabian dumplings (pelmeny, really) and mushrooms in cream sauce topped with broiler-crusted cheese; Ukranian borscht with a dollop of sour cream; herring with cubes of oniony fried potato; and meat crêpes with mushroom sauce—all downed with plenty of chilled vodka. Soups are a good bet; served in huge bowls, they appear frightfully rich but are actually more earthy/subtle than they look. The scarlet-colored borscht contains seven vegetables other than beets, so it's almost like a hot gazpacho; kharcho is herbacious cilantro-spiked lamb broth, and the chicken soup tastes appealingly restrained in spite of its being chock full of ingredients. Lamb chops are bathed in a spicy marinade prior to grilling and served with a potent tomato dipping sauce. Most entrees come with one of various shapes of well-browned fried potatoes, tangled with dill-specked sautéed onion. The spuds are fried in olive oil which gives them great flavor if not optimal crispness.

Other recommendations: Skip dry chicken tabaca and tough-skinned khinkali (Georgian dumplings), and opt for more complex fish preparations (such as stuffed trout) rather than simpler grilled fish.

Summary & comments: There are Russian baths all over town, but this is the cleanest and most modern, and its dining room is also a high-class operation. You needn't be a spa customer to eat here, but if you don't pay the $18 fee for use of the pool, jacuzzi, Finnish, Turkish, and Russian saunas/steam rooms, you won't get to eat in a bathrobe. The food is good-not-great, and no great bargain, but it's the best bathrobe eating I can think of, short of leftover Charles Southern Kitchen fried chicken pilfered from your fridge at 3 A.M.

Eva's

Zone 13   Northern Brooklyn
551 4th Avenue (near 16th Street),
    Park Slope, Brooklyn
(718) 788-9354

Ecuadoran	
★★★	
Inexpensive	
Quality 87 Value A	

Reservations:	Not accepted
When to go:	Anytime
Kind of service:	Waiter service at tables
Entree range:	$6–12
Payment:	Cash only
Service rating:	★★½
Friendliness rating:	★★
Transit:	M/N/R to Prospect Avenue
Bar:	Beer (weekends only)
Wine selection:	None
Dress:	Casual
Disabled access:	Good
Clientele:	Ecuadoran regulars who eat here daily
Open:	Every day, 11 A.M.–9 P.M. (later on weekends)

Atmosphere/setting: Dark, boxy little space with Spanish TV and jukebox (often running simultaneously).

House specialties: Anything with shrimp: ceviche de camarones (raw shrimp pickled in a limey marinade), sopa de camarones (a pungent, salmon-colored shrimp soup), arroz con camarones (shrimp with rice). The ceviche mixta (a combination of fish and shellfish) is also recommended. Daily soups are great bargains: sopa de torreja on Mondays (a homey, highly satisfying bowl full of bits of meat, vegetables, and egg); Tuesdays, a cilantro-flecked lentil soup of magnificent balance and depth; and Thursdays, the aforementioned shrimp soup. Also good: encebollado de pescado (a smooth fish-onion-yucca stew), chaulafan (like fried rice that went to grad school, introduced to Peru via Chinese immigrant laborers), fritada (a huge pile of good-chewy fried pork, circled by crunchy fried green plantains), guatita (tripe), yapingacho (minute steak and fried eggs capping piles of fried mashed potato), and churrasco (minute steak with french fries in delicious tomatoey gravy with sautéed onions and peppers).

Other recommendations: Don't miss Quaker (pronounced KWAKair), a thick, smooth oatmeal drink spiked with orange and passion fruit juices and cinnamon), or the wonderful batidos (milk shakes) of fruits like guanabana.

Entertainment & amenities: Pro-level karaoke sung by a debonair señor weekend nights.

EVA'S *(continued)*

Summary & comments: Ecuadorans have a certain touch with shrimp (tons of lime plays a big part) and rice, and when the two are combined, the result is downright amazing. Eva's is the best Ecuadoran restaurant in New York, but eating there can be a challenge for outsiders: the menu is not translated, and the staff speaks little English. But it's this very insularity that protects their authenticity; the ways of the old country are embraced and maintained here.

Famous Pita

<table>
<tr><td colspan="2">

Kosher/Israeli

★★★

Inexpensive

Quality 87   Value A

</td></tr>
</table>

Zone 14   Southern Brooklyn
935 Coney Island Avenue (near Newkirk
    Avenue), Brooklyn
(718) 284-0161

Reservations:	Not accepted
When to go:	Anytime
Kind of service:	Self-service
Entree range:	Half sandwiches from $3.50, plates up to $12
Payment:	Cash only
Service rating:	★★
Friendliness rating:	★½
Transit:	D/Q to Newkirk Avenue
Bar:	None
Wine selection:	None
Dress:	Casual
Disabled access:	Good for takeout only; poor for eat-in—three steps down to tables, small step at door
Clientele:	Hurried observant locals
Open:	Every day, 10 A.M.–3 A.M.; closed Friday and Saturday until an hour after sunset

Atmosphere/setting: A fluorescent-lit, bare bones joint with a long salad bar in front and a sunken dining room at the rear. Spinning logs of shwarma provide the main decorative focal point.

House specialties: Sandwiches in freshly homemade pita; sensational crispy, spicy falafel; extremely tasty—and phenomenally greasy—turkey shwarma (like gyro).

Other recommendations: Umba is an Iraqi hot sauce made from mangos. It's used as a secret seasoning in the shwarma, and you can squeeze some out of a bottle near the salad bar. Malawas (buttery flatbreads) cooked to order are terrific, and the chicken soup is very good.

Summary & comments: There's a lot of room for confusion at this glatt kosher, Israeli-style cafeteria. The price of any of the "main dishes" (sizes range from half pita to full plate) includes as much food from the salad bar as will fit on your sandwich (you can cheat by loading up the aluminum wrapper as well). But if you look closely at the bar, you'll spot several of those same "main dishes." So those who've ordered, say, shwarma, can scoop up vast numbers of falafel balls and smear on endless eggplant salad or hummus (all main dishes in their own right). So if you're vegetarian, order the cheapest possible sandwich, and lob on all the rest as well. If you're a carnivore (*and* are on cholesterol-lowering medication *and* work out at a health club four to six times a week), go for the hypercaloric shwarma—one of the few things *not* available from the bar—and add from there. The bar itself is all vegetarian, including great baba ghanoush, hummus, scallions, roast peppers, fried eggplant, and cole slaw.

Ferdinando's

Zone 13 Northern Brooklyn	Italian
151 Union Street (near Columbia Street),	★★★½
Red Hook, Brooklyn	Moderate
(718) 855-1545	Quality 90 Value A

Reservations:	Not accepted
When to go:	Anytime
Kind of service:	Waiter service at tables
Entree range:	$8–10
Payment:	Cash only
Service rating:	★★★
Friendliness rating:	★★★
Transit:	F to Carroll Street
Bar:	Wine and beer only
Wine selection:	Limited
Dress:	Casual
Disabled access:	Good
Clientele:	Half local Italians, half questing chowhounds
Lunch/Dinner:	Monday–Thursday, 9:30 A.M.–6 P.M.; Friday–Sunday, 9:30 A.M.–9 P.M.

Atmosphere/setting: A charmingly atmospheric old Sicilian cafe with tiled floors, painted tin ceiling, walls dotted with pictures of the old country, and rave reviews from all the major newspapers. Most of the food is on display up front, and you can point out your selections to the friendly waitress. The feeling is very informal and low-key.

House specialties: Panelle (a chickpea flour croquette best eaten as a sandwich on fluffy, crusty homemade rolls with silky ricotta and a dusting of good Parmesan cheese); thin slices of silky, tender, garlicky, smoky barbecued eggplant; deep fried—but ungreasy—breaded rice balls studded with ground meat, cheese, and peas (best smothered in mild marinara sauce); ultrafresh, perfectly marinated seafood salad. The warm peasant bread is homemade, often right out of the oven.

Other recommendations: Manhattan Special soda, the way-intense coffee soda usually found only in bottles, is available here on draft.

Summary & comments: This old-fashioned cafe is so honestly Sicilian that I once watched a homesick Palermo-born friend burst into tears upon his first bite. Stop by for a snack, or bring friends and turn several communal snacks into a meal; this is a place to order a bit of this, a bit of that, and pass it all around. Think tapas, order freely (it's inexpensive), and you can mix-and-match a memorable repast.

5 Stars Punjabi

Zone 15 Northwestern Queens	Indian
13-15 43rd Avenue (corner of 21st Street),	★★★★
Long Island City, Queens	Inexpensive
(718) 784-7444	Quality 91 Value A

Reservations:	Not accepted
When to go:	Anytime
Kind of service:	Waiter service at counter and tables
Entree range:	$4.99–11 (lunch buffet, $4.99)
Payment:	Cash only
Service rating:	★★★
Friendliness rating:	★★★★
Transit:	E/F to 23rd Street–Ely Avenue
Bar:	Beer only
Wine selection:	None
Dress:	Casual
Disabled access:	Poor; several steps
Clientele:	Locals and cab drivers
Lunch/Dinner:	Every day, 10 A.M.–5 A.M.
Lunch Buffet:	Every day, 11 A.M.–4 P.M.

Atmosphere/setting: A real antique diner, complete with turquoise and pink interior and seating in booths or at a long counter. Every surface in sight is either tiled or shiny. Located a block from the 59th Street Bridge, this is a magnet for Indo-Pak cab drivers headed back to Manhattan.

House specialties: The cuisine is Indian Punjabi (for great Pakistani Punjabi food from right across the border—that is, Brooklyn—see review of Bukhara Restaurant), known for its rich, dairy-heavy cooking and great beans and breads. Try the wonderful curries (chicken, lamb, or goat), butter chicken (a very complex recipe much loved in India but extremely rare here; it's creamy and colored—as per tradition—a preternatural shade of orange), anything with chickpeas (and various renditions of dal), mix pakora (vegetables battered and fried), samosa chat (fried potato turnovers smothered in gravy), eggplant, aloo gobhi (potatoes and cauliflower), luxuriously rich rice pudding made with partially ground rice and lightly spiked with cardamom. Tandoori breads (fresh, hot nan comes with the buffet) are exceptional, as you'd expect from a Punjabi kitchen.

Other recommendations: The sole fault is the sometimes funny-tasting raita—a yogurt and cucumber dip, here served with what the waitress identified as "crunchy things" floating in it.

138

5 Stars Punjabi *(continued)*

Summary & comments: Unlike New York's most famous Indian food "diner," Jackson Diner (see review), 5 Stars is an actual vintage diner, and the food is nearly as worthy (its peaks may not be quite as lofty as those of Jackson Diner, but J.D. doesn't always hit them itself these days). While it's a chowhound maxim to shun all-you-can-eats—where food languishes desicatively in steam table purgatory—5 Stars has figured out how to make it work. They serve saucy dishes that sit well, and rice and fried items are prepared in small batches and constantly replenished. They've even found a way to successfully offer tandoori chicken (which otherwise turns into Naugahyde within ten minutes) by leaving a few pieces at a time sizzling atop a hot platter. Genial waiters guide you through the offerings of this amazingly inexpensive all-you-can-eat. After 4 P.M., order from the menu, itself quite a bargain.

FORTUNE GOURMET

CAUTION

Zone 16   NE Queens
135-02 Roosevelt Avenue
    (near Prince Street), Flushing, Queens
(718) 321-9070

Chinese
★★½
Inexpensive

Quality 84   Value A

Reservations:	Not accepted
When to go:	For a snack or light lunch
Kind of service:	Waiter service at tables
Entree range:	$4.25–14.25
Payment:	Cash only
Service rating:	★★★
Friendliness rating:	★★★½
Transit:	7 to Flushing/Main Street
Bar:	None
Wine selection:	None
Dress:	Casual
Disabled access:	No
Clientele:	Taiwanese teenyboppers
Open:	Every day, noon–10 P.M.

Atmosphere/setting: A brightly lit, shiny tiled tiny corner place framed by huge glass windows. It's a trendy magnet for hip Chinese teenagers.

House specialties: Although there's a long menu of lunch and dinner items (see Other reccommendations, below), ice dessert dishes—made with ice shaved by an antique hand-powered contraption—are the specialty. There's a long list of combinable options such as taro, black jelly, longan, lichee, red or green beans, peanut paste, and potato ball. Lightly stir everything together with your spoon.

Other recommendations: Main dishes are reasonably priced and tasty in a simple, rough way—imagine Taiwanese diner cooking. Oniony oyster pancakes are moist with lots of smoky wok flavor; extra crunchy, slightly spongy scallion pancakes are even better (dunk into a mixture of soy and hot sauces). Black bean pork chops are very good, if a little fatty; rice sausage (a hard-to-find Taiwanese specialty, here translated—grotesquely—as "rice in intestine") is good, as is shredded pork with scallion. For brave souls, the name "smelly bean curd" hardly conveys the olfactory challenge of these cubes of fried fermented tofu, off-menu but considered a house specialty.

Summary & comments: This fast-foody little spot isn't the place for a full sit-down dinner; rather it's best for "one more bite" after a meal, a quick lunch or snack, or for ices after dinner. You can get ordering advice from the genial waiter who hangs out between the door and the kitchen window; he speaks good English, as do the cooks.

Fried World

Zone 6   Chelsea West
408 8th Avenue (between 30th and 31st
    Streets), Manhattan
(212) 967-0274

<table>
<tr><td>Fried</td></tr>
<tr><td>★★</td></tr>
<tr><td>Inexpensive</td></tr>
<tr><td>Quality 86   Value A</td></tr>
</table>

Reservations:	Not accepted
When to go:	Whenever you're feeling fried
Kind of service:	Self-service
Entree range:	$3.50–7
Payment:	Cash only
Service rating:	★★
Friendliness rating:	★★
Transit:	A/C/E to 34th Street/Penn Station
Bar:	None
Wine selection:	None
Dress:	Casual
Disabled access:	Good; rest rooms not accessible
Clientele:	Madison Square Gardeners at night, local workers by day
Open:	Every day, 24 hours

Atmosphere/setting: A generic Midtown self-serve joint with picnic tables for in-house munching. The block's an ultralow-rent restaurant row; next door are Blarney Stone and Wonder (sic) Wok.

House specialties: Chicken, fish, and shrimp—all fried.

Other recommendations: There are gloomy vats of steam table Asian-Latino fare. Not fried. Not good.

Summary & comments: It is, to be sure, a heady name to live up to, but Fried World truly is the planetary epicenter for fried stuff. Their's is a decidedly Asian frying aesthetic, so the juicy, crisp chicken, fresh, flakey fish, and tender, plump shrimp are greaseless and light-tasting with grainy breading more reminiscent of tonkatsu than Colonel Sanders. The crinkle-cut french fries, alas, taste like they've been imported from Freezer World. Also skip fried rice, soups, and stews if you know what's good for you; it's a Fried World, after all.

Gabriela's

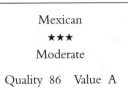

Zone 10   Upper West Side
685 Amsterdam Avenue, Manhattan
(212) 961-0574

Mexican
★★★
Moderate

Quality 86   Value A

Reservations:	For 6 or more
When to go:	Anytime
Kind of service:	Waiter service at tables
Entree range:	$6.95–12.95
Payment:	VISA, MC, AMEX
Service rating:	★★½
Friendliness rating:	★★★
Transit:	1/2/3/9 to 96th Street
Bar:	Beer, tequila
Wine selection:	Small
Dress:	Casual
Disabled access:	Fair; rest rooms not accessible
Clientele:	Locals
Brunch:	Saturday and Sunday, 11:30 A.M.–3 P.M.
Lunch/Dinner:	Monday–Thursday, 11:30 A.M.–11 P.M.; Friday and Saturday, 11:30 A.M.–midnight; Sunday, 11:30 A.M.–10 P.M.

Atmosphere/setting: The room, like the food, is brighter and slicker than your standard issue Mexican place; decor is cheerful and colorful with cactus murals on walls and mini-candelabras over tables. It's gringo-friendly without pandering.

House specialties: Rotisserie chicken, posole (a very satisfying huge bowl of pork and hominy corn soup), crema de elote y poblano (spicy, creamy corn soup), tamales, panucho yucateco (Yucatán-style thick stuffed tortillas with black bean paste), cochinita pibil (roast pork marinated in orange juice and numerous spices), tinga poblana (crispy tortillas topped with shredded pork), garnachas (tortillas filled with cheese, scallions, and hot peppers), licuados (fruit shakes), and aguas frescas (fresh fruit drinks). Be sure to also check out some of the five terrific varieties of tamales (one made with mushrooms is tucked under the "Vegetarian Platters" menu heading).

Summary & comments: This relatively upmarket establishment cooks some unusual dishes with uncommon panache. It's the only place for rare Yucatán-style specialties like panuchos yucatecos and Yucatán roast chicken, and there are also some touches from Oaxaca and Veracruz. Stick with more complex specialties from the platter part of the menu rather than simpler stuff like tortas, tacos, quesadillas, and enchiladas. Such antojitos (snacks) can be good here, but the kitchen is more consistent with more ambitious dishes.

Gaither's

Zone 14   Southern Brooklyn
1664 Atlantic Avenue (near Troy),
   Bedford-Stuyvesant, Brooklyn
(718) 771-1748

Southern
★★★★
Inexpensive

Quality 92   Value A

Reservations:	Not necessary
When to go:	Weekdays for takeout, weekend evenings for live music
Kind of service:	Waiter service at tables; takeout only in the afternoon
Entree range:	$5.25–12.50
Payment:	Cash only
Service rating:	★★★
Friendliness rating:	★★½
Transit:	A/C to Kingston-Throop Avenues
Bar:	Full service
Wine selection:	Limited
Dress:	Casual
Disabled access:	*Takeout:* server will come out to take order
	Bar: steps, but staff will assist
Clientele:	Locals
Open:	*Takeout:* Tuesday–Thursday, 10 A.M.–9 P.M.; Friday and Saturday, 10 A.M.–11 P.M.;
	Bar: hours vary; call ahead

Atmosphere/setting: Outside, the mean streets of Bed-Stuy. Inside, a safe, plush '60s-style inner-city cocktail lounge done up in red vinyl with an immense bar and a bandstand for live jazz. It's the kind of old-fashioned place where men wear hats and no nonsense is tolerated. Food from the adjoining kitchen is served here, but only at night. Next door, there's a takeout vestibule serving all afternoon (peer in to watch women in starched white blouses do delicious things to collard greens in a gleaming white-tiled kitchen that's more Memphis than Brooklyn).

House specialties: Hushpuppies—crisp outside, cakey inside—as good as any down South; luscious candied yams and mild-flavored cabbage; stellar fried chicken—juicy meat framed in ultralight, instant-melting crispness. Although cooked in the oven, not in smoke, the merely good ribs and chopped barbecue are served with a wonderfully redeeming sauce. Skip weirdly fluorescent macaroni and cheese and blah desserts.

Other recommendations: Authentic, smooth southern-style iced tea, poured from a large glass jar.

143

Entertainment & amenities: Live jazz and blues (call for info).

Summary & comments: Mrs. Gaither Bellamy isn't a soul food chef, properly speaking; soul food is about extracting deliciousness from humble ingredients. But Gaither's is an established, respectable place where *nice* ingredients are used (for example, lard is shunned—though there are bacon drippings in the gravy . . . one can't *help* that). Mrs. Bellamy is not cooking from deprivation; her kitchen offers meticulous, proper southern cuisine (contrast with its more down-home—but equally tasty—neighbor, Soul Food Kitchen—see review). Takeout's your best choice on weekdays, since the chefs go home early and the lounge serves leftovers. But weekend evenings, you can have the best of all worlds: live music and good food well into the night.

Grange Hall

Zone 4   Greenwich Village
50 Commerce Street, Manhattan
(212) 924-5246

American
★★★★
Expensive

Quality 91   Value B

Reservations:	Recommended
When to go:	Anytime
Kind of service:	Waiter service at tables and bar
Entree range:	Small dishes, $3.75–7; main dishes, $10.25–16.75
Payment:	AMEX
Service rating:	★★★★
Friendliness rating:	★★★½
Transit:	1/9 to Christopher Street/Sheridan Square
Bar:	Full service
Wine selection:	Decent range of Americans
Dress:	Nice casual or better
Disabled access:	Good (use Commerce Street entrance)
Clientele:	Very diverse, but all very glib and Manhattany
Brunch:	Saturday, 11 A.M.–3 P.M.; Sunday, 10:30 A.M.– 4 P.M.
Lunch:	Monday–Friday, noon–3 P.M.
Dinner:	Monday, 5:30–11 P.M.; Tuesday–Saturday, 5:30–11:30 P.M.; Sunday, 6–11 P.M.

Atmosphere/setting: Situated on a twisty, picture-postcard block in the most beautiful part of Greenwich Village, the exterior is most inviting and the interior is even more so: smart and hiply elegant, warmly lit and well-appointed but not at all pretentious. The retro decor ('40s sophistication with a twist) doesn't intrude, good jazz wafts romantically, and there's a striking mural (by young artist David Joel). All contribute to a setting perfect for low-key, urbane dining.

House specialties: Acorn squash, freshly made sausage, potato pancakes, yukon gold scalloped potatoes, oven-roasted organic chicken, cranberry-glazed pork chops, farm vegetable platter, soups, salads.

Other recommendations: The potato pancakes make an ideal bar snack if you stop by just for drinks.

Summary & comments: Grange Hall started out as the latest offering from a group known for their stable of theme eateries. This one was designed to be Upscale Retro Blue Plate, but Grange Hall has become loved on its own terms rather than as a contrived novelty. They've stocked the place with smart, funny, young servers and a great bar (good for solo dining and quite popular for martinis late into the night), and they serve a seasonal menu of savvily cooked Middle-American dishes. Simple ingredients are used, but the chef is far too sophisticated to let his food devolve into clichéd comfort food; everything's prepared with flare, and simplicity never lapses into dullness. This is the perfect spot for carnivores to bring vegetarians; in addition to well-cooked meat dishes there are numerous small vegetable plates that can accumulate into a meal (also, larger plates can be shared). It's all very mix-and-match. If you've been dipping deep into New York's unparalleled ethnic food scene and want to relax with a more familiar—but still exciting—menu, this is the place.

Grimaldi's Pizza

<table>
<tr><td></td><td>Pizza</td></tr>
</table>

Zone 13   Northern Brooklyn
19 Old Fulton Street (between Water
    and Front Streets), Brooklyn Heights
(718) 858-4300

Pizza
★★★½
Moderate
Quality 90   Value B

Reservations:	Not accepted
When to go:	Peak mealtimes and weekends are very crowded
Kind of service:	Waiter service at tables
Entree range:	$12–20
Payment:	Cash only
Service rating:	★★★
Friendliness rating:	★★½
Transit:	A/C to High Street
Bar:	Beer and wine only
Wine selection:	Minimal
Dress:	Casual
Disabled access:	Good
Clientele:	Questing foodies
Lunch/Dinner:	Monday, Wednesday–Friday, 11:30 A.M.–11 P.M.; Saturday, 2 P.M.–midnight; Sunday, 2–11 P.M.

Atmosphere/setting: Perpetually mobbed, boisterous cafe just up the block from one of the city's most picturesque Manhattan skyline views. Enjoy the airy vista, then duck inside and wait in line.

House specialties: Very carefully cooked brick-oven pizza; owner Patsy Grimaldi is a zealot, and he combs the city for the best ingredients. Any toppings ordered will be the finest available—you can't go wrong.

Summary & comments: Ingredient for ingredient, Grimaldi's (formerly Patsy's) makes some of the best pizza in New York. His buttery cheese and zestful sausage are from the legendary Corona Heights Pork Store, and the freshest tomatoes go into his sauce; his crust is impressively crusty and chewy in all the right spots. Yet there's something missing. It's difficult to put your finger on it, because all T's have been crossed and I's dotted. But in the end, there's the feeling that you've tasted ingredients (*great* ingredients), not an overall delicious pizza gestalt. Perhaps it's the sauce (very fresh but a tad bland and not quite cooked down enough), but in the end, the problem may be conceptual; this foodie magnet was conceived to please the gourmet palates of people wont to appreciate trees without regard for the forest. I'm nitpicking, of course; many discerning people love Grimaldi's. But check out Lento's or Patsy's (of East Harlem) for less perfect but more soulful pizza, and Nick's or La Pizza Fresca for equally high-class pies that satisfy on every level (see reviews for all).

Hall Street Kosher Cafe

CAUTION

Zone 13   N Brooklyn
9 Hall Street (at Flushing
    Avenue), Williamsburg, Brooklyn
(718) 802-9638

Kosher
★★★
Inexpensive

Quality 89   Value A

Reservations:	Not accepted
When to go:	Anytime
Kind of service:	Self-service
Entree range:	$4–7.50
Payment:	Cash only
Service rating:	★★★
Friendliness rating:	★★★★
Transit:	G to Flushing Avenue
Bar:	None
Wine selection:	None
Dress:	Casual
Disabled access:	Not accessible
Clientele:	Local workers
Open:	Monday–Thursday, 7:30 A.M.–7 P.M.; Friday, 7:30 A.M.–4 P.M.; Saturday and Sunday, closed

Atmosphere/setting: The Hall Street Kosher Cafe consists of a long trailer parked in an abandoned lot across from the Brooklyn Navy Yards. It's very Mississippi; when you enter and approach the steam tables, you might expect to encounter ribs and collard greens. But one glance at the staff—jolly, friendly fellows with curly sideburns, long beards, and yarmulkes—will tell you that ribs are most assuredly not on the menu.

House specialties: Latkes (potato pancakes) are thin and large—nearly schnitzel-sized—and the all-essential crisp-outside/tender-inside polarity has been exquisitely achieved. Kugel (sort of a baked potato pancake casserole) is uncommonly rich and tender; as your teeth glide smoothly through, the course grains yield with little resistance. Noodle kugel (mildly sweet baked noodle casserole) is made from unusually narrow noodles, and its sweetness is ingratiating, not cloying; the tender gefilte fish contains a subtle sweetness as well. Wonderful cheese blintzes consist of rich, vanilla-scented pot cheese spiraled between layers of a spongy crêpe (the crêpe's bland and the cheese is almost too intense to bear, so the symbiosis is perfect). Pickled vegetable salad is sprightly and fresh.

Other recommendations: There are disappointments to avoid: brown "Israeli-style" noodle kugel, dosed with caramel, is way too sweet, and flat-tasting knishes and desserts (not made here) are missable as well. Beware also of chef Mario's more experimental specials, such as a memorably unsuccessful nouvelle "french toast" (imagine a microwave-fried kaiser roll). But at these prices one can painlessly accept some fumbles along with the touchdowns.

Summary & comments: Mario is an Argentinian orthodox Jew who—despite speaking with an accent that's more Ruben Blades than Jackie Mason—cooks terrific kosher dairy specialties just like you'd eat in an Eastern European Jewish grandma's kitchen. While most Hall Street customers are religious Jews, all sorts of people come around—and all are treated with the same graciousness. Mario and his cohorts are simply nice people, and their food brims with this same kindness.

Hallo Berlin

Zone 8   Midtown West and
   Theater District
402 West 51st Street (near 9th Avenue),
   Manhattan
(212) 541-6248

Reservations:	Not accepted
When to go:	Anytime
Kind of service:	Waiter service at tables
Entree range:	$6.50–12.95
Payment:	No
Service rating:	★★
Friendliness rating:	★★★★
Transit:	C/E to 50th Street
Bar:	Beer and wine only
Wine selection:	A few Germans
Dress:	Casual
Disabled access:	Poor; big step up, rest rooms narrow
Clientele:	Beer-drinking revelers and timid office workers
Lunch/Dinner:	Monday–Saturday, 11 A.M.–11 P.M.; Sunday, 4–11 P.M.

Atmosphere/setting: This feels like a German beer garden set up inside a generic Midtown storefront—which, come to think of it, is exactly what it is. Tables are protected from the glare of a few innocent-looking light fixtures by oversized, gaily colored umbrellas festooned with flashing holiday lights. The tables themselves, covered with plastic red checkerboard tablecloths, are flimsy, as if they were temporary equipment dragged indoors each night. Vines are being trained to grow along a network of branches up against the ceiling, and hyper-kinetic oompah music blasts from some hidden speaker. This whole wacky scene is so full of contagious German good humor that the effect convinces. Clientele, as you'd imagine, is boisterous.

House specialties: Sausages (good, not great) include curry-dusted Berliner currywurst, bock knackwurst, bauernwurst, and fried bratwurst. Potato pancakes are tasty but thin, coarsely shredded and roughly fried; these are not cheek-pinching Grandma Helga's loving *kartofel* treats. Like the other offerings here, this is rough-and-ready bar food, so don't expect an edible epiphany. Fishy offerings include imported smoked pepperfish, herring fillets, and wine herring.

Other recommendations: This wouldn't be much of a beer garden without beer; Hallo Berlin has a decent selection, all served, surrealistically enough, in Jets

150

football mugs. Choices include Bitburger Pils and Köstritzer Black Lager on tap and Hacker Pschorr, Paulaner, and Erdinger Weiss in bottles. Teetotalers will be happy to find (aptly named) Elliot's Amazing Juices.

Summary & comments: The owner of "The Wurst Restaurant in NYC" first made a name for himself hawking sausages from a large green street cart while attired in liederhosen. This place has all the whimsy you'd expect from a such a character, though for sheer eccentricity he's surpassed by his waiter, an extremely friendly Pakistani fellow who's so easily flustered that his previous gig must have been at *Fawlty Towers*.

Happy Buddha

Zone 16   Northeastern Queens
135-37 37th Avenue (west of Main
    Street), Flushing, Queens
(718) 358-0079

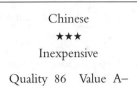

Chinese
★★★
Inexpensive

Quality 86   Value A–

Reservations:	Not necessary
When to go:	Anytime
Kind of service:	Waiter service at tables
Entree range:	$6.50–12.95
Payment:	AMEX, VISA, MC
Service rating:	★★★★
Friendliness rating:	★★★★★
Transit:	7 to Flushing/Main Street
Bar:	None
Wine selection:	None
Dress:	Casual
Disabled access:	Good
Clientele:	Local Chinese
Lunch:	Monday–Friday, noon–3 P.M.
Dinner:	Monday–Friday, 3–10 P.M.
Lunch/Dinner:	Saturday and Sunday, 11 A.M.–10 P.M.

Atmosphere/setting: Bright and cheery with large faux-marble tables and kitsch knickknacks (e.g., baby Buddha frolicking in an ever-flowing waterfall).

House specialties: Bamboo garden soup with bamboo pith (a completely new textural sensation; visualize melt-away gauze), black mushrooms, dried lily buds, and *wham* (their misspelling of ham—mock, of course, but startlingly ham-like); stuffed Chinese cabbage rolls (topped with white potato sauce); hibiscus fried rice (topped with shredded vegetables and strips of mock chicken); sautéed broad rice noodles (with bean sprouts, wham, mock beef—just like thin-cut tender slices of meat—and a few black beans); Szechuan chicken (fantastic fake chicken chunks in a spicy tomato sauce, ringed with very fresh broccoli); shredded Buddha delight with special sauce (in a nest of light, ungreasy fried taro; this is the same mélange that tops the hibiscus rice); soft spring rolls with nuts and mint leaves.

Other recommendations: Be careful; some items use similar sauces or vegetable combinations, so you can wind up with a monotonous meal. Order dishes whose descriptions are clearly dissimilar.

Entertainment & amenities: Most unusual for this traffic-choked neighborhood, Happy Buddha has its own free parking lot.

Happy Buddha (continued)

Summary & comments: Buddhist temples in China have, over the centuries, evolved a tasty vegetarian cuisine to suit their meatless regimen while simultaneously developing ingenious ways of simulating meat in order to please carnivorous temple visitors. When done right, the results can fool you into thinking you're eating actual flesh . . . and Happy Buddha does it right. As part of the overall salubriousness, no MSG is used.

The chef is capriciously inventive (though his sauces and dips are unexceptional), and the staff does its utmost to keep up with his ever-changing creations by handing out as many as three menus (anything on the lunch menu is available at dinner for a surcharge) and two photo books. The book with the most interesting looking things is, alas, for weddings only . . . and the waitresses are all married (I tried!). The staff, though constrained by a language gap, is very eager to please. They'll even offer to bring smaller portions if they believe you've overordered.

Healthy Tofu

Zone 16   Northeastern Queens
40-11 150th Street (between Roosevelt
    and 40th Avenues), Flushing, Queens
(718) 353-6962

<table>
<tr><td>Korean</td></tr>
<tr><td>★★★★</td></tr>
<tr><td>Inexpensive</td></tr>
<tr><td>Quality 93   Value A</td></tr>
</table>

Reservations:	Not accepted
When to go:	Anytime
Kind of service:	Waiter service at tables
Entree range:	$5.95–12.95
Payment:	Cash only
Service rating:	★★½
Friendliness rating:	★★★★
Transit:	Long Island Railroad (from Penn Station) to Murray Hill Station
Bar:	None
Wine selection:	None
Dress:	Casual
Disabled access:	Good
Clientele:	Mostly Korean women from the beauty parlor next door, some arriving with hair wrapped in plastic.
Open:	Every day, 10 A.M.–10 P.M.

Atmosphere/setting: A small dining room with checkerboard floors and humming fluorescent light fixtures. The walls are made of lacquered wood shavings, the ceiling plastered with lacquered Korean newspapers. All the magic is in the kitchen, where a sweet older Korean woman works gentle wizardry (and peers at customers through a one-way mirror, so behave yourself!).

House specialties: Homemade tofu, either hard (pretty soft, actually; served as pillowy, moist slices with the texture of fresh ricotta) or soft (tender, milky-curdy; served in soup). Both are revelations; who'd have imagined that plain tofu could be something to enjoy, let alone swoon over? Order the hard tofu either plain (mo dubu yangyeum) or with wasabi (mo dubu wasabi); soft tofu shines in kimchi daejigogi soondubu chigae, a roiling iron cauldron of smoky, spicy soup with just a bit of pork (kimchi heamul soondubu chigae substitutes seafood). In keeping with the health theme, a congee-like chunky rice gruel, kong juk, is almost completely unseasoned but deeply satisfying in an elemental way, like spa food. Haemul Pajun, an eggy pancake (here with octopus) is greaseless and perfectly textured—crunchy and soft in all the right places. The freebie appetizers are all uncommonly delicious and particularly exotic (like fried sea vegetable leaves that come on starchy but go out sweet, or a tangle of vegetable threads studded with unidentified flowering berries). Be sure to ask for some of their amazing rice; it's sticky, fortified with barley and black beans.

Other recommendations: Bulnak jungol (stir-fried whole octopus with tofu), pricey at $24.95, has been crossed off the menu, but, given a few days' advance notice, they'll prepare it.

Summary & comments: A restaurant called Healthy Tofu sounds like about as much fun as a trip to the dentist, but banish from your mind all images of spongy, tasteless cubes of ascetic white gelatin. I know, I know—you would not eat it in a box, you would not eat it with a fox, etc. But in this one humble storefront, give the green eggs and ham a shot, and just try to not be smitten. A few other places make tofu by hand, but they fail to achieve the pleasant nutty flavor and toothsome texture that makes you want to gobble more and more of the stuff, even when it's steamed and unadorned! The menu offers only unexplained dish names, but friendly, solicitous servers do their utmost to help and the tips above will get you started.

Hole in One

Zone 9   Midtown East
1003A 2nd Avenue at 53rd Street (2nd
    floor), Manhattan
(212) 319-6070

Reservations:	Not accepted
When to go:	Early evenings less crowded
Kind of service:	Waiter service at tables and bar
Entree range:	Small plates, $7.50–10; $30 cover charge
Payment:	VISA, MC, AMEX
Service rating:	★★★★
Friendliness rating:	★★
Transit:	E/F to Lexington Avenue or 6 to 51st Street
Bar:	Full service
Wine selection:	Minimal
Dress:	Your very best
Disabled access:	None
Clientele:	Well-heeled Japanese businessmen and their dates
Dinner:	Sunday–Friday, 7 P.M.–2:30 A.M.; Saturday, 7 P.M.–1 A.M.

Atmosphere/setting: The entrance is marked only by a discrete brass sign, in Japanese. But although Hole in One is well hidden and orthodontically pricey, and the clientele's almost entirely Japanese, it's not quite a private club. You're buzzed through an interior door (shout "Hole in One!" or "Whiskey!" into the intercom), pass up a flight of steps, and enter scotch heaven. This sleek window-less room provides seating for a few dozen at intimate tables and a long bar facing a sea of rare whiskey bottles. Unintentionally silly Scottish knickknacks—lots of golf clubs, for example—are scattered everywhere.

House specialties: Chicken shioyaki are miniscule strips of free-range chicken, each topped with a wisp of skin lovingly broiled to meet the Platonic ideal of salty crispness. The meat is so flavorful and juicy, the whole such a fantastic union—a deftly arranged yin/yang of crunch and tenderness—that it's as if you're tasting the combination of chicken skin and meat for the very first time. Your attention is drawn instantly to the mackerel sushi's consummately plump, texturally perfect rice grains; it seems as if each one has been painstakingly placed in position to ensure the most exquisite smoothness of bite. The fish is a mere scent, a floating perfumed halo. Baby eels are fried with stunning transparency; the batter's nearly invisible, and there's not an iota of residual grease. It's the eel flavor that shines through; frying is just a vehicle for primping and honing that flavor.

The result is crunchy perfection, a masterful accomplishment. There's also a haimish tangle of burdock, carrots, and shiitakes (chewy, elemental burdock is brilliantly counterpointed with melty mushrooms).

Other recommendations: This is by far the best bar for single malts in New York (perhaps in the entire country). Many bottles are extremely rare—some from distilleries long ago closed—and are priced accordingly. You can spend a fortune here; prices run from $14.50 to $1,000 per shot.

Summary & comments: This is definitely *not* a restaurant (it's a whiskey bar first and foremost); Hole in One serves small plates of Japanese food almost as an afterthought, but their quality simply cannot be surpassed. Ordering is as problematic as entering; there are no English menus, so you must rely on the aloof staff's attempts at translation. You'll pay dearly for the experience; the tiny plates cost $7.50 to $10 each, plus there's a $30 cover and a 20 percent service charge, and you're going to have to order a drink. But the food is exquisite; private clubs have traditionally snatched up the most talented Japanese chefs, and this is one of the only super premium Japanese businessman hangouts that admits outsiders (*if* you're well dressed and *if* you have substantial headroom on your platinum card).

Hop Lee

Zone 3   Chinatown, Little Italy, and
   Lower East Side
16 Mott Street (near Pell Street),
   Manhattan
(212) 962-6475

Reservations:	Accepted, but not necessary
When to go:	Anytime
Kind of service:	Waiter service at tables
Entree range:	$4.95–17
Payment:	VISA, DC, MC
Service rating:	★★★½
Friendliness rating:	★★★½
Transit:	J/M/N/R/Z/6 to Canal Street
Bar:	Beer only
Wine selection:	None
Dress:	Casual
Disabled access:	None
Clientele:	Local, aficionados
Lunch specials:	Monday–Friday, 11 A.M.–4 P.M.
Lunch/Dinner:	Every day, 11 A.M.–3 A.M.

Atmosphere/setting: From the glitzy exterior, this seems like a fancy Cantonese banquet hall. Upstairs there is, in fact, a nice party room for hire, but downstairs lies a more modest dining room where decor is pleasant if not luxurious. Floors are marble tiled, softly lit booths line the attractively papered walls, and ten tables (pink-linened and well spaced by Chinatown standards) dot the room's center. Everything's spotless.

House specialties: Straight-down-the-middle Cantonese cookery, from rich, unusually spicy black bean sauce (order with razor clams, which fetch half the price of clams at other places) to excellent noodle dishes (best with the exceptionally fresh seafood). The sizzling hot pots are excellent (beef tendon for the adventurous, regular beef for others), spiked with just the right amount of five-spice. At lunch, choose from a long list of $4.95 offerings; standouts include tender squid with pickled mustard greens and, especially unusual, mixed Chinese sausages with vegetables. It's rare to get to try a variety of these sausages in a simple stir fry; they're intriguingly intense and herby, the height of luxury for just five bucks. All lunch specials come with a scary-looking gray house soup that's actually fragrant nectar with black-eyed peas lending a rich oxtail-ish taste.

Summary & comments: Hop Lee (or 16 Mott, for those who follow the tradition of referring to restaurants on this street by address) is a triple threat, serving morning dim sum, cheap lunch specials, and classic Cantonese fare late into the night. The cooking's dependably first-rate; the kitchen turns out slick yet soulful dishes permeated with plenty of smoky wok flavor. A sumptuous feast can be had for under $20 per person, a simple but worthy supper for half that, and waiters are uncommonly friendly. New cuisines on the block like Taiwanese, Shanghai, and Malaysian are capturing all the attention lately, but this low-profile gem deserves a place on every aficionado's Chinatown short list.

Iammo Bello

Italian
★★½
Inexpensive

Quality 84   Value A

Zone 11   Upper East Side
39 East 60th Street, Manhattan
(212) 935-9418

Reservations:	Not accepted
When to go:	Anytime
Kind of service:	Self-service
Entree range:	$4–7.50
Payment:	Cash
Service rating:	★★★
Friendliness rating:	★★★
Transit:	N/R to 5th Avenue or 4/5/6 to 59th Street
Bar:	None
Wine selection:	None
Dress:	Casual
Disabled access:	None
Clientele:	Local workers
Lunch:	Monday–Friday, 11:30 A.M.–4 P.M.; Saturday, 10 A.M.–3 P.M.; Sunday, closed

Atmosphere/setting: A quick-moving queue snakes through this subterranean cafeteria, past myriad steam tables manned by hyperkinetic servers. All remaining space is crammed with long tables full of harried ravenous eaters, forks and jaws working at prodigious pace. It's all so manic that one feels as if a meek request to pass the salt might elicit a hail of shakers flung at you from all directions.

House specialties: Wonderful heros like chicken, veal, eggplant, or meatball parmigiana (with good strong Parmesan cheese rather than the usual clots of bad mozzarella), scrumptious chicken francese (hot only on Thursdays, other days it's available cold at the antipasto bar), delicious homey lasagna, soups, well-fried calamari (Fridays only). Skip the deftly flavored pastas if you demand al dente (impossible to achieve in a steam table), but you'll be missing a pretty decent alfredo sauce.

Other recommendations: Available from a separate concession in the back are various fancy pizzas (including one with nicely grilled vegetables) as well as regular slices, intriguingly different from—though not exceptionally superior to—the usual Gotham slice. Up front the abundantly stocked self-service cold antipasto bar costs $5.75 a pound.

Summary & comments: Iammo Bello means "come here, handsome" in Italian, but this no-frills kinetic cafeteria depends on cooking rather than homely looks. This obviously is not the most subtle of kitchens, but there's a time for subtlety and a time for rough, lusty satiation. Here there's also the bonus satisfaction of having enjoyed a really good $6 meal in a neighborhood filled with mediocre $30 lunches.

IHAWAN

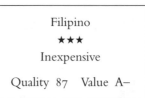

Zone 15   NW Queens
40-06 70th Street (near Roosevelt Avenue), Woodside, Queens
(718) 205-1480

Filipino	
★★★	
Inexpensive	
Quality 87 Value A−	

Reservations:	Not accepted
When to go:	Anytime
Kind of service:	Waiter service at tables
Entree range:	$4.50–15
Payment:	VISA, MC, AMEX, D
Service rating:	★★★
Friendliness rating:	★★★
Transit:	7 to 69th Street
Bar:	None
Wine selection:	None
Dress:	Casual
Disabled access:	None
Clientele:	Questing chowhounds (both Filipinos and non-Filipinos)
Open:	Thursday–Tuesday, 11 A.M. −8:30 P.M.; Wednesday, closed

Atmosphere/setting: Ihawan seems like the humblest of operations when you first spot its back-street location and enter through a cramped takeout area. But there's more. Make your way past harried cooks and waiters to the upstairs dining room (via an unmarked stairway—it's like going up to a friend's apartment), where you'll be surprised to find an incongruously expansive sunny dining room. Wall-to-wall carpeting, bright blue tablecloths and tiny border lights give the room a modern, fresh look, and sound absorbent ceiling panels help keep noise levels low. It's a whole other world up here, and the secret's out; the place is usually nearly full with Filipino families and intrepid chowhounds from both inside and outside the neighborhood.

House specialties: Sensational barbecued pork, in a sauce that's something like teriyaki (but a bit less sweet and a *lot* more garlicky) served with rice or on a stick. Crunchy and chewy in all the right places, it's some of the best barbecue you'll ever have, regardless of nationality. The chicken barbecue is nearly as good, and plump, peppery barbecued sausage (langonisa) is screamingly delightful. All barbecue is served with achara, an appealing condiment of pickled green papaya with carrots, raisins, and red bell pepper. Also good: crispy pata, a whole haunch of pork (sometimes mistranslated as pig's knuckle); to achieve stellar crispiness, it goes through a rigorous preparation of boiling, freezing, and then frying.

161

Other recommendations: There's a long (and untranslated) menu of traditional Filipino foods, few of them noteworthy. Stick with simple noodle dishes (pancit) or vegetables like laing (collards in coconut milk) if you absolutely require more than rice to accompany the barbecued meats (avoid fish; freshness is unpredictable). The refreshingly unsweet melon (canteloupe, really) drink is well worth a try.

Summary & comments: This is a brisk, skillful Filipino assembly-line kitchen, very efficient and very well run. Half the neighborhood seems to be working here in some capacity, and the other half is eating. Desserts are served, but you'll do better by walking down the block to new Krystal's Cafe (69-02 Roosevelt Avenue, (718) 898-1900), a really good Filipino bakery, for things like purple yam cake (with an otherworldly—but natural!—color and tuberous filling that tastes like the richest buttercream) as well as savory snacks like chicken empanadas (pastry pies).

Il Buco

Zone 5   East Village
47 Bond Street, Manhattan
(212) 533-1932

Reservations:	Necessary
When to go:	Anytime
Kind of service:	Waiter service at tables
Entree range:	$12–24
Payment:	Cash only
Service rating:	★★½
Friendliness rating:	★½
Transit:	6 to Bleecker Street or F to 2nd Avenue
Bar:	Full service
Wine selection:	Extensive
Dress:	Chic
Disabled access:	Good
Clientele:	Euro types, couples, management's kissy friends
Dinner:	Tuesday–Thursday, 6 P.M.–midnight; Friday and Saturday, 6 P.M.–1 A.M.; Sunday, 5–11 P.M.; Monday, closed

Atmosphere/setting: Antique store by day, restaurant by night, woody atmospheric Il Buco has an old European farmhouse feeling quite unlike any other spot in the city. You eat at rough candlelit tables surrounded by old furnishings, all for sale. It's tremendously romantic in its rustic way.

House specialties: Changing seasonal menu, but risottos, grilled baby octopus, blood orange and fennel salad, innovative pastas, flourless chocolate cake, and plum cake are delicious fixtures.

Entertainment & amenities: The wine cellar allegedly was the inspiration for Edgar Allan Poe's "Cask of Amontillado" story, and it's got atmosphere galore; ask to have a peek.

Summary & comments: Il Buco switched chefs shortly before this book went to press. New chef Jody Williams is steering the menu more squarely toward Italian, though some French and Spanish dishes remain. While not widely known, Il Buco is much loved by a discerning few, and the smallish place fills up most nights. This is an especially good locale for special occasions—long tables can be reserved either in the middle of the main room or in a rear alcove. A word about service: some staffers are downright caustic with attitude while others are quite friendly. In general don't expect much in the way of accommodation; this restaurant does things its own way. Don't get mad; just lose yourself in the romantic ambience and the evocative, smartly cooked food.

The Indonesian Consulate Cafeteria

Indonesian
★★★★
Inexpensive
Quality 92   Value A

Zone 11   Upper East Side
5 East 68th Street, Manhattan
(212) 879-0600

Reservations:	Not accepted
When to go:	Anytime
Kind of service:	Self-service
Entree range:	Prix fixe, $5 ($1 supplement for soup)
Payment:	Cash only
Service rating:	★★½
Friendliness rating:	★★★
Subway:	6 to 68th Street
Bar:	None
Wine selection:	None
Dress:	Nice casual
Disabled access:	Not accessible
Clientele:	Indonesian businessmen, abashed drop-ins
Lunch:	Monday–Thursday, 11 A.M.–2 P.M.; some Fridays, 11 A.M.–2 P.M. (call to check); Saturday and Sunday, closed

Atmosphere/setting: You walk down the stately steps of the Indonesian consulate into the building's basement. Open the massive iron door, buzz to be admitted through another set of doors, pass a receptionist (tell her you're there for lunch), go through still another door, and head straight toward what appears to be a large closet. In the center of this closet there's a single long table covered with a cheap plastic cloth at which dignified Indonesian men in suits are eating from paper plates. To the right, in a small alcove, a good-humored Indonesian woman is juggling dozens of pots and pans on her huge antique stove. The smell is positively hypnotizing. Tell her you want to try *everything*, and go have a seat at the table (grab some plastic utensils from the big central bucket and water from the water cooler) and await bliss.

House specialties: The menu changes every day; you'll be served tastes of five or six different things, all piled high on your plate. Possibilities include chicken or fish in spicy peanut sauce, spicy potatoes, tempe concoctions, a vegetable hodgepodge, and lots of perfectly cooked rice. The sole complaint is that the sambal (fiery Indonesian chutney) is usually commercial—but at least it's a good brand.

The Indonesian Consulate Cafeteria *(continued)*

Other recommendations: There's optional soup for an extra buck (raising your tab to a whopping $6). Go for it.

Summary & comments: Not only is this by far the finest Indonesian food in town (perhaps in the entire country), it's also a regional style (Sundanese) hard to find cooked this well even in Indonesia. The cuisine will please skittish eaters; its exoticness lies in the spicing and condiments, as the staples are relatively familiar. The chef cooks pretty spicy, but rarely does she apply *serious* heat as you'd find in, say, Thai restaurants.

While nobody minds well-behaved outsiders stopping by, this lunchroom is not particularly seeking our business, either. Keep conversation low and be patient about waiting for your food. Remember, this is not a Real Restaurant.

Note: There's also a cafeteria in the Indonesian U.N. Mission at 325 East 38 Street, but it's nowhere near as good.

Jackson Diner

Zone 15   NW Queens
37-47 74th Street,
   Jackson Heights, Queens
(718) 672-1232

Reservations:	Not accepted weekends; policy varies on weekdays
When to go:	Weekends are the most crowded, but also the most consistent
Kind of service:	Waiter service at tables
Entree range:	$6.75–8.95
Payment:	Cash only
Service rating:	★★★
Friendliness rating:	★★★
Transit:	7 to 74th Street/Broadway or E to Roosevelt Avenue/Broadway
Bar:	None
Wine selection:	None
Dress:	Casual
Disabled access:	Good
Clientele:	Local Indians, questing chowhounds
Lunch:	Every day, 11:30 A.M.–4 P.M.
Dinner:	Monday–Friday, 4–10 P.M.; Saturday and Sunday, 4–10:30 P.M.

Atmosphere/setting: This used to be a plain old luncheonette, and it still looks like one in spite of various attempts at decorative touch-ups (track lighting, peach-colored walls). Long tables are covered with sticky red checkerboard plastic tablecloths, each with its own worn plastic water pitcher.

House specialties: Both northern and southern Indian dishes are offered, and there are winners on both sides of the menu. Samosas (fried potato and pea turnovers) are a revelation, worlds better than the greasy, bland versions served most everywhere else; masala dosa (huge crunchy lentil crêpe stuffed with potatoes, peas, and cashews) are nearly as good; murgh tikka palakwala (chunks of tandoori chicken in a sauce of creamed spinach, ginger, cumin, and tomato) cannily isolates a single flavor facet of spinach; goat or lamb biryani (rice pilaf) are hidden at the bottom of the menu but shouldn't be missed (goat's better). Simple tandoori chicken is juicy and well marinated. There are many good vegetarian entrees, most of them featuring eggplant, okra, peas, potatoes, and/or homemade cheese.

JACKSON DINER *(continued)*

Other recommendations: The chutneys (sauces) and dal (beans) that accompany most dishes are good enough to eat by themselves. Skip the temptingly cheap lunch buffet and order from the menu. You've traveled this far . . . why skimp?

Summary & comments: This remains the best Indian restaurant in New York in spite of recent inconsistency (even off days are still pretty darned good). Jackson Diner has shmancy sister restaurants in Manhattan and Long Island, but even at quadruple the price neither comes close. Flavors come alive in this kitchen; dishes that elsewhere seem one-dimensional here taste remarkably vivid and alluring. Jackson Diner is located in the heart of Little India, and you'll find myriad shops and spice stores nearby (come for lunch if you want to shop, as they close early).

Jade Palace

Chinese

★★★★

Inexpensive

Quality 91   Value A−

Zone 16   Northeastern Queens
136-14 38th Avenue, Flushing, Queens
(718) 353-3366

Reservations:	For parties of 4 or more, dinner only
When to go:	Early for dim sum
Kind of service:	Waiter service at tables
Entree range:	Dim sum plates, $2–5
Payment:	VISA, MC, AMEX
Service rating:	★★★
Friendliness rating:	★★
Transit:	7 to Flushing/Main Street
Bar:	Beer and wine only
Wine selection:	Minimal
Dress:	Casual
Disabled access:	Good, but only if you arrive early for dim sum
Clientele:	Chinese families, questing dim sum freaks
Dim sum:	Every day, 8 A.M.–4 P.M.
Lunch:	Every day, 11:30 A.M.–4 P.M.
Dinner:	Every day, 4 P.M.–midnight

Atmosphere/setting: Attractive suburban-beige interior.

House specialties: All the dim sum is first rate, from standbys like har gow (shrimp dumplings) and taro cakes to slightly more exotic fare like the various sticky rices (one in a clear plastic bowl, the other wrapped in a lotus leaf). There are a few really unusual specialties, best of which is the memorable (if unlikely sounding) New Zealand clams topped with egg custard. Some nice touches, such as the large chunks of roast pork in those rice noodle tube thingees that normally contain only ground meat.

Summary & comments: Every New York dim sum lover must at some point in his life make a pilgrimage to Flushing and eat at Jade Palace; it's as simple as that. As always, it's best to come as early as possible and sit near the kitchen (by the time the cart ladies have wheeled their offerings around the room, stuff has cooled). Dim sum gets busy, and you'll feel some pressure not to linger, but that's simply part of the deal. Staff is pretty friendly; some servers have better English skills than others, but help is only a manager away. Afterwards, stop in for a fresh juice across the street at Sweet-n-Tart Cafe (see review).

Jean's

Zone 17   Southern Queens
188-36 Linden Boulevard (near Farmer's
    Boulevard), St. Albans, Queens
(718) 525-3069

Jamaican
★★½
Inexpensive

Quality 85   Value A

Reservations:	Large groups only
When to go:	Anytime
Kind of service:	Waiter service at tables
Entree range:	$6–11
Payment:	AMEX, MC, VISA, D
Service rating:	★★★
Friendliness rating:	★★★½
Transit:	E/J/Z to Jamaica Center, then take the 4 bus
Bar:	Beer only
Wine selection:	Limited
Dress:	Casual
Disabled access:	Good; rest rooms not accessible
Clientele:	Local Jamaicans
Breakfast:	Monday–Saturday, 7 A.M.–1 P.M.; Sunday, closed
Lunch:	Monday–Saturday, 11:30 A.M.–3 P.M.
Dinner:	Monday–Saturday, 3–11 P.M.

Atmosphere/setting: Jean's consists of two restaurants. Up front, there's a relaxed cafe with waiter service, its coffee-shop ambience brightened by Jamaica travel posters. In the rear lies, incongruously, a full-sized fast food–style takeout counter. This proud neighborhood landmark is immaculate and friendly.

House specialties: Amazing fried sweet plantains, bursting with flavor; tender, mild curried goat; stewed chicken; curried shrimp; Jamaican chop suey; and soups ranging from red peas to cow foot. Drinks are super intense; even the sorrel (usually a tame, tangy beverage) packs a spicy wallop. Breakfasts are served with fried or boiled dumplings and plantains. Skip the roti (the bread is too doughy).

Summary & comments: This is particularly wholesome-tasting Island cooking; Jean's may lack the refined, personal touch of Wangah Hut (see review), but their homier Jamaican style pleases in a simpler, more modest way.

Joe's Bar and Grill

Italian	
★★	
Inexpensive	
Quality 85	Value A

CAUTION

Zone 14   S Brooklyn

255 Avenue U (near West 4th
Street), Bensonhurst, Brooklyn

(718) 372-9595

Reservations:	Not accepted
When to go:	Anytime
Kind of service:	Waiter service at tables and bar
Entree range:	$4.25–11.50
Payment:	Cash only
Service rating:	★★
Friendliness rating:	★★★
Transit:	F or N to Avenue U
Bar:	Full service
Wine selection:	House
Dress:	Casual
Disabled access:	Good
Clientele:	Hardcore drinkers and gamblers, plus an occasional diner
Lunch/Dinner:	Wednesday–Sunday, 11:30 A.M.–10:30 P.M.; Monday and Tuesday, hours vary (call ahead)

Atmosphere/setting: A seedy old wood-paneled barroom with some utilitarian tables and chairs and dusty softball trophies towering behind the whiskey bottles. Some of the city's last surviving Damon Runyon characters have claimed the near end of the bar for their own, downing shots and coffee while arguing loudly over racing forms (Joe's provides Lotto forms at the tables for more lightweight clientele). The chef-waiter-manager cooks in his domain in a rear corner, the kitchen turf demarcated from the rest of the room by low temporary walls.

House specialties: Exceptional fried calamari and amazing small rice balls (greaselessly crisp with interiors redolent of strong cheese and bits of salami; the rice itself melts in the mouth). Potato croquettes are nearly as exquisite, but the real specialty here is capuzzelle, or whole lamb head, in a light crust of bread crumbs. The cheek meat is rich and moistly tender, but aficionados consider eyeball and brain the headiest pleasures.

Other recommendations: Avoid overcooked pastas, though there's something to be said for a plate of spaghetti and shrimp made with (tasty) *fried* shrimp. The veal is just OK, and heros—though otherwise tasty—are marred by the house's lackluster tomato sauce.

Summary & comments: Any place that serves your half lamb's head (split longitudinally, wise guy) with the eye facing up has got to be pretty serious, and Joe's is pretty serious. Don't confuse it with Joe's of Avenue U (a famous—and overrated—nearby focacceria); this Joe's has been here longer (they claim), and, while the menu is uneven, what's cooked well is cooked very well indeed. This sort of place is nearly extinct; when the old horseplayers at the bar go, there'll be no one left to eat lamb head, and the chef will have to bone up on sun-dried tomatoes and arugula. Go before it's too late.

Joe's Shanghai

<table>
<tr><td></td><td>Chinese
★★★½
Moderate</td></tr>
</table>

Zone 3   Chinatown, Little Italy, and
   Lower East Side
9 Pell Street (near Bowery), Manhattan
(212) 233-8894

Quality 90   Value A

Zone 16   Northeastern Queens
136-21 37th Avenue, Flushing, Queens
(718) 539-4429

Reservations:	For parties of 10 or more
When to go:	Arrive before 6 P.M. to beat crowds
Kind of service:	Waiter service at tables
Entree range:	$6.25–19.95
Payment:	Cash only
Service rating:	★★½
Friendliness rating:	★★½
Transit:	7 to Flushing/Main Street (Zone 16); J/M/N/R/Z/6 to Canal Street (Zone 3)
Bar:	Beer only
Wine selection:	None
Dress:	Casual
Disabled access:	Queens, good; Manhattan, fair (step to dining room)
Clientele:	*New York Times* readers (Manhattan), locals and questing chowhounds (Queens)
Open:	*Manhattan:* Every day, 11 A.M.–11:15 P.M. *Queens:* Every day, 11 A.M.–10:30 P.M.

Atmosphere/setting: Many critics have snubbed Joe's interiors as no-frills Chinatown decor, but that's unfair. While seating is a bit cramped and big tables are shared with strangers (it's part of the ritual), the styling (identical in all locations: print carpets, spotlights, brown and beige wood with deep green highlights) is actually quite nice. Atmosphere-wise, they attain a comfortable middle ground between holes-in-walls and over-the-top gold-splashed Hong Kong banquet halls.

House specialties: Crab meat steamed buns, stewed pork meatballs in a succulent sauce (a.k.a. "lion's head"), shredded pork with pickled cabbage soup, anything with mushrooms, shrimp fried rice cake, hot and sour soup, pork shoulder (with honey glaze), Shanghai-fried flat noodles, shredded turnip shortcakes, soya (mock) duck, turnip buns and steamed bread (weekends only), fish fritters (incredibly fresh minced fish fried greaseless and crunchy . . . dip in a pile of salt, pepper,

172

and MSG), and, for the adventurous, soup with duck blood and black mushrooms (delicate and smoky, with lots of wok flavor).

Summary & comments: By all means, start with the crab meat steamed buns—amazing soup-filled dumplings. Wait for them to cool a bit, then delicately transfer (whatever you do, don't puncture the dough; you'll lose the soup!) one to a spoon into which you've pooled a bit of gingery soy sauce and a dab of hot sauce. Nibble a hole in the skin, suck the soup, then down the dumpling. Don't fall for the typical Chinese restaurant dishes, though; try to stick with the Shanghai specialties (i.e., anything unfamiliar). Probe the harried but affable waiters for tips, or ask about good-looking dishes passing by. The Flushing branch is much better than the popular Manhattan one; the new third location in Elmhurst is not recommended.

Johnny's Famous Reef

Zone 18 The Bronx	Seafood
2 City Island Avenue (at the very end of the island), City Island, the Bronx	★★
	Moderate
(718) 885-2086	Quality 84 Value A

Reservations:	Not accepted
When to go:	Sunday afternoons are the traditional time to come; crowd-o-phobes should pick another time (but the teeming crowd is half the fun)
Kind of service:	Self-service
Entree range:	$5–18
Payment:	Cash only
Service rating:	★★½
Friendliness rating:	★★½
Transit:	6 to Pelham Bay, take the 29 bus
Bar:	Full service
Wine selection:	Very limited
Dress:	Casual
Disabled access:	Accessible from street entrance but not parking lot; rest rooms, however, are accessible only from parking lot
Clientele:	All types from all areas of the city
Lunch/Dinner:	Sunday–Thursday, 11 A.M.–11 P.M.; Friday and Saturday, 11 A.M.–1 A.M.

Atmosphere/setting: Outdoors, an enormous concrete patio with picnic tables. Strafing, screaming flocks of seagulls and mobs of hyper kids don't distract much from the unforgettable view of Long Island Sound, a vista so bucolic that it's nearly impossible to believe that you're (barely) inside NYC limits. This is an enjoyable spot to bring a family or a date on a summer weekend day, and tons of people of every color, age, and class have been doing so for as long as anyone can remember. The interior is a time capsule: Brooklyn seaside fish shack cafeteria circa 1958, designed on the Nathan's model—a series of stations (fried stuff, drinks, etc.) are demarcated by garish yellow signs listing the dishes served there (and admonishing customers not to tip the servers). The dining area is Leftover Deco: yellow formica tables and orange chairs in a jagged, once-futuristic space. It's deliciously noisy and chaotic.

House specialties: Fried everything: lobster tails, shrimp, scallops, porgy, smelts, filet of sole, whiting, soft shell crabs, frog's legs, clams, oysters, and squid. It's not fancy cooking by any means (though the price is about 30 percent higher than you'd like . . . you wanna view, you gotta pay), but they've been at it for forty years, so they've really got it down.

Other recommendations: To break up the frying monotony, there's a raw bar, steamed clams or shrimp, clam chowder, and look-but-don't-eat corn on the cob.

Summary & comments: City Island feels a lot more New England than Gotham, but Johnny's, perched at the far tip of the island, is pure New York—though the New York of an era long past. Staunchly unrefurbished, the place is fading to funkiness, but the food itself remains reliably fresh. As with that more famous seaside attraction, Coney Island, this nostalgic slightly shabby scene—suffused with the memories of countless Sunday afternoon outings—will appeal to some more than others.

Kabab Cafe

Zone 15   NW Queens
25-12 Steinway Street, Astoria, Queens
(718) 728-9858

Egyptian
★★★½
Inexpensive

Quality 90   Value A

Reservations:	Helpful for large groups
When to go:	Anytime
Kind of service:	Waiter service at tables
Entree range:	$6–11
Payment:	Cash only
Service rating:	★★★★★
Friendliness rating:	★★★★★
Transit:	N to Astoria Boulevard or G/R to Steinway Street
Bar:	None, but BYO allowed
Wine selection:	None
Dress:	Casual
Disabled access:	Good
Clientele:	A sitcom-like cast of regulars
Lunch/Dinner:	Tuesday–Sunday, noon–midnight; Monday, closed

Atmosphere/setting: A humble but very cozy little cafe with ingeniously crafted folk-art tables, wall paintings, and various Egyptian trinkets. Chef-owner Ali is a riot and an impeccable host, and you are eating in his kitchen.

House specialties: There's always excellent falafel, baba ghanoush, and hummus, and the foul madamas (garlicky fava bean stew) is made to order. Other standard offerings include freshly made kofta (ground lamb with spices), lamb and chicken kebabs, grilled fish, salads, and sautéed vegetables (all with a sprinkle of cumin). Other than that, the menu changes daily; often a stewed meat with potatoes, some sort of soup, or whatever else you can persuade Ali to make.

Summary & comments: Ali is a trained chef and will cook almost anything you ask for (it needn't be Middle Eastern, either; for example, his pasta rocks). While from the outside this looks like your typical falafel-hummus-kebab joint, and all that stuff *is* wonderful here, Kabab Cafe is also the only source in NYC for traditional Egyptian fare like aiga (vegetable cutlet) and melokhia (a viscous and garlicky green soup). Not everything's available everyday, but shmoozing with Ali to devise an order is half the fun. It's best to let him improvise; you'll be served a sort of tasting menu with a little bit of this, a little bit of that. If he likes you, he might whip up some hummus with lime instead of lemon and a monolith of grilled bread topped with a leaf or two of fried basil . . . tall food comes to Queens. Note: this is one of the most inconsistent restaurants I know (hence the relatively mild quality rating), but spectacular highs more than compensate for the errant blah meal.

KAM CHUEH

Zone 3   Chinatown, Little Italy, and
     Lower East Side
40 Bowery (south of Canal Street),
     Manhattan
(212) 791-6868; (212) 791-6866

Chinese	
★★★½	
Moderate	
Quality 91	Value B+

Reservations:	Large groups only
When to go:	Late
Kind of service:	Waiter service at tables
Entree range:	$3.75–18
Payment:	Cash only
Service rating:	★★½
Friendliness rating:	★★★½
Transit:	J/M/N/R/Z/6 to Canal Street
Bar:	Beer only
Wine selection:	None
Dress:	Casual
Disabled access:	Poor; small step up, rest rooms not accessible
Clientele:	Good blend of Chinese and occidental mavens
Open:	Every day, 11:30 A.M.–4:30 A.M.

Atmosphere/setting: Contented fish swim spunkily through crystal clean water in front window display tanks. Humans are accommodated in an only slightly less congenial habitat: the brightly lit dining room goes for an upscale look with faux-marble tiles and glittery cheap chandeliers.

House specialties: Razor clams (or jumbo shrimp) in superb black bean sauce, salt and pepper squid (basically top-notch fried calamari sans tomato dipping sauce), chunks of excellent medium-rare T-bone steak with flowering chives, sautéed mixed vegetables (order with off-menu foo yee sauce, a briny fermented bean curd), snow pea leaves (when this super-expensive, super-delicate vegetable is in season), intense hot and sour soup, satisfying winter melon soup, flowering chives with clams, huge crabs with either ginger-scallion or black bean sauce.

Other recommendations: You can't go wrong ordering from the smaller specials menu that is full of exotic baby vegetables and fancier preparations many restaurants refuse to translate into English. Don't order egg rolls and such; the menu lists a few Chinese American workhorses, but the chef's clearly not happy about it.

Entertainment & amenities: Each table is covered with a thick wad of white plastic sheeting; don't miss the meal-end spectacle when your waiter bundles up the remains inside the topmost sheet and hauls it back to the kitchen on his back, leaving behind a new layer of clean virgin plastic.

KAM CHUEH *(continued)*

Summary & comments: Kam Chueh descends from Cantonese royalty; it's the estranged brother of the late, lamented Shing Kee, Chinatown favorite of many cognoscenti. Their menu is nearly identical and the cooking comes pretty close (their black bean sauce should be declared a cultural landmark by the city). This is an after-hours hang; it's quite the scene at two or three o'clock in the morning as gigging musicians and snazzily dressed young Chinese clubbers converge here. One could go earlier, but it wouldn't feel quite the same.

Kang Suh

Zone 6   Chelsea West
1250 Broadway (enter on 32nd Street),
  Manhattan
(212) 564-6845

Korean	
★★½	
Moderate	
Quality 84 Value B	

Reservations:	Accepted but not required
When to go:	Anytime
Kind of service:	Waiter service at tables
Entree range:	$6.95–18.95
Payment:	VISA, MC, AMEX, D, DC, JCB
Service rating:	★★★
Friendliness rating:	★★★
Transit:	B/D/F/N/Q/R to 34th Street/Herald Square or 6 to 33rd Street
Bar:	Beer, sake, and wine only
Wine selection:	Very limited
Dress:	Casual
Disabled access:	Good
Clientele:	Youthful Koreans
Open:	Every day, 24 hours

Atmosphere/setting: The second floor is a fun, loud, fluorescently lit expanse of booths and tables, each beneath a giant ventilation hood. The more sedate downstairs area (incandescent lights, red carpet, wooden tables, large sushi bar) is closed at night, giving late eaters even more of the feeling of having been booted upstairs to Korean Dinerland.

House specialties: In keeping with the modest ambience, comfort foods are best here, particularly dduk bokeum, a Korean childhood favorite of sticky rice cakes (in three different shapes) with an incendiary hot pepper paste that doesn't quite cover a charming underlying sweetness. Gal bi jjim (stewed short ribs with chestnuts and jujube) is perhaps the most accessible dish on the menu and also one of the most delicious; the succulent meat's falling-apart tender and a deep-flavored, slightly sweet sauce makes the perfect foil (but where are the chestnuts?). Noodle dishes like jab chae (clear noodles with vegetables and beef) are winners, as are the barbecued short ribs (kalbi) and chicken that are considered house specialties (Kang Suh grills the old-fashioned way, over live coals). Pa jun (savory pan-fried rice flour vegetable/seafood cakes) are gloppy-crunchy, supercaloric, and thoroughly addictive; skip the fancier versions with stuff like oysters. In fact, skip anything that sounds fancy here. This fast, deft kitchen turns out consistently good eats with vibrant lusty flavors, but don't ask them to make anything requiring much fuss.

Other recommendations: Also in keeping with the modest ambience, the panchan (assorted freebie appetizers) are strictly vestigial; even the kimchee is pedestrian. For memorable panchan (and a much more grown-up atmosphere), try Woo Chon (see review).

Entertainment & amenities: Half-priced parking is available in the garage next door upon validation in restaurant.

Summary & comments: Don't let the setting fool you . . . you'll pay as much here as at more expensive-seeming places (especially for at-table barbecue, which carries a two-order minimum at nearly twenty bucks per order). But budget diners do have some $7 to $10 entrees to choose from.

KARAM RESTAURANT

	Lebanese
	★★★★
	Inexpensive
	Quality 92 Value A

Zone 14   Southern Brooklyn
8519 4th Avenue (between 85th and 86th
   Streets), Bay Ridge, Brooklyn
(718) 745-5227

Reservations:	Not accepted
When to go:	Anytime
Kind of service:	Self-service
Entree range:	$3.50–10
Payment:	Cash only
Service rating:	★★★
Friendliness rating:	★★★
Transit:	R to 86th Street
Bar:	None
Wine selection:	None
Dress:	Casual
Disabled access:	Poor
Clientele:	White collar Lebanese
Open:	Every day, 6 A.M.–1 A.M.

Atmosphere/setting: This is a glary little takeout stand with a few bare-bones self-service tables. Meats revolve in the window, high display cases groan with enticing foods and desserts, and you can help yourself at the beverage case. The clientele is mostly well-to-do Middle Easterners (white collar Lebanese have lived in this neighborhood for decades) who might otherwise be eating in more expensive places but who flock here when homesick for authentic, masterful Lebanese cooking.

House specialties: Chicken shwarma sandwiches, rotisserie chicken, hummus, tabbouleh, moujadara (lentils, rice, and sweet fried onions, served cold), shish taouk (chicken shish kebab), tongue (briskety, slow-cooked, and totally unrubbery), herby and pungent spinach pies, lahambajin (ground lamb and spices on toasted pita), closed meat pies, nutty, lemony eggplant salad. For the brave, there's spinal cord in an understated garlic and parsely sauce spiked with cinnamon and delicately sautéed brain.

Other recommendations: Don't skip dessert. Try anything with phyllo dough, such as baklava; or, if you don't mind rose water (the ubiquitous perfumey-soapy flavor in Middle Eastern desserts), try mhalabia, an aromatic milk pudding. Also: great mini pies stuffed with walnuts and honey or with cheese.

Summary & comments: Karam really makes you reexamine your restaurant preconceptions. What looks like a generic falafel joint actually serves the finest

Lebanese food in the city. If you can tune out the commotion (or, better, revel in it), you'll enjoy—for under $10—Lebanese deliciousness that can't be bought at any price in Manhattan. The chicken shwarma (like most things here, better ordered as a sandwich than in a platter) deserves honors in the Food Hall of Fame. They cut off shavings from a spinning, shaggy mass of fresh, succulent marinated chicken, lather it with the most amazing, intense garlic sauce (a dead ringer for Catalan allioli) and insert strips of crunchy pink (lightly) pickled turnip, all rolled—not stuffed—in grilled pita and toasted and pressed, like a Cuban sandwich. Many other offerings are nearly as good. It's worth the trip.

Kasturi

Zone 7   Chelsea
  East and Gramercy
83 Lexington Avenue (between 26th and
  27th Streets), Manhattan
(212) 685-4346

Indian
★★
Inexpensive
Quality 75   Value A–

Reservations:	Not accepted
When to go:	Anytime
Kind of service:	Self-service
Entree range:	$3–7
Payment:	Cash only
Service rating:	★★
Friendliness rating:	★★★½
Transit:	6 to 28th Street
Bar:	None
Wine selection:	None
Dress:	Casual
Disabled access:	Poor (steps)
Clientele:	Cab drivers, locals
Open:	Every day, 24 hours

Atmosphere/setting: A utilitarian basement eating hall with large-screen TV and primitive wall murals (signed with a beeper number). Order at the steam table counter.

House specialties: This is a rare source for Bangladeshi fish curries. The one simply called "fish curry" is skinny whole papa fish (carnivorous, I'm told) in a rich tomatoey curry with late-onset heat. There are also crispy french fried wedges of buffalo fish doused in an acidic sauce with lots of onion. Everything's served with mounds of rice reheated in the microwave.

Other recommendations: Tandoori items, biriyanis, and breads are not recommended; other curries vary. You'll do much better ordering from the prepared dishes at the steam table than ordering from the menu—with the exception of the samosas which are splendid only when fried to order.

Summary & comments: It's hard to find good Indian fish for a reasonable price; while Kasturi's fare is more consistent in its reasonableness than in its goodness, most days those curries are quite tasty and service is very friendly. Though many local Indian restaurants are Bangladeshi-owned and Bangladeshis and Bengalis are famous for their fish preparations, regrettably few choose to cook them.

KATE'S JOINT

◆ CAUTION

Zone 5   East Village
58 Avenue B, Manhattan
(212) 777-7059

Vegetarian
★★
Moderate

Quality 83   Value B

Reservations:	Parties of 6 or more
When to go:	Anytime
Kind of service:	Waiter service at tables and bar
Entree range:	$8–10
Payment:	VISA, MC, AMEX, D, DC
Service rating:	★★
Friendliness rating:	★★
Transit:	F to 2nd Avenue
Bar:	Beer and wine
Wine selection:	Small
Dress:	Casual
Disabled access:	Good
Clientele:	Neighborhood bohemians
Brunch:	Saturday and Sunday, 10 A.M.–4:30 P.M.
Lunch/Dinner:	Monday–Friday, 9 A.M.–11 P.M.; Saturday and Sunday, 10 A.M.–11 P.M.

Atmosphere/setting: Informal, mellow bohemian cafe with brooding, dark-colored walls and a good view of the East Village sidewalk parade.

House specialties: Grilled vegetable hero, soups, hummus (chickpea spread) with roasted garlic, mock-meat dishes (especially chile con tofu carne).

Other recommendations: Specials can be hit-or-miss.

Summary & comments: There are few vegetarian restaurants of merit in New York, but this is a notable exception. Chef-owner Kate Halpern cooks with a deft, knowing touch; her grilled vegetable hero is a knockout, her hummus assertively pungent and garlicky, and her mock meat dishes (made from carefully marinated tofu) are both delicious and convincingly meat-like. Her trick? She likes meat and cooks it for herself all the time. As a result, Halpern has the easy panache of a well-rounded chef, rather than the usual ascetic veggiecook primness. Kate's Joint was a pioneer in the new restaurant row that's cropped up on formerly seedy Avenue B; while the neighborhood is still borderline, it's no longer dangerous. Expect the usual spacy vegetarian restaurant servers (it must be the meat deprivation).

KERVAN

	Turkish
	★★★★
	Moderate
	Quality 94 Value B

Zone 20   Nearby in New Jersey
360 Lawton Avenue (near Anderson and
    Grant Avenues), Cliffside Park
(201) 945-7227

Reservations:	Accepted
When to go:	Anytime
Kind of service:	Waiter service at tables
Entree range:	$9–17
Payment:	VISA, MC, AMEX, D, DC, JCB
Service rating:	★★★★
Friendliness rating:	★★★★
Transit:	NJ Transit bus 159 from gate 200 of Port Authority Terminal to intersection of Anderson and Grant Avenues
Bar:	Full service
Wine selection:	Decent variety of inexpensive
Dress:	Casual
Disabled access:	Good; rest rooms tight
Clientele:	A potentially explosive mix of local Turks, Armenians, and Jews (miraculously, they all get along)
Lunch:	Every day, noon–6 P.M.
Dinner:	Every day, 6–10:30 P.M.

Atmosphere/setting: Very 1960s upscale suburban: linen tablecloths and napkins, mirrored walls, worn nice carpets, expensive large chairs, and ornate cheap chandeliers. There's a spotless open kitchen toward the rear displaying the appetizer plates; head back there before ordering and ask chef-owner Nazmi or one of his assistants what's what.

House specialties: Nearly everything cooked here is the finest version I've ever tried, but the crème de la crème is their scrumptious Iskender kebab—chunks of donner (a.k.a. gyro, a.k.a. shwarma, here made of veal and lamb) topped with garlicky, buttery croutons and doused in homemade yogurt and a tomato sauce so perfect you'll wish they served spaghetti. Other kebabs include juicy, spicy adana made from ground beef and lamb and incredibly tender and flavorful lamb chops. Even the chicken kebab—often dry and bland elsewhere—is worthy, well-marinated and removed from the flame in the nick of time. Slightly less exquisite are relatively plain shish kebab and kach kach kebab (adana in tomato sauce; a pale cousin to the Iskender)

Backing up to the appetizers, or mazza: The smoked eggplant in Turkish eggplant salad is hardly chopped or otherwise fooled with; the small portion exudes

185

concentrated deliciousness. Grape leaves are fresh and plump, and lebni—a thick yogurt spread (as with most mazza, scoop it up with bread) heavy with garlic and walnuts—is downright ambrosial. Nutty hummus is very lemony and fluffy and the tabbouleh properly aromatic and fresh with lots of parsley; ezme—a scarlet paste of crushed fresh vegetables, walnuts, and red pepper, is heavenly, as are boreks, which appear here as tiny delicate pastry twists redolent of strong cheese. Even rice—buttery and with crunchy pot-stickings mixed in—is a peak experience (it comes with the kebabs, but order an extra portion), and long, beautifully meaty, crunchy french fries are just as good.

Save room for dessert: pastries such as baklava, like the mazza, are tiny in scale, delicate and brimming with focused flavor. Order with Turkish coffee and dollops of kaymak, the exceedingly thick, rich cream that's a dead ringer for the clotted cream Brits serve at tea (a little goes a long way).

Other recommendations: Drink Ayran (a thin, quenching yogurt drink), anise-flavored raki (a strong liquor that when cut with water—which is advisable—turns milky white), or a soft drink; the tap water in this part of Jersey is nearly undrinkable, and it would be a pity to tarnish a perfect meal.

Summary & comments: There's no first-rate Turkish food to be found in the five boroughs (Cafe Istanbul—see review—is an exception, but it's more a specialist than a mainstream Turkish kitchen). Magnificence awaits in Jersey, however; for those willing to go a bit out of their way. Kervan cooks the cuisine about as well as any mere mortal could stand; it's regarded with awe even by locals blessed with many Turkish restaurants to choose from. Nazmi Cardak is a masterful chef, able to evoke deep, intense flavors, and the exceptionally friendly and accommodating staff ably steers you through his offerings, suggesting half portions of kebabs and off-menu appetizer samplers. Those samplers, together with various mixed grill options, are terrific bargains; bring a large group and you can easily try most of the menu.

Killmeyer's Old Bavaria Inn

German

★★★★

Moderate

Quality 91   Value B

Zone 19   Staten Island
4254 Arthur Kill Road (near Sharrott's
    Road), Staten Island
(718) 984-1202

Reservations:	Not accepted
When to go:	Anytime
Kind of service:	Waiter service at tables
Entree range:	$10–30
Payment:	MC, VISA
Service rating:	★★½
Friendliness rating:	★★½
Transit:	Ferry to the 74 bus toward Tartanville
Bar:	Full service
Wine selection:	Limited
Dress:	Nice casual
Disabled access:	Good
Clientele:	Locals
Lunch:	Monday–Saturday, 11 A.M.–4 P.M.
Dinner:	Monday–Thursday, 5–10 P.M.; Friday and Saturday, 5–11 P.M.; Sunday, 2–10 P.M.

Atmosphere/setting: This building is thought to date back to the eighteenth century. It's approached via Sharrott's Road, a barely paved route through the Clay Pit Ponds State Preserve, a setting so bucolic that the time travel sensation sets in long before you reach this surrealistically Bavarian relic. The main dining room's stage features an oom-pah duo—two older guys in liederhosen and feathered caps who announce tunes with thick Brooklyn accents—and the enormous 150-year-old bar (of hand-carved wood, with intricate details), along with the ceiling fans, antique light fixtures, and dark green–painted tin ceiling lend a Wild West-meets-Würzburg decorative spin. Naturally, there's an outdoor beer garden with picnic tables, cobblestones, and a large bandstand/dancing area.

House specialties: The enormous slow-roasted Fred Flintstonian veal haunch is the most expensive item on the menu at $30, but it could feed half of Bedrock. All portions are large enough to share; try the Farmer's Feast, which offers tastes of perfectly grilled bratwurst (crunchy—almost burnt—outside but juicy inside), unforgettable smoked pork chops, and silky roast pork in a thick gravy (perfect for dunking the accompanying starchy bread dumplings). Potato pancakes are blissful—very crunchy, with starchy, oniony interiors—and sauerkraut and herby, tangy pickled cabbage are top-notch as well. The menu features

187

plenty of fancy, creamy dishes like chicken in wine and mushroom sauce, turkey croquettes in herby cream sauce, and biere suppe (beer soup served over cubes of black bread), as well as large, crispy, expertly fried wiener schnitzels. For dessert: creamy Barenjager ice cream has the liqueur blended in, and, of course, there's warm apple strudel.

Other recommendations: The immense beer collection is one of the finest on Staten Island and well-priced, too. Erdinger's dark malty wheat beer is on tap, and the bottle list includes dozens of top-notch German lagers (try a tangy Schneider Weisse, strong Aventinus, or ultrasmoky Schlenkerla), as well as some excellent Belgians.

Entertainment & amenities: Bands—leaning heavily toward polka, but including a smattering of rock and jazz—play in the beer garden on summer evenings; during colder weather, it's synthesized oom-pah with the indefatigable Brooklyn twosome in the main dining room.

Summary & comments: Staten Island is the most old-fashioned borough, but Killmeyers lags by centuries rather than mere decades. Well-run and carefully maintained but never modernized; it's no stretch at all to imagine travelers hitching their horse-drawn carriages here for dinner. Though tucked into the furthest corner of the island, it's well worth a visit from Manhattan for the superb German cooking alone.

La Espiga

Zone 15   Northwestern Queens
La Espiga Original
42-13 102nd Street, Corona, Queens
(718) 779-7898

Zone 15   Northwestern Queens
La Espiga Bakery II
32-44 31st Street (between Broadway and 34th Avenue), Astoria, Queens
(718) 777-1993

Reservations:	Not accepted
When to go:	Anytime
Kind of service:	Waiter service at counter
Entree range:	$4–5
Payment:	Cash only
Service rating:	★★
Friendliness rating:	★★
Transit:	7 to 103rd Street–Corona Plaza; N to Broadway (Bakery II)
Bar:	None
Wine selection:	None
Dress:	Casual
Disabled access:	Poor (Corona): steps up and rest room not accessible; better (Astoria): rest room not accessible
Clientele:	Mexican workers
Breakfast:	*Astoria:* Every day, 9–11 A.M.
	Corona: Every day, 7–11 A.M.
Lunch/Dinner:	*Astoria:* Every day, 11 A.M.–10:30 P.M.
	Corona: Monday–Saturday, 11 A.M.–11 P.M.; Sunday, 11 A.M.–10 P.M.

Atmosphere/setting: Absolutely bare-assed minimum. These people are not fooling around—this is serious Mexican soul food and nothing else. La Espiga I has more elbow room for eating in but is also more remote. La Espiga II, right under the N train, is easier to get to, but it's smaller and less friendly.

House specialties: Pambazos are a Mexico City specialty extremely hard to find in this country. A torta bun (Mexican hard roll) is fried along with its eventual filling of diced chorizo sausage and potatoes until the bread becomes red and crunchy. Cheese and lettuce are added, and the result is magical. Everything's good here—enchiladas suizas, flautas, tacos, tortas, you name it. Sometimes you can even find the rarest of rareties: quesadillas with huitlacoche, a mild succulent black fungus that grows on corn.

Other recommendations: The Mexican pastries are interesting, if not overwhelmingly delicious. Serve yourself with the tongs and bring trayfuls to the register.

Summary & comments: These places call themselves bakeries, but, as their slogan goes, they "ain't just bread." The two outlets play musical chefs, so it's hard to keep track of which is best at any given moment. But year in and year out, Las Espigas have remained the most dependable venues for authentic Mexican eats.

La Hacienda

Zone 12   Harlem, Morning-
    side Heights, and Washington Heights
219 East 116th Street (between 2nd and
    3rd Avenues), Manhattan
(212) 987-1617

Mexican
★★½
Inexpensive

Quality 85   Value A

Reservations:	Not accepted
When to go:	Anytime
Kind of service:	Waiter service at tables
Entree range:	$6–12
Payment:	Cash only
Service rating:	★★
Friendliness rating:	★★
Transit:	6 to 116th Street
Bar:	Beer only
Wine selection:	None
Dress:	Casual
Disabled access:	Not accessible
Clientele:	Locals
Open:	Every day, 11 A.M.–11:30 P.M.

Atmosphere/setting: Like the mess hall in a big Mexican hacienda: cavernous, slightly gloomy, and lots of fun.

House specialties: Tacos are generously portioned and well dressed (with particularly fresh, aromatic red and green salsas); order them with tender goat (barbacoa) or, even better, with exemplary extra-spicy chorizo (also good in torta sandwiches). Quesadillas here take the form of fried doughy pockets; weekends only, they're available with off-menu huitlacoche (a succulent black fungus that grows on corn, a particularly rare delicacy). Both antojitos (snacks like tamales, nachos, and flautas) and entrees (standards like mole poblano and enchiladas suizas as well as extremely unusual specialties like Yecapiztla aged beef and garlic shrimp cooked with brandy) are recommended here.

Other recommendations: This is one of the few Mexican places where you'll want to order dessert; they do a nice job with fresas con crema (strawberries with sour cream) and ensalada de frutas (fruit salad).

Entertainment & amenities: Live mariachi music weekends, 4–11 P.M.

Summary & comments: Perhaps because the immigrant population is so new to New York, Mexican restaurants here can be vexingly inconsistent. La Hacienda has remained one of Manhattan's very top spots for several years, but even this neighborhood landmark (almost totally undiscovered by outsiders) has its off days. Give them a try, though; good days are very very good.

La Pizza Fresca

<table>
<tr><td colspan="2">Italian/Pizza</td></tr>
<tr><td colspan="2">★★★★</td></tr>
<tr><td colspan="2">Moderate</td></tr>
<tr><td colspan="2">Quality 93   Value A</td></tr>
</table>

Zone 7   Chelsea East and Gramercy
31 East 20th Street (between Broadway
   and Park Avenue), Manhattan
(212) 598-0141

Reservations:	Parties of 3 or more
When to go:	Anytime
Kind of service:	Waiter service at tables
Entree range:	$7.95–14.95
Payment:	VISA, MC, AMEX, DC
Service rating:	★★★½
Friendliness rating:	★★★
Transit:	N/R to 23rd Street or 6 to 23rd Street
Bar:	Beer and wine only
Wine selection:	Extensive Italian
Dress:	Casual chic
Disabled access:	Good
Clientele:	Locals, local workers
Lunch:	Every day, noon–3:30 P.M., Saturday, noon–4 P.M.; no lunch Sunday
Dinner:	Monday–Saturday, 5:30–11 P.M.; Sunday, 5–10:30 P.M.

Atmosphere/setting: Stylishly modern and sleek, with white stucco walls and handsome wood-burning oven on proud display.

House specialties: Amazing Neapolitan pizzas, such as cime di rapa (with broccoli rabe, sausage, and buffalo mozzarella) and margherita (tomato, buffalo mozzarella, Parmigiano Reggiano, olive oil, and basil); genuinely homestyle Italian pastas such as gnocchetti al pesto genovese (handmade potato gnocchi with pesto) and penne all'arrabbiata (with red pepper and garlic spiced tomato sauce). All salads are first-rate, and espresso and capucino (made from Illy brand coffee) are among New York's best.

Summary & comments: These folks are the only New York members of the Naples-based La Vera Pizza Napoletana (the sanctioning body for heavyweight pizza-makers), and they bake immaculately authentic, beautifully prepared, brick-oven pizza Neapolitan style, topped with imported buffalo mozzarella that's incredibly buttery and subtle (other ingredients are just as heavenly). The pastas are equally good, made just like Over There. This kitchen can do almost no wrong, but skip dessert—only the tiramisu is made in-house, and the chef's heart isn't in it.

La Porteña

Zone 15   Northwestern Queens
74-25 37th Avenue (between 74th and
    75th Streets), Jackson Heights, Queens
(718) 458-8111

Argentinian
★★★★
Moderate

Quality 91   Value A

Reservations:	Weeknights or for 5 or more
When to go:	Anytime
Kind of service:	Waiter service at tables
Entree range:	$7.50–15.95; mixed grill for two, $25.95
Payment:	VISA, MC, AMEX
Service rating:	★★★
Friendliness rating:	★★½
Transit:	7 to 74th Street/Broadway or E to Roosevelt Avenue/Broadway
Bar:	Beer and wine only
Wine selection:	Good South Americans
Dress:	Casual
Disabled access:	Good; rest rooms not accessible
Clientele:	Locals
Lunch:	Monday–Friday, noon–3:30 P.M.
Dinner:	Monday–Friday, 3:30 P.M.–midnight
Lunch/Dinner:	Saturday and Sunday, noon–midnight

Atmosphere/setting: The grill beckons inside the front window (take a good look at what's cooking on your way in), and many other items are on display in a refrigerator case just below. The dining room is warm and vibrant, furnished in kitsch Argentinian cowboy: woody walls festooned with lassos and other such gewgaws, and ceiling fans with antique lighting fixtures hanging from ceiling beams. Gruff waiters dress up like gauchos in broad leather belts studded with Argentinian coins; their neckerchiefs are color coded to indicate rank (waiters = red, busboys = light blue, waterboys = dark blue).

House specialties: La Porteña is famous for its meaty chorizo ("pork sausage" on the menu), and the blood sausage is also tops. The popular mixed grill platter includes both, as well as skirt steak, short rib, sweetbreads, and tripe. Sirloin steak is a humongous 18-ounce slab for $14 that drapes over the sides of the plate and is served (as are all grilled meats) with either huge platters of hand-cut fries or moist rice cooked in rich broth. The meats (which include filet mignon, shell steak, pork chops, roast chicken, and more) pick up considerable smoky flavor from the charcoal and are often served a tad more done than stipulated, so order accordingly. There's a lot of Italian blood in Argentina, so much of the nonmeat menu consists of pastas, milanesas, and such; the gnocci ("gnoquis" on the menu) and canelones (spinach and cheese–stuffed pasta tubes topped with bechamel or tomato sauce) are particularly good. The puffy potato and onion omelet (reheated, Castillian style) is also recommended.

Other recommendations: Empanadas (pastry turnovers stuffed with vegetables, meat, or fish) are becoming trendy in Manhattan, but La Porteña's put others to shame; they—like everything else—taste even better dunked in the awesome chimichurri (a green sauce of parsely, garlic, and lemon that's always swathed on). There are a number of good salads (with ingredients like watercress, avocado, heart of palm, prawns, and red onion), and this is spud heaven—choose from steamed, mashed, french fried, or Spanish-style potatoes (fried slices), with or without chopped garlic *(provenzal)*. When the room's crowded, stick with mashed or steamed—the cooks sometimes rush the frying on busy nights, with soggy results. Nice onion soup, based on a rich chicken stock, is served French style with cheese on top (not Gruyère, though).

Entertainment & amenities: The restaurant offers discount parking at 37-18 75th Street (between Roosevelt and 37th Avenues).

Summary & comments: New York's most respected Argentinian grill has come a long way since its origins as a humble butcher shop; as they've grown popular, the owners have kept reinvesting, and this is now one of Jackson Heights's trendiest restaurants. Quality hasn't wavered at all and prices remain unbelievably low, especially considering the excellent beef. How many pricey Manhattan steakhouses can boast such a delicious array of side dishes, much less an entire menu of Italian entrees and pastas?

La Xelaju

Zone 17   Southern Queens
87-52 168th Street (just north of
    Hillside Avenue), Jamaica, Queens
(718) 206-1457

Guatemalan

★★★★

Inexpensive

Quality 91   Value A

Reservations:	Not accepted
When to go:	Anytime
Kind of service:	Waiter service at tables
Entree range:	$5–8
Payment:	Cash only
Service rating:	★★½
Friendliness rating:	★★½
Transit:	F to 169th Street
Bar:	None
Wine selection:	None
Dress:	Casual
Disabled access:	Good
Clientele:	Guatemalans from all over the area (friendly, but a bit surprised to be joined by outsiders)
Open:	Every day, 9 A.M.–10:30 P.M.

Atmosphere/setting: With dishes priced so low (you'll feast for under $10), there's not much slack in this restaurant's budget for decoration. Nonetheless, the sweet, kindly Morales family has managed to make their bare storefront feel homey, a refuge for local Guatemalans and for anyone who wishes to feel Guatemalan for a day.

House specialties: Tacos (really more like flautas; homemade tortillas rolled around meaty filling and deep fried, topped with dabs of good tomato sauce); salpicón, a strangely Thai-like salad of cold ground pork with ground radishes; tender tamales wrapped in a banana leaf; revolcado (pork parts in a seductive, complex sauce); and carne cecina, a thin steak with wonderful beans. Atol corn drink (either "de elote" from fresh corn or "de maiz" from dried) is amazing (but rich; almost a meal in itself), but best of all are the handmade tortillas; plump and mesmerizingly flavorful, they're the apotheosis of corn.

Other recommendations: There are dishes you'll recognize from Mexican restaurants, but the versions here are subtly skewed. In addition to those tacos, there are chiles rellenos, enchiladas, tostadas, and chorizos, all prepared the Guatemalan way.

Summary & comments: This is likely the only Guatemalan restaurant in New York, and we'll never need another. Señora Morales reigns over her frying pans with the offhand absorption of a master, and everything she cooks is beyond scrumptious. As in many Latin American restaurants, most dishes are only made on weekends, but on any given night it would be more than worth the trip for those tortillas alone. If the food and ambience are supremely homey, so is the service. Expect long waits and a certain amount of well-intended confusion.

LENTO'S

CAUTION

Zone 13   N Brooklyn
833 Union Street (between 6th
    and 7th Avenues), Park Slope, Brooklyn
(718) 399-8782

Italian/Pizza
★★★
Moderate

Quality 91   Value B

Reservations:	Parties of 6 or more
When to go:	Anytime
Kind of service:	Waiter service at tables
Entree range:	$6.50–17.95
Payment:	VISA, MC, AMEX
Service rating:	★★½
Friendliness rating:	★★★
Transit:	2/3 to Grand Army Plaza or M/N/R to Union Street
Bar:	Beer and wine only
Wine selection:	Limited
Dress:	Casual
Disabled access:	Good
Clientele:	Locals
Lunch:	Every day, 11:30 A.M.–5 P.M.
Dinner:	Sunday–Thursday, 5–11:30 P.M.; Friday and Saturday, 5 P.M.–1:30 A.M.

Atmosphere/setting: One of the most spacious, atmospheric, high-ceilinged eateries in the neighborhood; this used to be a carriage house.

House specialties: If you like very thin crust pizza, this is the pie of your dreams. The crust is razor thin and impeccably crisp, the cheese fresh and full-flavored, and the sauce tangy. Though you'd swear the delicate flavor and hypercrisp texture were imparted by baking in a brick oven, that's not the case. Believe it or not, it's a standard oven—clearly there are secret techniques involved in the construction of a Lento's pie. However they do it, the result is so delicious, with all elements merging to pure harmony, that it would spoil the exquisite equilibrium to add toppings. And, indeed, while the toppings are worthy, it's the cheese pizza that rules.

Other recommendations: Heroes, especially the parmigiana ones, are excellent; entrees and pastas vary.

Summary & comments: Lento's has been serving pizza (in their original Bay Ridge location, still operating at 7001 3rd Avenue, (718) 745-9197) since the days when it was a Prohibition-era speakeasy catering not to Zagat-clutching foodies but to a local neighborhood clientele. Having baked pizzas according to their unique, idiosyncratic methods for so many decades, the kitchen's able to turn out outrageously harmonious pies with a confident shrug. Balance this perfect comes not from trying but by doing.

Little Portugal

Zone 21 Nassau County, Long Island	Portuguese
241 Mineola Boulevard (south of Jericho	★★★½
Turnpike), Mineola, Long Island	Inexpensive
(516) 742-9797	Quality 91 Value A

Reservations:	Not accepted
When to go:	Anytime
Kind of service:	Waiter service at bar and tables
Entree range:	$5.75–12.95
Payment:	VISA, MC, AMEX, D, DC, JCB
Service rating:	★★½
Friendliness rating:	★★½
Transit:	Taxi from Long Island Railroad Mineola Station
Bar:	Full service
Wine selection:	Small Portuguese list; try Presidente, a good, tart, vinho verde
Dress:	Casual
Disabled access:	Good in front of bar; back dining room and rest rooms up two steps
Clientele:	Portuguese immigrants, old and young
Lunch/Dinner:	Monday–Friday, noon–10 P.M.; Saturday, noon–11 P.M.; Sunday, noon–9 P.M.

Atmosphere/setting: This bar is just *exactly* like being in Portugal, down to the sugar—an extra-large helping, in packets shipped in from Lisbon). Satellite TV blasts Portuguese shows, wistful old men chain smoke at the bar, and Portuguese yuppies (puppies?) gather after work for darts and beer. The American pop music issuing from the jukebox is just one more authentic touch. Eat at the bar itself, at one of a few small tables nearby, or in the boxy back room. If smoke and noise bug you, go eat in the more refined main restaurant. In summertime, barbecue is cooked and served on the outdoor patio.

House specialties: There are always a couple of meat dishes and a couple of fish dishes, plus a soup (which you shouldn't miss; Portugal's one of the very best soup countries). Specials change daily, but look for things like stuffed baby squid, roast chicken, rice with mixed seafood, fried sardines, grilled fish or steak, and pork with clams. Portions are huge, prices low, and flavor reliably scrumptious.

Summary & comments: Little Portugal has two faces: first (and best), there's a bar area (plus back room) filled with smoke and TV soccer matches and nasal Portuguese inflections where bartenders fling huge lovingly prepared plates of very traditional home cooking at you for under ten bucks. And then there's the restaurant itself where non-Portuguese go for expensive, fancified cooking in an elegant, safe, spoon-fed-for-outsiders, Epcot Portuguese Pavilion ambience. It's not hard to figure out where the staff tries to direct outsiders. You've got to prove yourself worthy to eat in the bar part, the *real* part. Walk in confidently. Nod and smile at the bartender. Don't gawk, don't hesitate, just head in (the entrance is right off the sidewalk; the main restaurant is set back from the road) and take a seat in the bar's back room. After you're seated, send emissaries back to the bar to read the blackboard, decode what they can from the Portuguese and (apologetically) ask the bartender to explain the remainder. Don't be too demanding; he's friendly but busy, and it's not his job to do the "welcome to our cuisine" shtick— that's what the main restaurant is for. If you become a regular, you may be permitted to order a few things off the fancy menu at bar prices.

MABAT

<table>
<tr><td></td><td>Kosher/Israeli</td></tr>
<tr><td></td><td>★★★★</td></tr>
<tr><td></td><td>Moderate</td></tr>
<tr><td></td><td>Quality 92   Value B</td></tr>
</table>

Zone 14   Southern Brooklyn
1809 East 7th Street (near Kings
   Highway), Flatbush, Brooklyn
(718) 339-3300

Reservations:	Not accepted
When to go:	Anytime
Kind of service:	Waiter service at tables
Entree range:	$5.95–16.95 (mostly toward the high end)
Payment:	Cash only
Service rating:	★★★
Friendliness rating:	★★★
Transit:	F to Kings Highway or D/Q to Kings
Bar:	None
Wine selection:	None
Dress:	Nice casual
Disabled access:	Fair; one step up, rest rooms not accessible
Clientele:	Well-heeled, Sephardic Jews
Lunch/Dinner:	Sunday–Thursday, noon–12:30 A.M.; Friday, closed; Saturday, open one hour after sunset

Atmosphere/setting: A boxy but inviting cafe, painted in vibrant colors. The open grill spills forth whiffs of garlic and sizzles of flame-seared meat, and the room feels alive with the bristling excitement of mavens (all-knowing connoisseurs) who know they're about to eat very, very well. The scene here is sophisticated—kosher chic, if you will—and people dine fashionably late. Mabat cooks Israeli style, not eastern European Ashkenazic, so while this place is glatt kosher, don't even *think* of looking for pickles and rye bread.

House specialties: Lamb, beef, chicken, or sweetbread skewers and steaks relentlessly marinated and impeccably broiled; sinaya, a luscious blend of grilled turkey, fried onions, and mushrooms on a bed of doctored-up tahini; lamb soup (spoon in spicy, slimy hilbeh, made from fenugreek); Moroccan-style pastry flutes filled with ground meat; roasted marinated onions.

Other recommendations: The hugely aromatic, gaspacho-esque hot sauce is irresistible; you'll want to lard (pardon the expression) it onto everything.

Summary & comments: Much kosher meat in New York is so tough and tasteless that it's practically a religious asceticism for observant Jews to choke the stuff down. Mabat, on the other hand, is one of the best steakhouses in town, kosher or not. It ain't cheap (what's more, there are no menus to tell you prices; this is something of a Yemenite high rollers' hangout, so money is no object), but

MADAT (continued)

the food—and the scene in general—is so evocative that you'll feel utterly transported. The spicing, the marinade, and the condiments are all very different from what most are used to, so a meal here makes a great change of pace (you'll receive kind help in ordering this unfamiliar stuff from the fashionable young servers). While meat's the thing, there are interesting sides and appetizers that change daily; head to the display counter and point at whatever looks good.

Margon Restaurant

	Latin American
Zone 8 Midtown West and Theater District	★★
136 West 46th Street, Manhattan	Inexpensive
(212) 354-5013	Quality 84 Value A

Reservations:	Not accepted
When to go:	Anytime
Kind of service:	Self-service
Entree range:	$5.25–7.25 (breakfast, $2)
Payment:	Cash only
Service rating:	★★½
Friendliness rating:	★★★
Transit:	B/D/F/Q to 47–50 Streets/Rockefeller Center or N/R/S/1/2/3/7/9 to 42nd Street/Times Square
Bar:	None
Wine selection:	None
Dress:	Casual
Disabled access:	None
Clientele:	Local workers
Breakfast:	Monday–Friday, 6 A.M.–10:30 P.M.; Saturday, 6:30 A.M.–10:30 A.M.
Lunch:	Monday–Friday, 10:30 A.M.–4 P.M.; Saturday, 10:30 A.M.–2:30 P.M.; Sunday, closed

Atmosphere/setting: A harshly lit, bare-bones, hustle-your-tray-through-the-line basement cafeteria.

House specialties: Roast chicken, octopus salad, rice and beans, fried plantains; all the standard-issue Latino luncheonette fare, but much tastier than usual.

Summary & comments: If you need to catch a quick lunch in Midtown, this place will get you in and out in a jiffy (don't sweat long lines—they move quickly), but patrons' fast-shoveling forks belie the high quality of the food. Everything's very fresh and made with care. There are precious few good Latin lunch counters left, and friendly, efficient Margon is a proud bastion.

Mavalli Palace

Zone 7   Chelsea East and Gramercy
46 East 29th Street, Manhattan
(212) 679-5535

Indian	
★★★½	
Moderate	
Quality 89	Value A

Reservations:	Accepted
When to go:	Anytime
Kind of service:	Waiter service at tables
Entree range:	$6.75–14.95
Payment:	VISA, MC, AMEX, DC
Service rating:	★★★½
Friendliness rating:	★★★
Transit:	6 to 28th Street
Bar:	Full service
Wine selection:	Small
Dress:	Nice casual
Disabled access:	Good, but rest rooms not accessible
Clientele:	Indian families, businessmen
Lunch:	Tuesday–Sunday, noon–3 P.M.
Dinner:	Tuesday–Sunday, 5–10 P.M.; Monday, closed

Atmosphere/setting: Quiet, relaxing, and surprisingly elegant—perfect for a date—considering the reasonable prices. Beautiful wood floors, uncommonly well spaced tables, and blessedly low noise levels.

House specialties: Sukka alu (mildly spicy potatoes with green curry leaves), chanamasala (chick peas with pomegranate), alu gobhi (cauliflower and potatoes sautéed with tomatoes and spices), onion rava masala (rice crêpe filled with potatoes, peas, and onions), masala dosa (similar, with lentil crêpe), kancheepuram iddly (fluffy spiced lentil cakes), uttappam (a spongy-crunchy pancake with various toppings), and thalis (decorative metal pans bearing tastes of many items).

Other recommendations: Great South Indian munchies: don't miss the masala cashew nuts (fried and spicy) and pappadum (the ubiquitous spicy lentil crackers—here baked, not fried).

Summary & comments: You won't miss the meat, promise. South Indians have cooked vegetarian for millenia, and they've got it figured out (those with meat and potatoes–sized appetites might enjoy one of several combination plates or thalis). Mavalli's concerned service, stylishly low-key ambience, and subtle, refined—and novice-friendly—cooking combine to make this a top Manhattan Indian pick.

Menchanko-Tei

Japanese	
★★★	
Moderate	
Quality 86	Value B

Zone 9   Midtown East
131 East 45th Street (between Lexington
and 3rd Avenues), Manhattan
(212) 986-6805
Zone 8   Midtown West and
Theater District
39 West 55th Street (between 5th and 6th Avenues), Manhattan
(212) 247-1585

Reservations:	45th Street: Accepted; 55th Street: Only for parties of 5 or more
When to go:	If possible, avoid the 1 P.M. rush
Kind of service:	Waiter service at counter and tables
Entree range:	$7.25–13
Payment:	VISA, MC, AMEX, DC
Service rating:	★★½
Friendliness rating:	★★½
Transit:	S/4/5/6/7 to 42nd Street/Grand Central (Zone 9); E/F to 5th Avenue or B/Q to 57th Street (Zone 8)
Bar:	Full service, with several sakes, Japanese beers, and spirits like shochu
Wine selection:	House
Dress:	Nice casual
Disabled access:	Difficult (rest rooms not accessible) at both branches
Clientele:	Japanese businessmen and noodle aficionados
Breakfast:	*55th Street:* Tuesday–Sunday, 7–9:30 A.M.
Lunch/Dinner:	*Both locations:* Monday–Saturday, 11:30 A.M.–12:30 A.M.; Sunday, 11:30 A.M.–11:30 P.M.

Atmosphere/setting: Noodles are taken very seriously here, and the dignified decor immediately signals that there ain't no fooling around. 55th Street Menchanko-Tei has stylish Midtown Japanese restaurant ambience: low ceilings, nice wood floors, halogen lights, some cursory Oriental tchotchkes, a low bar in front of an open (sparkling) kitchen and a long line of tables for two and four (there's also a more peaceful dining room in back that's painted a friendly mustard yellow). The 45th Street branch—airier and more Western—is also designed with a careful touch; higher ceilings, green carpet, potted plants, and a small dining spillover area upstairs near the rest rooms. Clientele in both is mixed but predominantly Japanese.

204

House specialties: Several variations on souply themes. Menchanko itself is an egg noodle soup of profound delicacy; it can optionally be prepared with a miso base and additions can include hot pickled vegetables, fish balls, or a kitchen sink version called tokusei menchanko, dominated by chunks of fresh, flaky salmon that assertively flavor the delicate broth. There are two ramen soups, both topped with a succulent slice of yakibuta pork: hakata is a white broth (gingery and simple, but with great balance), and kikuzo is soy-based (and the plainest of all, but no less worthy). Zousui soups are made with plump, perfectly cooked grains of rice rather than noodles; Kimchi Zousui is particularly good and it's quite spicy from the hot pickled cabbage. Nagasaki saraudon is frizzy thin fried noodles with a sweetish seafood sauce; Nagasaki chanpon is the same, but in soup.

Other recommendations: There are a handful of non-noodle options, few of them in a class with the soups. Onigiri (rice balls wrapped in nori seaweed, containing stuff like umeboshi, salmon, and preserved cod fish roe) are perhaps too subtle for the unaccustomed palate. Oden are small appetizer plates; check out kinchaku—a deliciously exotic cake of fried tofu stuffed with sticky rice paste in a soothing broth/sauce. There are also side orders of things like yakibuta (pork), menma (tender bamboo shoots with a slightly caramelized flavor), or kimchi (hot pickled cabbage) to be had. Ask for some yuzu-kosho—a red pepper paste flavored with Yuzu fruit—to spoon into the soups.

Summary & comments: Fans of the film *Tampopo* will feel at home here in NYC's best Japanese noodle bar, where noodle soups are made with incredible care for a discerning clientele. These loyal customers come often; the 55th Street branch will sell regulars a full bottle of booze to keep on reserve (they have three months to drain it). Soups are served in heavy iron kettles, with a wooden ladle for transference to your bowl. Slurp loudly (silent noodle scarfing is an insult to the chef), but get out quick; despite the deliciousness, the well-appointed decor, the polite service, and the nonbargain prices (soups run as high as $13), this type of restaurant is considered fast-food, so lingering is discouraged. The oden are better at 55th Street (which sports an expanded dinner menu), but the soups may be slightly more complex at 45th Street (considered by many the superior location). There's a third branch (unreviewed) at 257 World Trade Center Concourse, (212) 432-4210.

Metropolitan AME Church

Southern

★★★½

Inexpensive

Quality 89   Value A

CAUTION

Zone 12   Harlem, Morningside Heights, and Washington Heights
58 West 135th Street, Manhattan
(212) 690-1834

Reservations:	Not accepted
When to go:	Anytime
Kind of service:	Self-service
Entree range:	Complete dinners well under $10
Payment:	Cash only
Service rating:	★★
Friendliness rating:	★★★★★
Transit:	2/3 to 135th Street
Bar:	None
Wine selection:	None
Dress:	Nice casual
Disabled access:	Good
Clientele:	Congregation members and locals
Open:	Friday and Saturday, 11:30 A.M.–6:30 P.M.; Sunday–Thursday, closed

Atmosphere/setting: The process is the setting: walk through a narrow
alley just west of this century-old church to reach the building's back entrance,
which leads into the dining hall. There, you'll report to an older woman sitting at
a neatly covered table. She'll take your order, painstakingly completing a form that
you then bring to the kitchen window for presentation to one of several other
older women (dressed in starched whites) who'll painstakingly confirm that Lady
Number One has in fact circled the correct items. In time, your (styrofoam) plate
will be presented—jam-packed to overflowing—for carrying back to one of
many very long institutional-type tables where you'll eat among friendly members of the congregation and neighborhood regulars. Prayer is strictly optional,
though it's hard not to invoke a deity or two upon first tasting the pork chops.

House specialties: Manhattan's best smothered pork chops are very thoroughly cooked yet amazingly juicy (how do they do it?), and the smothering
sauce is downright transportive. I like it a lot that plain unsmothered pork chops
aren't even an option. Baked chicken is also tender, with rich corn bread stuffing.
Other mains include fried chicken and fish, oxtails, pig feet, and turkey wings
(avoid the sole dud: tough oven-baked—not pit-smoked, alas—ribs). The sides are

206

more than half the fun: tomatoes with okra (as well as corn and onion) are great simple, wholesome fare; perfect-textured black-eyed peas, definitive macaroni and cheese, and soft, flavorful collard greens are also fine choices. The corn bread tastes skillet-cooked with no sugar or vanilla added. For dessert, sweet potato pie achieves an ideal balance of spice and sweetness; its extremely toothsome filling (deep orange in the pie's center, growing ever darker toward the nearly blackened edge) works perfectly with the crisp crust (slices are $1.75 each, whole pies are *less than six dollars!*).

Other recommendations: Chitterlings are an increasingly hard-to-find dish even here in Harlem. Naturally, this place serves 'em.

Summary & comments: Everyone down South knows about church suppers, but it's a custom few New Yorkers have been exposed to. Yet visitors to the dining hall at Metropolitan AME (African Methodist Episcopal) Church, where hearty weekends-only meals have been served for decades, would never guess that they were viewing a rare, displaced tradition; the crowds of friendly, hungry customers (mostly older folks) make this as vibrant a supper as any in Mississippi. The cooking hasn't been diluted by dislocation, either; here you can eat the undiluted Real Thing . . . which means you'll need to bear in mind that unrepentantly old-fashioned soul food chefs like these church ladies haven't caught on yet about low-sodium or low-fat cookery.

MILAN'S RESTAURANT

Zone 14   Southern Brooklyn
710 5th Avenue (between 22nd and 23rd
    Streets), South Park Slope, Brooklyn
(718) 788-7384

Slovakian
★★★★
Inexpensive

Quality 92   Value A

Reservations:	Not accepted
When to go:	Anytime
Kind of service:	Waiter service at tables
Entree range:	$3.50–6.50
Payment:	Cash only
Service rating:	★★½
Friendliness rating:	★★★
Transit:	M/N/R to 25th Street
Bar:	None
Wine selection:	None
Dress:	Casual
Disabled access:	Good
Clientele:	Local Slovaks (many of them tipsy from the rollicking bar next door)
Lunch special:	Monday–Friday, noon–3 P.M.
Lunch/Dinner:	Sunday–Thursday, noon–9 P.M.; Friday and Saturday, noon–10 P.M.

Atmosphere/setting: An almost painfully clean, gleaming white interior with green highlights, hanging philodendrons and widely spaced tables. Tucked away around a corner is a hidden dining room, a breathtakingly discongruous space with gorgeous oak floors and tables and decorative wood panels with Slovakian phrases. You ain't in Brooklyn anymore.

House specialties: There are a few hard-to-find Slovakian specialties such as halusky (similar to spaetzle and served with either rich, funky sheep's cheese or, less appealingly, sauerkraut) or szeged goulash with dumplings (chunks of pork in a soothing, creamy sauce studded with bits of tender cabbage; the dumplings here are the typical Czech/Slovak monsters—entire slices of steamed bread). There are two other goulashes (both great): Hungarian, and Hot Hungarian. The rest of the menu consists of familiar Eastern European fare like potato pancakes (thin, light, and incredibly crusty), also available "stuffed with beef" (fantastic—the "beef" is actually tender goulash, and its toothsome sauce almost saturates the pancakes). Pierogi ("pirohy" at Milan's) are expertly fried, but blintzes are bizarrely sprayed with fake whipped cream and topped with thin chocolate syrup. Skip also blandly mild kielbasa as well as compot (it's not the Polish drink; this is just canned fruit with the syrup). Soups are good but unexciting.

Other recommendations: The Slovak Combination Plate gives you a taste of halusky, pierogi, and potato pancake for under five bucks. Since the cheese halusky are really too rich for an entire entree anyway, this is a good way to try just a bit.

Summary & comments: Milan's is one of the best bargains in Brooklyn (especially considering their $5.20 lunch special), and service is friendly in spite of the language barrier. Food from this part of the world can taste dull and heavy unless it's cooked with extraordinary care; such care is applied here more often than not.

Mocca Hungarian

CAUTION

Zone 11   Upper East Side
1588 2nd Avenue (between 82nd
   and 83rd Streets), Manhattan
(212) 734-6470

Hungarian
★★½
Moderate

Quality 85   Value B–

Reservations:	For parties of 4 or more
When to go:	Anytime
Kind of service:	Waiter service at tables
Entree range:	$10–14
Payment:	Cash only
Service rating:	★★½
Friendliness rating:	★★★
Transit:	4/5/6 to 86th Street
Bar:	Full service
Wine selection:	Limited (mostly Hungarian)
Dress:	Casual
Disabled access:	Good
Clientele:	Brooding older Hungarians and younger bargain hunters
Lunch:	Every day, 11:30 A.M.–4 P.M.
Dinner:	Every day, 4–10:30 P.M.

Atmosphere/setting: A faded Eastern European dining hall. Some will be charmed by touches such as clunky chandeliers hanging from painted tin ceilings, starchy white tablecloths and plain sturdy wooden chairs; others might find the place slightly dreary. Generous use of blond wood saves the room from the common Eastern bloc drab decor, but, still, this is a scene designed for eating, intellectual discussion, and conspicuous world-weariness, not special occasion revelry or candlelit romance.

House specialties: Stuffed cabbage is extremely satisfying, but, even better, try an off-menu variation called szekely gulyas that presents cabbage and filling separately along with some sour cream; it's transporting, evocative cooking. Bean soup is redolent of garlic, pork, and paprika (the three pillars of Hungarian cuisine); wiener schnitzel is greaseless and delicate, a classic, served with paprika-heavy home fries and herbacious creamed spinach. Homey chicken paprikash with spaetzle has a beautifully creamy sauce; freebie cucumber salad (dusted with paprika, of course) perfectly balances sweet and tart. Best dessert choices are the amazing cheese strudel—with just the right amount of lemon zest added to rich pot cheese—and tender apricot and walnut crêpes (palacsinta) served hot.

Other recommendations: Gyongyos Bedeci, a dry Hungarian pinot noir, is a good wine choice.

Summary & comments: All manner of characters stock the place, from ultrastern waitresses to shabby old Hungarian men with wistful aristocratic eyes. The phone—sitting right next to the sullen, matronly manager—rings, and she groans, with unfathomable ennui, "TEL-uh-fon" after each ring. The food's much like the ambience: very authentic and evocative, charming if you like that sort of thing, and sometimes just a bit tired. The $13.95 pretheater special is a steal.

Molly's

<CAUTION>

Zone 7 Chelsea East and
   Gramercy
287 3rd Avenue, Manhattan
(212) 889-3361

Pub
★★★
Moderate

Quality 87   Value B

Reservations:	Policy varies, but worth a try
When to go:	Anytime
Kind of service:	Waiter service at bar and tables
Entree range:	$10.50–18.95
Payment:	VISA, MC, AMEX, D, DC, JCB
Service rating:	★★½
Friendliness rating:	★★
Transit:	6 to 23rd Street
Bar:	Full service
Wine selection:	Very limited
Dress:	Casual
Disabled access:	Fair
Clientele:	Locals
Lunch:	Every day, 11 A.M.–4 P.M.
Dinner:	Every day, 5 P.M.–midnight

Atmosphere / setting: Classic Irish pub; woody and snug, complete with working fireplace. Lots of booths and tables (the largest, a round table seating eight, is handy for afterwork get-togethers).

House specialties: The best cheeseburger and shepherd's pie in Manhattan; also very good chicken pot pie, nondeluxe steak, mashed potatoes, and most fried items.

Other recommendations: Avoid specials; stick with the main menu. Ask for fried onions on your cheeseburger (they're sensational), and request the special walnut dressing on your salad.

Summary & comments: Typical pub food here is great, but Molly's also transcends type with touches like a surprisingly worthy bread basket and fresh (gasp!) not-overcooked vegetable sides. Guinness stout, properly creamy and not over-chilled, is among Manhattan's best as well.

MOUSTACHE PITZA

Zone 4   Greenwich Village
90 Bedford Street (between Grove and
    Barrow Streets), Manhattan
(212) 229-2220

Zone 5   East Village
265 East 10th Street (between 1st Avenue and Avenue A), Manhattan
(212) 228-2022

Middle Eastern
★★★½
Inexpensive

Quality 87   Value A–

Reservations:	Not accepted
When to go:	Anytime
Kind of service:	Waiter service at tables
Entree range:	$7–12
Payment:	Cash only
Service rating:	★★
Friendliness rating:	★★★
Transit:	1/9 to Christopher Street (Zone 4); L to 1st Avenue (Zone 5)
Bar:	Full service
Wine selection:	Limited
Dress:	Casual
Disabled access:	Good; small step on 10th Street
Clientele:	*Bedford Street:* couples and mellow turtlenecks *10th Street:* more body piercings and kids on unicycles
Open:	Every day, noon–11:30 P.M.

Atmosphere/setting: Each branch sports decor to suit its neighborhood: the Bedford Street Moustache—situated on one of Greenwich Village's prettiest blocks—has expansive windows and a burnished, low-lit, cozy chicness, while the 10th Street location is more stark and bricky. This latter proudly displays a gorgeous handmade Iraqi rug that's been passed from branch to branch since the first Moustache opened in Brooklyn (still in operation but under new ownership and not recommended).

House specialties: Outrageous sandwiches are made with baked-to-order crispy-chewy pita bread. Into this manna is stuffed things like spicy merguez sausage, superb falafel, or tender leg of lamb with lemon mint mayonnaise. Delectable "pitzas" are served on a crust of the same fresh bread with toppings like garlic shrimp and scallops, eggplant, capers, lemon chicken, merguez, or cheese with sundried tomatoes and basil. Lahambajian (pita topped with perfectly seasoned minced lamb) is a must, but typical Middle Eastern salads such as hummus, tabbouleh, baba ghanoush, and foul are just OK (lentil and bulghur salad with fried onions is better). Best dessert is basboussa, a honey-soaked (but not overly sweet) cake made of coarse, chewy cornmeal topped with almonds. Have it with Turkish coffee.

Other recommendations: Loomi, a citrus drink, tastes a bit like furniture polish at first, but it grows on you.

Summary & comments: Moustache management has hit upon a successful formula: made-to-order preparation of some original-but-accessible dishes that taste just a bit exotic. Be aware that the proud motto here is "Slow food." Either relax into the groove or dine elsewhere.

Mr. Broadway Kosher Deli

Zone 8   Midtown West and
        Theater District
1372 Broadway, Manhattan
(212) 921-2152

Deli
★★★½
Moderate
Quality 87   Value A

Reservations:	Accepted
When to go:	Lunchtime gets crowded; late afternoons are quiet
Kind of service:	Waiter service at tables
Entree range:	$4.25–21.75
Payment:	VISA, MC, AMEX, D, DC
Service rating:	★★★
Friendliness rating:	★★★
Transit:	B/D/F/N/Q/R to 34th Street/Herald Square
Bar:	Beer and wine
Wine selection:	Small (kosher)
Dress:	Casual
Disabled access:	Fair
Clientele:	Locals, businesspeople
Open:	Monday–Thursday, 9 A.M.–9 P.M.; Friday, 9 A.M.–3 P.M.; Sunday, 11 A.M.–9 P.M.; Saturday, closed

Atmosphere/setting: From the front, this looks like just another of the area's many kosher fast food spots. But the rear is classic Jewish deli, a tumultuous hall with darting waiters, tables crammed with pickles and cole slaw, and regulars who look like they eat a *lot* of pastrami trying to squeeze their way through the tight floor plan.

House specialties: Outstanding garlicky baba ghanoush (eggplant salad), potato knishes, couscous, kasha varnichkes (oniony buckwheat with bowtie noodles), potato pancakes (deep fried, but good), homemade french fries, chicken soup with matzo balls, falafel, derma (rich, spicy stuffing in sausage casing), fried "Moroccan cigars" (pastry flutes stuffed with finely minced meat), homemade gefilte fish.

Other recommendations: There's a top-notch self-service Middle Eastern salad bar up front (for takeout at $3.99 a pound or to accompany falafel and shwarma sandwiches—falafel's better, by the way).

Summary & comments: Mr. Broadway Kosher Deli is known by many names: It's also Me Tsu Yan Kosher Chinese Restaurant and Chez Lanu (a Hebrew pun), serving North African dishes. The confluence of cuisines makes for some strange culinary juxtapositions, from customers smearing hummus on their hot-dogs to the Moroccan couscous served with a homely piece of eastern European roast chicken riding indecorously atop. For both Middle Eastern and deli special-ties, Mr. Broadway is a winner. The kitchen somehow manages to turn out per-fectly balanced baba ghanoush and flaky potato knishes without watering down the soulfulness of chicken soup or tender gefilte fish. Corned beef is of paramount importance in a Jewish deli; their's is good and well-cut, though a bit too lean (everything's a tad lighter than usual here . . . perhaps it's the Sephardic influence). Chinese dishes—glatt kosher, like everything else—are handily available to those for whom Chinatown isn't an option. This place is relatively new and thus unpedigreed in NYC deli history, but the more venerable delis seem grimily past their primes while Mr. Broadway thrives.

NEW PASTEUR

Zone 3   Chinatown, Little Italy, and
    Lower East Side
85 Baxter Street, Manhattan
(212) 608-3656; (212) 608-4838

Vietnamese	
★★★½	
Inexpensive	
Quality 87	Value A

Reservations:	Suggested
When to go:	Avoid the peak hours of 8–10 P.M.
Kind of service:	Waiter service at tables
Entree range:	$3.75–9
Payment:	Cash only
Service rating:	★★★
Friendliness rating:	★★½
Transit:	J/M/N/R/Z/6 to Canal Street
Bar:	Beer and wine only
Wine selection:	House
Dress:	Casual
Disabled access:	Fair
Clientele:	Aficionados
Open:	Every day, 11 A.M.–10 P.M.

Atmosphere/setting: Spare cramped dining room with little decoration to detract from the memorable cooking. Be prepared to share tables.

House specialties: Any of the phos (elemental beef-based soups), barbecued beef (with vermicelli or on its own), shrimp rolls, fried spring rolls, barbecued shrimp on sugar cane, iced coffee.

Summary & comments: Vietnamese food is "hot" in Manhattan, and chichi startups are opening all over town. Yet year after year homely New Pasteur (formerly Pho Pasteur) outclasses most with the sheer skillfulness of its cooking. The barbecued beef is a marvel of gastronomic engineering, an entire beefy symphony compressed into each small nugget (wrap them in lettuce leaves along with mint, cucumber slices, sprouts, and carroty fish sauce; the Vietnamese eat most everything this way). If New Pasteur is full, as it often is, head up the block to larger and more decorative Nha Trang—whose food is nearly as good.

New Siu Sam Yuen

Zone 3   Chinatown, Little
  Italy, and Lower East Side
5 Catherine Street (between Bowery
  and East Broadway), Manhattan
(212) 925-2663

Chinese
★★
Inexpensive

Quality 85   Value A

Reservations:	Not accepted
When to go:	Anytime
Kind of service:	Waiter service at tables
Entree range:	$2.75–9.25
Payment:	Cash only
Service rating:	★★½
Friendliness rating:	★★★
Transit:	B/D/Q to Grand Street or F to East Broadway
Bar:	Beer Only
Wine selection:	None
Dress:	Casual
Disabled access:	Good; rest rooms not accessible
Clientele:	Exclusively Chinese locals
Open:	Every day, 9 A.M.–midnight

Atmosphere/setting: Small meat-chopping counter up front, plain tables in the back. Typical tiny Chinatown hole-in-wall.

House specialties: Barbecued baby pig, roast pork, soy chicken, roast duck, Chinese sausage, stuffed beef intestine; anything cut at the counter up front. A bit of pureed ginger comes alongside for dipping.

Other recommendations: Skip the rest of the menu; gingery congee's pretty good, but most everything else is sloppily prepared.

Summary & comments: You can sporadically find baby (a.k.a. suckling) pig in a few other Chinatown places, but here it's consistently available and consistently excellent. As per Chinese tradition, the skin is roughed up prior to roasting, making it particularly crisp. There's so little fat (especially if you're fortunate enough to order when the cutters have worked up to the piglet's prime middle section) that the skin easily separates from the moist, flavorful meat. It's served with a thick hoisin sauce. The other roast meats are also excellent, and you can order up to three of them over rice for $3.50 (accompanied by a dishwater-like soup that will convince optimists to skip the rest of the menu and stick with the meat).

THE NICE RESTAURANT

Zone 3   Chinatown, Little Italy, and
   Lower East Side
35 East Broadway, Manhattan
(212) 406-9510

Chinese	
★★★½	
Moderate	
Quality 91	Value B

Reservations:	Suggested
When to go:	Anytime (earlier is better for dim sum)
Kind of service:	Waiter service at tables
Entree range:	$7.25–24; dim sum, $1.80–3.50
Payment:	AMEX
Service rating:	★★★½
Friendliness rating:	★★½
Transit:	B/D/Q to Grand Street or F to East Broadway
Bar:	Beer only
Wine selection:	None
Dress:	Nice casual or better
Disabled access:	Upstairs room not accessible; downstairs (closed Monday and Friday) one step up
Clientele:	Chinese businessmen
Lunch/Dinner:	Every day, 11 A.M.–4 P.M. and 4–10 P.M.

Atmosphere/setting: Not as over-the-top as some of the more garish Hong Kong–style pavilions, the Nice is done up in burgundy red, and stuffed with uniformed waiters and dignified managers—elegant but not ostentatious. Noise levels run high, but it's an excited buzz, emanating from avid eaters.

House specialties: Minced conch and seafood with coconut curry sauce in conch shell; crispy seafood roll, minced squab with pine nuts in lettuce leaf; baby veal chops hot pot; tofu, minced chicken, and salted fish casserole; sautéed snow-pea shoots with shredded dried scallops; stewed abalone in oyster sauce; crispy shrimp with walnuts.

Other recommendations: At dim sum: special order—from a manager—garlic har gow (shrimp dumplings). They contain just a whisper of garlic, which dovetails beautifully with the nutty shrimp.

Summary & comments: The top end of Cantonese cuisine recalls France with its great complexities of flavor, intricate presentation, attention to aroma and after-taste, and striking juxtapositions. The Nice Restaurant consistently attains these lofty heights; order well and you'll taste fancy Cantonese/Hong Kong banquet cooking at its best. Any of the above list of sensational—and mostly off-menu—specialties will leave doubters forever convinced that Chinese food is much more than General Tso. The Nice puts on one of Chinatown's better dim sums, too. Arrive early, avoid fried things, and don't forget to special order those amazing garlic shrimp dumplings.

Nick's Pizza

Zone 17   Southern Queens
108-26 Ascan Avenue (near Austin
  Street), Forest Hills, Queens
(718) 263-1126

Pizza
★★★½
Moderate

Quality 92   Value B

Reservations:	Not accepted
When to go:	Anytime
Kind of service:	Waiter service at tables
Entree range:	Pizzas, $10 and $12; calzones, $4.75 and $11.75; salads, $3.75–5.75
Payment:	Cash only
Service rating:	★★
Friendliness rating:	★★
Transit:	E/F to 75th Avenue
Bar:	Beer and wine only
Wine selection:	The usual cheap stuff
Dress:	Casual
Disabled access:	Good
Clientele:	Locals and pizza pilgrims
Lunch/Dinner:	Monday–Thursday, 11:30 A.M.–9:30 P.M.; Friday, 11:30 A.M.–11 P.M.; Saturday, 12:30–11 P.M.; Sunday, 12:30–9:30 P.M.

Atmosphere/setting: Pale blue-gray interior with painted tin ceilings and wall trim, wood floors, nice formica tables for two, and an enormous gleaming coffee machine. Very focused lighting lends a modern, almost swanky look at night; during the day, tall windows provide plenty of sunlight.

House specialties: Great brick-oven pizza, featuring New York's finest homegrown mozzarella, sausage, and pepperoni from the Corona Heights Pork Store. Thinly sliced, flavor-packed prosciutto and tender roast peppers are best on a white pizza made with either ricotta, mozzarella, or both (the combo's best; for still more complexity, try half red, half white). Made-to-order calzones—crunchy crust stuffed with cheese and your choice of any pizza toppings—are equally good, and the cannoli may be the best thing of all.

Other recommendations: Salads are well prepared; there's classic Caesar (with anchovies) and very fresh mixed greens. The special house salad (with arugula, watercress, sun-dried tomatoes, and roasted peppers) is good, but order overly sweet honey dijon dressing only on the side.

Summary & comments: Nick's creamy, subtle mozzarella and soft, flavor-packed sausage come from the same top provider as Grimaldi's (see review), but

Dear Gigi,

This is the book where I found out about Sakagura, so I thought that it would be an appropriate gift for the occasion. I also hope that it will be one small addition/recommendation

to keep you around my!

I have really enjoyed working with you the past few years, and I really appreciate your hard work/ever curiosity. I understand I'm not the most informed re: palette and classopenim (how will it miss your) — unless you got — and the "Return of the big food look with your next move

though — (and P.O. of fun)

to take — all the best

Adam (V.!)

though not as famous as Patsy Grimaldi, Nick makes better use of these primo ingredients. Nearly perfect tomato sauce is an important factor, and his crust—almost burnt in spots—is a thing of wonder; few others get it so charry-bumpy-crispy. Save room for beyond-great cannolis. Service has its quirks; while the team-waitering staff is cordial and efficient, managers are notoriously unaccommodating. But perhaps one must be a bit unyielding to make pizza this good. Pizza Fresca (see review) bakes a more sophisticated Neapolitan-style pie, but Nick's is the top American (i.e. New Haven) style brick oven in town. If hallowed names like Pepe's and Sally's mean anything to you, you'll want to make the trip (it's only fifteen minutes from Manhattan on the express F train).

Caveat: The good mozzarella very occasionally runs out, and second (or worse) grade cheese is put into service. That's show biz.

Noodle 88

Chinese
★★
Inexpensive

Quality 83   Value A

Reservations:	Not accepted
When to go:	Everything's freshest—but most hectic—at lunchtime
Kind of service:	Self-service
Entree range:	$3.75–7.95
Payment:	Cash only
Service rating:	★★½
Friendliness rating:	★★
Transit:	A/C/E to 34th Street/Penn Station
Bar:	None
Wine selection:	None
Dress:	Casual
Disabled access:	Very cramped and difficult, but possible
Clientele:	Chinese laborers in sweatshirts and Chinese businessmen in suits, plus a small scattering of non-Chinese area workers
Open:	Monday–Saturday, 7 A.M.–9 P.M.

Atmosphere/setting: Garment District side street no-frills cafeteria, identical to innumerable others—except this one is always packed.

House specialties: That rarest of rarities: respectable Midtown chow fun (best with either beef or beef and vegetables), or perhaps even better, beef rice cakes (like chow fun, but with disks of compressed rice rather than noodles), which hipper customers order topped with a fried egg. Mapo tofu (bean curd in a spicy meat sauce with peas) is OK, soups are fine and well-varied, but skip the "rice plates" menu of Chinese American dishes and definitely avoid the dumplings; order instead by pointing at the good stuff—the off-menu authentic Chinese offerings displayed at the counter (all very fresh—made in small batches and constantly replenished). Here you'll find more interesting preparations like roast pork, scrambled egg with shrimp and scallion, duck blood, pig knuckles, watercress with garlic. The vegetables (bok choy is a perennial) are especially recommended.

Summary & comments: It's always been hard to find authentic Chinese fare outside of Chinatown. While there are plenty of dismal joints in the Garment District serving lunch to Chinese laborers, Noodle 88 is of an entirely different class. It's very clean and well run, and while service is on the fast-food model (order at the counter and carry your tray back to a table), the open kitchen reveals a battery of serious chefs working with some care. You will not by any means be served high-class Cantonese cuisine (to give you an idea, fried spam is often a special), but it's good, it's real, and it's inexpensive, and for Midtown Chinese that's an unbeatable combination. The most telling endorsement: while this is a place purposed to serve bargain-priced lunches to bottom-echelon workers, that clientele vies for seating with increasing numbers of well-dressed Chinese execs.

North Star Pub

Zone 1   Lower Manhattan
93 South Street (between Water
    and Fulton Streets), Manhattan
(212) 509-6757

	Pub
	★★
	Moderate
	Quality 82 Value C

Reservations:	Not accepted (but parties of 4 or more can call 15 minutes ahead to get on the waiting list)
When to go:	Weekday lunches are crowded, so come before 12:30 P.M. or after 1:30 P.M.
Kind of service:	Waiter service at bar and tables
Entree range:	$9–12.95
Payment:	VISA, MC, AMEX, DC
Service rating:	★★★★
Friendliness rating:	★★★★
Transit:	A/C/J/M/Z/2/3/4/5 to Broadway–Nassau/ Fulton Street
Bar:	Full service
Wine selection:	Very limited
Dress:	Casual
Disabled access:	Ring bell at South and Fulton Streets; rest rooms not accessible
Clientele:	Businessmen and tourists
Open:	Every day, 11:30 A.M.–10:30 P.M.

Atmosphere/setting: Amid all the contrived Ye Olde Shticke that makes South Street Seaport such a tourist trap, this much-loved British-style pub is a surprisingly real haven from the cuteness. Management may have started out intending this as a theme joint, but it feels so genuinely English that it's come to boast a fiercely loyal clientele of expat Brits as well as Anglophile downtown office workers.

House specialties: Shepherd's pie, burgers, fish and chips, chicken curry, good Mondays-only steak and kidney pie.

Entertainment & amenities: Manager's witty North Star Notes newsletter.

Summary & comments: Is "good English pub food" an oxymoron? Well, the North Star's kitchen won't be feted by the James Beard House Anytime soon, but food here is fresh, deftly prepared, and a great value in a neighborhood where clip joints abound. When crowded, grab a bite at the bar or standing at the perimeter counter by the windows (order from a bartender). The beer's fine (though over-chilled), but in spite of the reasonable prices, a couple of pints and a bite can add up startlingly fast, so order with care if price is an object. Smart, funny servers are a big plus.

NyoNyA MAlAysiAN CuisiNE

CAUTION

Zone 3   Chinatown,
   Little Italy, and Lower East Side
194 Grand Street, Manhattan
(212) 334-3669; (212) 334-6701

Malaysian
★★½
Moderate
Quality 83   Value B+

Reservations:	Accepted (except weekends after 7:30 P.M.)
When to go:	Anytime
Kind of service:	Waiter service at tables
Entree range:	$8–17
Payment:	Cash only
Service rating:	★★½
Friendliness rating:	★★½
Transit:	B/D/Q to Grand Street or J/M to Bowery or 6 to Spring Street
Bar:	Beer only
Wine selection:	None
Dress:	Casual
Disabled access:	Good; rest rooms not accessible
Clientele:	Southeast Asians and aficionados
Open:	Every day, 11 A.M.–11:30 P.M.

Atmosphere / setting: Like most of the offspring of Flushing's Penang restaurant, Nyonya is designed as a woody cabin more reminiscent of, say, Wyoming than Malaysia. Incongruous though this may be, it does make an agreeable enough setting.

House specialties: The menu's nearly identical to that of Penang in Flushing (see review), so order the usual Malaysian classics like roti canai, saté (the accompanying peanut sauce is even better here—not as sweet), Hainanese chicken rice (boiled chicken accompanied by a pile of gingery rich rice cooked in the broth), and mee siam noodles (thin pasta studded with shrimp and nuggets of crunchy pork skin). But here skip the tamarind skate and the coconut rice, and be even more careful about ordering more expensive seafood dishes. Keep it modest; noodles, soups, and simple seafood preparations.

Summary & comments: The owners of wonderful Penang keep churning out new restaurants. These McMalaysian cookie-cutter places sport similar menus (prices adjusted according to neighborhood) and decor. Although none hold a candle to the original, Nyonya on Grand Street is the most reliable of the brood. At best, it's nearly as good as the Mothership, but the place has a bad inconsistency problem. Careless lapses occur; the peanut pancake may be badly out of balance, the coconut rice cheaply flavored, the tea tepid. It's difficult to predict which things will be best on which days, so order many small items rather than risk disappointment with an expensive dish or two. Nonetheless, Nyonya is still pretty darned good—if you've never made a pilgrimage out to Flushing's Penang, you won't know what you're missing—so this, Manhattan's most authentic Malaysian, is well worth a try.

Pa Do Whae House

Korean	
★★★½	
Moderate	

Zone 16   Northeastern Queens
161-23 Crocheron Avenue (near
    Northern Boulevard),
    Flushing, Queens
(718) 461-3377

Quality 90   Value A

Reservations:	Not accepted
When to go:	Anytime
Kind of service:	Waiter service at tables
Entree range:	$8.95–20
Payment:	Cash only
Service rating:	★★½
Friendliness rating:	★½
Transit:	Long Island Railroad (from Penn Station) to Broadway Station
Bar:	Beer only
Wine selection:	None
Dress:	Casual
Disabled access:	Fair; step up, but all on one level
Clientele:	Local Koreans
Lunch:	Every day, noon–3 P.M.
Dinner:	Every day, 11 A.M.–11:30 P.M.

Atmosphere/setting: Zillions of Korean eateries dot Northern Boulevard, and there's not the slightest indication from outside or inside that this one's at all distinctive. The most remarkable visual element is a bank of fish tanks gurgling away by the door. It's comfortable, but only in the most generic sort of way. This restaurant is anonymous both literally and figuratively: its name is not to be found in English letters on the sign, on menus, or on business cards. As a result, the few non-Korean customers must refer to it as "that place."

House specialties: Lavish bargain-priced platters of sashimi make for a fun celebratory meal, but the reasonable lunches are hard to beat; main plates like clam soup, fish teriyaki, lunch box, or tempura are accompanied by a multitude of delicious little dishes. Beyond that, there's great pa jun (large seafood pancake), sublime salmon teriyaki, homey potato pancakes, and fish soups.

Other recommendations: The mind-bogglingly generous array of free starters (tasty little plates—*panchan*—such as kimchee, potato pancakes, pickles, outstanding congee-like seafood rice soup, and crab and mayo hand-rolls, just to name a few) are alone worth the trip. Even the barley tea *(bori-cha,* served hot or cold) is extra tasty here.

Pa Do Whae House *(continued)*

Summary & comments: When it comes to accommodating skittish non-Koreans, this place flunks with flying colors; little English is spoken, some specials are untranslated, and those unaccustomed to eating this kind of food will receive little guidance from the staff. No one's impolite, mind you; it's just that a bit of self-sufficiency is required (learn the ropes first at more occidental-friendly spots like Bo or Kang Suh—see reviews).

Pastrami King

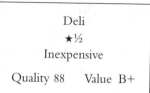

Zone 17   Southern Queens
124-24 Queens Boulevard (near
    82nd Street), Forest Hills, Queens
(718) 263-1717

Deli
★½
Inexpensive

Quality 88   Value B+

Reservations:	Accepted
When to go:	Anytime
Kind of service:	Waiter service at tables
Entree range:	$6.95 for pastrami sandwich
Payment:	AMEX, MC, VISA, DC
Service rating:	★★
Friendliness rating:	★★★
Transit:	E/F to Kew Gardens/Union Turnpike
Bar:	Beer and wine only
Wine selection:	Limited
Dress:	Casual
Disabled access:	Good
Clientele:	Locals, tourists, foodies
Breakfast:	Every day, 9–11 A.M.
Lunch:	Every day, 12:30–2:30 P.M.
Dinner:	Every day, 2:30–10 P.M.

Atmosphere/setting: You've got to give them credit for not masquerading as a real deli; this place resembles nothing so much as a deli concession set incongruously in an airport VIP waiting room. No sour-faced old waiters bearing platters of kugel; it's all cool and mute and bland (much like the kitchen's non-pastrami offerings).

House specialties: Pastrami sandwiches. That's it.

Other recommendations: None whatsoever.

Summary & comments: Ignore the sweetish deep-fried potato pancakes, the desiccated steam table ziti with meat sauce, the franks (split lengthwise and grilling in perpetuity on greasy rollers). Eschew the weirdly yellow knishes, and for God's sake don't go near the noodle pudding (studded with icky maraschino cherries). Understand: this is not really a deli, it's a pastramiteria, so all else is vestigial. That said, even the pastrami sandwiches can be quibbled with by pastrami purists (there are lots of 'em in this part of Queens): the meat's sliced to order by machine, not by hand, and the rye bread should be denser. But nonetheless, this pastrami is memorably tender and intense; its rich flavor goes long and wide.

Patsy's Pizza

Zone 12   Harlem, Morningside
    Heights, and Washington Heights
2287 1st Avenue, Manhattan
(212) 534-9783

Pizza
★★★½
Inexpensive
Quality 92   Value A

Reservations: Not necessary, but a good idea for big groups
When to go: Anytime
Kind of service: Waiter service at tables (takeout next door)
Entree range: Whole pizzas, $9–12
Payment: Cash only
Service rating: ★★
Friendliness rating: ★★
Transit: 6 to 116th Street
Bar: None
Wine selection: None
Dress: Casual
Disabled access: Good
Clientele: Locals, questing chowhounds
Lunch/Dinner: Monday–Thursday, Saturday, 11:30 A.M.–
                           midnight; Friday, 11:30 A.M.–1 A.M.;
                           Sunday, 1–11 P.M.

Atmosphere / setting: Though this ancient landmark has been in dire need
of renovation for decades, the new owner steadfastly refuses to fix up the place.
The pizza-making room (which doubles as a takeout stand) is dingy and harshly
lit but permeated with the collective spirit of a century of great pizza, so it would
be a pity to lose that atmosphere (I hope they never eliminate the big pile of coal
in front of the oven). Next door there's a somewhat less intimidating room offering table service by the bumbling but friendly amateur waiter—if you can find
him. This neighborhood gets rough at night, but you won't be the only pizza pil-
grim nervously darting in from a double-parked car or taxi to cop a quick slice
o' bliss.

House specialties: Fantastic, utterly unself-conscious brick-oven pizza
(artisanly baked, with charry crust, buttery fresh cheese, and a tomato sauce that
beautifully links both together) from an ancient coal-burning oven.

Entertainment & amenities: A semi-broken black and white television
blasting Spanish programs (takeout area only)

Summary & comments: While this is the only top-notch brick-oven pizzeria that will serve slices, you should really get a whole pie in order to experience
the full grandeur (order slices from pies that have been sitting and you may face

less crusty crust). Pizza chef Jose may soon institute a full menu of Italian food; if so, don't miss it (Frank Sinatra, who loved this place dearly, once tried to hire Jose away to be his personal chef, but formidable previous owner Carmella fended him off, and Jose remains to this day). Across the street, open during warm weather only, Rex's is an eccentric secret spot for some of the city's best Italian ices (avoid strawberry, though).

Important note: the other Patsy's Pizzas in Manhattan have merely licensed the name; they're unrelated and not recommended.

Pearson's Texas Barbecue

Zone 15   Northwestern Queens
5-16 51st Avenue (between Vernon
    Avenue and 11th Street),
    Long Island City, Queens
(718) 937-3030

Barbecue	
★★★	
Inexpensive	
Quality 88	Value C

Reservations:	Not accepted
When to go:	Anytime
Kind of service:	Self-service
Entree range:	$3–5.95
Payment:	Cash only
Service rating:	★★
Friendliness rating:	★★
Transit:	7 to Vernon/Jackson (rear of train)
Bar:	Beer only
Wine selection:	None
Dress:	Casual
Disabled access:	Good; bathrooms narrow
Clientele:	Locals, questing chowhounds
Open:	Hours change seasonally; call ahead

Atmosphere/setting: The interior has a hip, shiny-tiled, fast-food ambience. In nice weather, make a beeline for the back door that opens onto a gravel patio nearby the humongous pit (with heaps of firewood stacked everywhere). Sit and eat at picnic tables beneath big umbrellas. Kids can run around and you'll feel like you're a thousand miles from Manhattan (though the Empire State Building looms startlingly close to your left as you head out the front door).

House specialties: All manner of barbecued meats, cut to order. Best: brisket and pork ribs. Sandwiches are stuffed into spongy Portuguese rolls and dosed with sauce.

Other recommendations: Fries and onion rings are merely functional; savory, not sweet, corn bread (made from coarse corn meal and studded with tiny chunks of cheese) is better, and cole slaw and potato salad are particularly good. There are some good beers to be tried, best of all the products of Pierre Celis, an Austin-based expat Belgian master brewer. Check out Celis White, a slightly sweet brew flavored with an almost subliminal touch of coriander and orange peel.

Summary & comments: After the failure (and subsequent fire) of their Manhattan location, Stick To Your Ribs changed names to Pearson's. There followed a period of decline, but now everything's tasting better than ever. This is Texas-style barbecue, which means the meat is cooked unadorned, with sauce added only upon serving. The meat isn't tough but neither is it supposed to be falling-off-bone tender; it's chewy and rough, and the spicy sauce makes a good counterpoint. This good 'cue lies just one subway stop east of Grand Central Station. Here's how to get there: When you get off the train, walk down Vernon with your back to all the stores. Make your first right onto 51st Avenue, and the restaurant's on the left near the end of the block (you'll pick up the smoky scent long before you arrive).

Penang Cuisine Malaysia

Zone 16   Northeastern Queens
38-04 Prince Street, Flushing, Queens
(718) 321-2078; (718) 321-3838

Malaysian	
★★★½	
Moderate	
Quality 91	Value A–

Reservations:	Parties of 5 or more
When to go:	Peak mealtimes and weekends are very crowded
Kind of service:	Waiter service at tables
Entree range:	$3.75–16.95
Payment:	Cash only
Service rating:	★★½
Friendliness rating:	★★★
Transit:	7 to Flushing/Main Street
Bar:	None
Wine selection:	None
Dress:	Casual
Disabled access:	Good; rest rooms not accessible
Clientele:	Local Southeast Asians and food pilgrims from all over
Lunch/Dinner:	Every day, 11 A.M.–midnight

Atmosphere/setting: Generic interior, surprisingly humble considering that this is the place that spawned a Malaysian food wavelet. The long sloping ramp inside leading up to the door is often jammed with supplicants at peak hours, so go early or late. Larger tables sport lazy susans, and smart scarfers bring large groups so that many dishes can be tried.

House specialties: Top appetizer is roti canai (a ribbony mess of ultrathin crêpe-like stuff; tear off bits and dunk into a small dish of luxurious chicken and potato curry). Don't miss it—there are those who trek out from Manhattan to sup exclusively on two or three orders of the stuff. Another popular starter, saté (skewered chunks of broiled chicken or beef), comes with a complex sweet dipping sauce made the traditional way with fresh peanuts (rather than peanut butter, a common shortcut). There are excellent noodle dishes such as Singapore rice noodles (not the jive fluorescent yellow curry powder number served in Cantonese places; this version is brown, very dry, with slivers of fatty barbecued pork and a faint dose of five-spice), mee goreng (fried egg noodles with tomatoes, cabbage, potatoes, garlic, and shrimp), and lardy penang chow kueh teow noodles. Among entrees, try stingray in tamarind sauce (the dried stingray, reminiscent of bacalau, is slightly fermented and dosed with smelly belachan—shrimp paste—so it stinks to high heaven but tastes deliriously good), fried pompano fish (also with shrimp paste), beef rendang (chunks of falling-apart-tender beef stewed in a thick brown sauce spiked with cardamom), Hainanese chicken rice (homey boiled chicken—dose it with chili sauce—served with rice cooked in the broth), and anything else the waiter suggests (show intrepid zeal, though, or risk receiving gringo suggestions). Beware of the more expensive seafood specialties—some of them aren't worth their premium.

Other Specialties: Who says Asians don't excel at desserts? Peanut pancake (that same crêpe-like bread stuffed with butter, finely chopped peanuts, and peanut butter) is sublime, as are shaved ice desserts (ABC or chendol are good choices) containing various combinations of liquid brown palm sugar, black gelatinous cubed things, palm, evaporated milk, ice, corn, green squiggly things, red and black beans, syrups, and coconut milk; loosely stir it all together.

Summary & comments: Penang has a glitzy, trendy spin-off in Soho (not as good or authentic), and cousin Penangs and Nyonyas have come to dot the city. When great places get expansion fever, both the parent and its progeny invariably go to pot, but Flushing Penang has, much to its credit, maintained high standards.

Malaysia, the crossroads of the food world, has incorporated into its cooking the best culinary qualities of nearby India, China, Thailand, and Vietnam—along with some European touches from the British colonizers. Malaysians, some of the most food-savvy people in the world, enjoy a cuisine that's extremely broad and uniquely delicious when prepared correctly. As of this writing, Flushing's Penang is the only reliable source for the Real Thing.

PEPE ROSSO TO GO

	Italian
	★★★½
	Inexpensive
	Quality 91 Value A

Zone 2   Soho and Tribeca
149 Sullivan Street (just south of
   Houston Street), Manhattan
(212) 677-4555

Reservations:	Not accepted
When to go:	Off hours (to beat the crowds)
Kind of service:	Self-service
Entree range:	$5.95–7.95
Payment:	Cash only
Service rating:	★★★
Friendliness rating:	★★★
Transit:	C/E to Spring Street
Bar:	None
Wine selection:	None
Dress:	Casual
Disabled access:	Not accessible, but servers will come to the door to take your order (and there are outdoor tables)
Clientele:	Homesick young Italians (often no English is to be heard here)
Open:	Every day, 11 A.M.–11 P.M.

Atmosphere/setting: Why take Pepe Rosso to go when it's so nice to stay? This miniscule eatery is charmingly warm with exposed brick walls, strings of sun-dried tomatoes hung from a gorgeous antique ceiling, and brown paper bag lamp shades softening the light. There are a few small tables as well as sidewalk seating in warm weather.

House specialties: Sandwiches on crusty baguette or homemade focaccia, homestyle pastas (particularly recommended: gnocchi with several cheeses), and organic salads. Any dessert made in-house is worth ordering, especially the luxurious melon tart. Orders are filled with lightning speed.

Summary & comments: The sign by the cash register lays down the law: *No diet coke, no decaf, no skim milk; only good food is served here!* Pepe Rosso does profound, unpretentious Italian homestyle cooking. Their most unaffected creations can intoxicate; a sandwich of air-cured beef (bresaola), goat cheese, arugula, and truffle oil conveys Deep Ideas via the extraordinary balance of these few ingredients. They are sparsely portioned ingredients, at that; this is real Italian cooking, not the lard-it-on *abbondanza* school of Italian American food. Things might be *too* homey for some—some overly experimental specials may be less well conceived than regular menu offerings (though everything's smartly executed from fine ingredients), the tarts are sometimes slightly burnt (but an endearing kind of slightly burnt) at the edges, fusilli primavera contains quantities of olive oil more to Neapolitan taste than American, and you're expected to bus your own plates. If you're put off by such quirks, head instead to any of a zillion pricey Manhattan Italian spots. But you won't easily find Pepe Rosso's charm or knowing touch for even ten times the price.

Petite Abeille

Zone 6   Chelsea West
107 West 18th Street, Manhattan
(212) 367-9062

Belgian	
★★½	
Inexpensive	
Quality 86	Value A

Reservations:	Not accepted
When to go:	Anytime
Kind of service:	Waiter service at tables (plus self-service at counter)
Entree range:	$5.75–8.75
Payment:	AMEX, D
Service rating:	★★
Friendliness rating:	★★
Transit:	F to 14th Street or L to 6th Avenue
Bar:	None
Wine selection:	None
Dress:	Casual
Disabled access:	Good—staff helps with step
Clientele:	Local, business, expat Belgians
Brunch:	Saturday and Sunday, 9 A.M.–4 P.M.
Open:	Monday–Friday, 7 A.M.–7 P.M.; Saturday and Sunday, 9 A.M.–6 P.M.

Atmosphere/setting: Boxy but pleasant, with a distinctly European flair. There's a counter for takeout and drinks.

House specialties: Waffles (unadorned, per Belgian tradition), carbonade (hearty sweet and savory beef stew with prunes), steump de carrot (homey carrot-flecked mashed potatoes), various sausage dishes, quiches, salads, and sandwiches.

Other recommendations: Do not miss your chance to buy prized Belgian Cote d'Or Chocolate; it's not officially imported to this country (*shhhh*), and this is one of the only places you can find it.

Summary & comments: It's hard to decide if you're eating in a tony establishment masquerading as a cheap lunchroom, or if this is simply a super high quality coffee shop. Don't expect gastronomic miracles, just skillfully cooked Belgian comfort food, unusual (for New York) but very accessible and easy to enjoy. You can't beat the price. They offer a primitive version of waiter service, but you'll do best by pitching in with trips to the counter to select things. There's a full-service Petite Abeille in Greenwich Village (466 Hudson, (212) 741-6479), with longer hours, a different menu, and particularly worthy pommes frites, but the staff can be peevish.

Pho Bac

Zone 15   Northwestern Queens
82-78 Broadway (near Elmhurst
   Avenue), Elmhurst, Queens
(718) 639-0000

<table>
<tr><td>Vietnamese</td></tr>
<tr><td>★★★★</td></tr>
<tr><td>Inexpensive</td></tr>
<tr><td>Quality 93   Value A</td></tr>
</table>

Reservations:	Accepted (but not necessary)
When to go:	Anytime
Kind of service:	Waiter service at tables
Entree range:	$4–13.95
Payment:	Cash only
Service rating:	★★★★★
Friendliness rating:	★★★★★
Transit:	G/R to Elmhurst Avenue
Bar:	Beer only
Wine selection:	None
Dress:	Casual
Disabled access:	Good; short step up
Clientele:	Locals
Open:	Every day, 10:30 A.M.–11 P.M.

Atmosphere/setting: Set in a shopping strip (between the newest branch of Joe's Shanghai and overrated Singa's Pizza) with the rare convenience of its own parking lot, Pho Bac itself is a plain but brightly inviting room.

House specialties: Spicy-sour shrimp soup, pho bo vien (the traditional Vietnamese beef soup with noodles and meat balls), shrimp on sugarcane stick, spring rolls with grilled pork on rice vermicelli, grilled pork chop, sesame beef (available on its own or with vermicelli), simmering fish in caramel sauce, simmering prawns in pasty coconut cream, fried rice (made with an especially short-grained rice), lemon grass fried fish, chicken lemon grass, grilled marinated fish, beef stew (like French stew but spicier), asparagus and crabmeat soup with lots of crab; again, very French), peppered salt crab (four entire blue crabs stir-fried in butter for six bucks!). Unlike some Chinatown Vietnamese places, fancier and more expensive dishes are recommended as well as simpler fare.

Other recommendations: If you don't mind a drink that smells like sweaty feet, sulphurous durian fruit (much loved by many Asians) milk shakes are very well made here, as are ones made from soursop (a much milder fruit, slightly acidic).

Summary & comments: Manhattan Vietnamese places keep getting more and more chi-chi and fusiony, and while a few Chinatown places like New Pasteur (see review) hold the fort on the real, unadulterated cuisine, none can hold a candle to this place, the labor of love of owner-waiter-cashier-menu decoder Bac Njuyan. It's not easy to find an ethnic restaurant that's authentic, great, *and* helpful to newcomers, but Bac will patiently explain everything and show you how to wrap food the traditional Vietnamese way, inside a lettuce leaf with mint, coriander, carroty fish sauce, and cucumber slices. Between the coddling and the awesome quality, even the most skittish eater will be delighted.

Warning: Don't confuse this with Pho Bang, the Vietnamese place out in the parking lot; it's not nearly as good.

Pho Cong Ly

Zone 3   Chinatown, Little Italy, and
   Lower East Side
124 Hester Street (near Chrystie
   Street), Manhattan
(212) 343-1111

Vietnamese
★★½
Inexpensive

Quality 86   Value A

Reservations:	Not accepted
When to go:	Anytime
Kind of service:	Waiter service at tables
Entree range:	3.75–7.50
Payment:	Cash only
Service rating:	★★★½
Friendliness rating:	★★★★
Transit:	B/D/Q to Grand Street
Bar:	None
Wine selection:	None
Dress:	Casual
Disabled access:	Poor; high step up, rest rooms not accessible
Clientele:	Locals, starving artists
Open:	Every day, 10 A.M.–9 P.M.

Atmosphere/setting: A sunny little hole-in-the-wall with friendly service.

House specialties: Pho (pronounced like "funk" without the "nk," and with voice rising as if asking a question), the proud Vietnamese meat soup, is stellar here. It comes stocked with your choice of various cuts of beef; the topmost menu choice (pho xe lua) is a kitchen-sink combo that includes tendon and tripe along with various thin-cut beefy slices. Squeeze lime and toss in sprouts and bits of fresh Thai basil. The chef is heavy on the star anise, an authentic touch that's toned down in most other places. The other big winner is chicken curry (misspelled "chicken cary"), available with egg noodles, rice noodles, vermicelli, or rice. The starch makes a great foil for the tender, sauce-saturated chicken, and chunks of taro also absorb lots of smooth coconutty curry.

Other recommendations: Ultracrisp fried spring rolls are mirror shiny but a bit bland. Iced coffee and salty lemonade are good (as usual at Vietnamese places), and the freebie green tea is a particularly fragrant brand.

Summary & comments: For pho and chicken curry, Pho Cong Ly's a real find, especially considering the price. The bathroom's accessible only through the kitchen, and as you pass by, you'll be surprised to discover that the fellow who brought your water and cleared your soup bowl is also the chef. He and the manager-waiter do their genial best with limited English skills.

Piccola Venezia

CAUTION

Zone 15   NW Queens
42-01 28th Avenue (at 42nd Street),
   Astoria, Queens
(718) 721-8470

Italian
★★★★
Expensive

Quality 93   Value D+

Reservations:	Necessary
When to go:	Avoid lunch (same menu, same stratospheric prices)
Kind of service:	Waiter service at tables
Entree range:	$17.95–33.95
Payment:	AMEX, VISA, MC, DC
Service rating:	★★★★
Friendliness rating:	★★★
Transit:	R to Broadway
Bar:	Full service
Wine selection:	Extensive (mostly Italian)
Dress:	Elegant casual to dressy
Disabled access:	Good
Clientele:	Politicians, movie stars, and neighborhood folks who've been eating here for decades
Lunch/Dinner:	Wednesday–Monday, noon–10:30 P.M.; Tuesday, closed

Atmosphere/setting: Spirited conviviality amid old-world graciousness. This is a real class joint, from the quality table linens to the marble paneling and uniformed waiters, and it's filled to the rafters meal after meal with celebratory eaters (and celebrity eaters, too; there are more celeb sightings here than in nearly any Manhattan eatery). Venetian scenes decorate the walls, but the management is actually Istrian (part of Yugoslavia, though the region was once under Venetian rule).

House specialties: While masterful food is to be had here, if you seek a meal as sensational as its price tag, you'll need help. The following is a user's manual to Piccola Venezia's arcane menu stratagems. First of all, definitely cop a veal, especially the oversize veal porterhouse (thick, tender, and beautifully seared from expert broiling beneath an old-fashioned red-hot salamander). Veal chop giardiniera is also worthy, and the veal franchaise is stunning. Fusi (a twisty Istrian pasta) is best with exquisite grappa sauce or a traditional Istrian veal sauce. Fried calamari, roasted peppers, tricolor and house salad, tripe, chicken campagnola (basically chicken marsala with mushrooms), and oniony sautéed Venetian liver are all dependably first-rate. Fried stuff (zucchini, potatoes, etc.) and other sides can be delicious (spinach mixed into mashed potatoes is a particular favorite) but vary wildly depending on which cook has been assigned the task. Wholesale seafood

242

wildly depending on which cook has been assigned the task. Wholesale seafood quality in Astoria has waned considerably in recent years, and this place's fish has likewise grown a tad inconsistent. While nothing's ever bad, choices like mussels in white wine sauce are recommended only when the mussels are particularly good, and fish in general varies with supply; trust your waiter to advise or else steer clear.

Regular menu items—particularly osso bucco—are best when offered as specials. One difference—aside from freshness—is the sauce; specials are often served with a luscious Istrian brown sauce, while their regular menu equivalents are in a less characterful red. Other specials not to be missed include venison, rabbit, veal valdostano—veal cooked in cognac sauce with cheese and eggplant or asparagus—and Istrian sauerkraut soup, but avoid contadinas and other mixed grills (it's hard to optimally time each element), risotto, and beware the pesto— ambrosial when fresh, it's frozen in winter and occasionally in summer as well.

Piccola Venezia was not always such an expensive ticket; it's a regular neighborhood restaurant that over the years has grown exorbitant. So while the plainer preparations are perfectly fine, they may not be exciting enough to merit their cost, especially if you've come for a festive, special meal. Avoid potential disappointments such as the two lobster tail selections (whole lobster, when a special—e.g., wonderful lobster fra diavolo—is much more interesting), cold antipasto plate (just the usual cast of characters), minestrone soup, and filet mignon. Some whole-fish dishes— seafood quality doubts aside—can be a bit pedestrian as well. And definitely skip the ho-hum desserts.

Other recommendations: There's a fine line between specials and dishes served only to those in the know; off-menu standbys like roast loin of pork, scallops casino, stuffed artichokes, and shrimp and clams in vodka sauce seem to appear magically to those who ask. In fact, if they're in the mood, the kitchen will whip up most anything you crave, though some shmoozing with the maître d' may be required.

Entertainment & amenities: Valet parking.

Summary & comments: Piccola Venezia, the most senior of several Astoria Istrian-Italians, has a fanatically devoted clientele (there's one particularly loyal fellow who eats here literally every single night). These folks know the waiters (old pros all) and count on them for guidance on matters of pesto freshness, seafood quality, etc. Newcomers are warmly served, but the staff may not go the extra mile for fresh faces. Unless you manage to establish a particular rapport with your waiter, stick with the above suggestions, the culminated insights of several knowledgeable insiders.

Picholine

Zone 10   Upper West Side
35 West 64th Street (between Columbus
  Avenue and Central Park West),
  Manhattan
(212) 724-8585

Reservations:	Required
When to go:	Preshow
Kind of service:	Waiter service at tables
Entree range:	$25–33 (tasting menus, $65–85)
Payment:	VISA, MC, AMEX
Service rating:	★★★★
Friendliness rating:	★★★½
Transit:	1/9 to 66th Street
Bar:	Full service
Wine selection:	Excellent (waiters offer thoroughly non-snobbish suggestions)
Dress:	Elegant casual
Disabled access:	Good
Clientele:	Early, mostly businesspeople, some suburbanite pre-Lincoln Center; later (and weekends), younger and more varied
Lunch:	Tuesday–Saturday, 11:45 A.M.–2 P.M.; Sunday and Monday, closed for lunch
Dinner:	Sunday, 5–10 P.M.; Monday–Saturday, 5:30–11:45 P.M.

Atmosphere/setting: There are three dining sections: the rear room is both intimate and festive, done in burnished orange with dark olive trim, hung with paintings and tapestries, with seating at tables and banquettes and effective sound absorbtion cleverly built into the decor; a narrow middle room, brighter and noisier, adjoins a small front serving area that is smoker's Siberia.

House specialties: Start with delicate white bean gazpacho (soups are dependably good), appetizers of light sheep cheese gnocci with morrel sauce, grilled octopus, or calamari. Entree winners include wild mushroom and duck risotto (one of the best and most unpretentious risottos in town), rack of expertly grilled lamb (served with artichokes, preserved tomato, and potato goat cheese gratin), dayboat seafood selection (prepared differently each day), or an occasional special of exquisitely flaky whole fish for two. For dessert, don't miss sublime baked-to-order Valhrona chocolate soufflé, accompanied by creamy

244

coconut ice cream. Flavored breadsticks (part of a nice bread selection) are a signature, as is the generous *amuse-gueule* of biscotti and chocolates. But save room for the greatest treat of all: Picholine's incredible cheese cart (see below).

Other recommendations: The kitchen's sole fault is its uninspired sauces, a serious flaw indeed when broad flavor strokes miss their mark yet are too assertive to ignore. The successful entrees are those that transcend their sauces (grilled things—such as rack of lamb or Tuesdays-only rabbit au riesling—and other such hearty fare) and those served sans sauce (whole fish, risotto).

Summary & comments: Picholine, very much a known quantity in New York's top restaurant echelon, might seem a surprising inclusion in a collection of offbeat and lesser-known eateries. But as part of a rank where trendiness, showiness, and snobbishness often stand in for deliciousness, Picholine stands out. Here, smart cooking doesn't seek to call attention to its own cleverness; this is how a really good grandma cafe might cook if it could afford to do so on a grand scale. The thoughtful, unobtrusive servers have been known to counter-suggest less expensive wine, and will, upon request, hurry ticket holders out in time for nearby Lincoln Center.

But let's cut to the cheese. Maître Fromagier Max McCalman rounds up more than fifty luscious varieties at a time (many not to be found elsewhere), and putts his cart around the rooms, reeling off effusive descriptions of the rich, earthy Spanish *tortas del casar,* delicate Italian *quartirolos* (made from tired cow's milk) and the odd raw milk *Trappiste.* Few realize that customers are welcome to stop in for cheese alone; if the dining room's full, there's usually seating at the bar alongside other *chèvre*-chomping devotees. ("We've become quite the cheese destination," McCalman beams.)

The Pink Teacup

CAUTION

Zone 4   Greenwich Village
42 Grove Street (between
    Bleecker and Bedford Streets),
    Manhattan
(212) 807-6755

Southern
★★★
Moderate

Quality 86   Value C

Reservations:	Not accepted
When to go:	Great $6.25 lunch special, weekdays, 11 A.M.–2 P.M.
Kind of service:	Waiter service at tables
Entree range:	$8–15
Payment:	Cash only
Service rating:	★★½
Friendliness rating:	★½
Transit:	1 to Christopher Street
Bar:	None
Wine selection:	None
Dress:	Nice casual
Disabled access:	Good; rest rooms not accessible
Clientele:	Locals (mostly long-time regulars)
Open:	Sunday–Thursday, 9 A.M.–midnight; Friday and Saturday, 9 A.M.–1 A.M.

Atmosphere/setting: Like the genteel southern tea parlor of an aging, slightly loopy aunt: dowdily homey, filled with knickknacks and overstuffed cushions, the whole just a tad worn and shabby.

House specialties: The state of the art in fried pork chops; also, salmon croquettes (made with canned salmon, as per tradition), wonderful fried smoked bacon, ham, and sausage, great collard greens and black-eyed peas (stir in Tabasco). Breakfast, available at all times, is the best meal: grits (especially cheese grits) are primo and home fries nearly as good. For dessert, sweet potato pie is a better choice than the cakes.

Summary & comments: Lots of diners do wrong here by ordering the menu's less distinguished offerings. Stick with breakfast, pork chops (try them with eggs and grits for breakfast), smoked meats, collard greens, and black-eyed peas, and you'll be mightily satisfied.

Pio Pio

Zone 15 Northwestern Queens	Peruvian
84-13 Northern Boulevard (between	★★★
84th and 85th Streets), Jackson Heights,	Moderate
Queens	Quality 88 Value B
(718) 426-1010	

Reservations:	Large parties only
When to go:	Weekend nights are crowded
Kind of service:	Waiter service at tables
Entree range:	$4–18
Payment:	VISA, MC, D
Service rating:	★★★
Friendliness rating:	★★★
Transit:	7 to 74th Street/Broadway, Q33 bus to 83rd Street and Northern Boulevard
Bar:	Full service
Wine selection:	Limited Peruvian and Italian (plus sangria)
Dress:	Casual
Disabled access:	Good
Clientele:	Peruvians from all over, mostly young and stylish
Lunch/Dinner:	Wednesday–Monday, noon–11 P.M.

Atmosphere/setting: The somewhat cheesy indigo and mustard facade belie Pio Pio's softly lit, strikingly atmospheric interior. This soaringly handsome space, with cascading water, halogen spot lighting, brick walls hung with colorful Peruvian paintings, and stylishly grungy exposed concrete, is quite unlike any other restaurant in this part of Queens, known more for spare storefront dining than for dramatic design. There's an upstairs dining room with wood floors and Spanish-style iron window gates. All in all, it's an evocative, hip setting that will make you hanker for a trip to Peru.

House specialties: Rotisserie chicken; juicier, fresher, meatier, and tenderer than almost anywhere else. This is not a notably crisp-skinned bird, but the exceptionally harmonious and complex marinade penetrates deeply into the meat. It's accompanied by dipping sauces of impressive potent complexity that you'll want to dunk everything in, especially the tostones (fried starchy green plantains). Smooshed as per tradition to provide maximal surface area for extra crunchiness, these tostones are absolutely perfect; as with the equally wonderful french fries and fried sweet plantains, what little oil you taste is impeccably fresh.

Other recommendations: To supplement the poultry and fried stuff, Pio Pio makes great salads (with avocado or prawns) and ceviches (seafood pickled in lime), and they're justifiably proud of their pisco sours (cocktails with fresh lime and egg white). But skip the what's-wrong-in-this-picture salchipapas con papas (french fries studded with frankfurters) if you know what's good for you.

Summary & comments: Peruvian-style chicken—distinctive for its long and devilishly complex marination—can be had at a number of other restaurants (e.g. Manhattan's Flor De Mayo and El Pollo), but others don't come close. The trio of Pio Pios (sister branches at 62-30 Woodhaven Boulevard, Rego Park, Queens, and 1329 St. Nicholas Avenue in Washington Heights offer great food but merely functional decor) has electrified the local Peruvian community; though fairly new, word has spread quickly. Amazingly, the Pio Pio kitchens managed from day one to cook with a mature, sure-handed deftness seldom seen in more experienced places; management has helped by going out of their way to track down superior poultry—these chickens are astoundingly plump and flavorful. The clientele—mostly young, second-generation Peruvians—packs the place on weekend nights when this becomes quite the scene; everyone dresses up as if for a nightclub, and you'll wait for a table.

Punjab

Indian
★★
Inexpensive

Quality 81   Value A

Zone 5   East Village
114 East 1st Street (between Avenue A
    and 1st Avenue), Manhattan
(212) 533-9048

Reservations:	Not accepted
When to go:	Anytime
Kind of service:	Self-service
Entree range:	$2–4
Payment:	Cash only
Service rating:	★★
Friendliness rating:	★★
Transit:	F to 2nd Avenue
Bar:	None
Wine selection:	None
Dress:	Casual
Disabled access:	None
Clientele:	Indo-Pak (and environs) taxi drivers
Open:	Every day, 24 hours

Atmosphere / setting: About the flimsiest excuse for an eating establishment that one could possibly imagine. Squeeze between the taxi drivers in this narrow musty basement shop, walk past shelves laden with spices, tapes, and Indian comic books, and behold the refrigerated case laden with trays of vegetarian curries. Point at whatever appeals, and the counterman will nuke and hand you a styrofoam plateful, which you can take out or eat on the narrow ledge.

House specialties: All vegetarian, and all surprisingly good: samosa chat (fried potato and pea dumplings smothered in sauces and chutneys), tender aromatic chickpea curry, earthy spinach (or spinach and cheese) curry, other vegetable curries.

Summary & comments: It's cheaper than cooking for yourself, it's healthy (this vegetarian fare, made off-premises, is notably ungreasy and wholesome), and it's delicious. This ain't the apex of Indian vegetarian cuisine, mind you—for that, try Mavalli Palace or Chowpatty (see reviews)—but it's fine home cooking. Chowing on the ledge here next to turbaned taxi guys amid the scents of exotic spices and soaps and sounds of Punjabi music (which strangely resembles ska) is a great New York experience, one that few outside the neighborhood (or even inside the neighborhood) know about. If you prefer to dine while seated (and thus miss half the fun), bring takeout to nearby DBA Bar (41 1st Avenue, (212) 475-5097), the city's preeminent locale for high-end beer.

RINCONCITO PERUANO

Zone 8   Midtown West and
    Theater District
803 9th Avenue (between 53rd and 54th
    Streets), Manhattan
(212) 333-5685

Peruvian

★★★½

Inexpensive

Quality 92   Value A

Reservations:	For large parties only
When to go:	Anytime (weekends more choices)
Kind of service:	Waiter service at tables
Entree range:	$6–15
Payment:	VISA, MC
Service rating:	★½
Friendliness rating:	★★★½
Transit:	C/E to 50th Street
Bar:	None
Wine selection:	None
Dress:	Casual
Disabled access:	Good; rest rooms not accessible
Clientele:	Peruvians from all over, locals
Lunch/Dinner:	Monday–Friday, 11 A.M.–11 P.M.; Saturday and Sunday, 10:30 A.M.–11 P.M.

Atmosphere/setting: A little touch of Jackson Heights, Queens, in Manhattan. The interior is spruced up to the extent that income from $6 entrees allows. Although they seem to have learned restaurant management from a correspondence course, the mom-and-pop owners are lovely people (food this good doesn't come from cold-hearted cooks), and the good vibes that enliven the food permeate this humble parlor. Peruvians flock here, as do intrepid Anglos.

House specialties: Tamales are the very epitome of corn; papas a la huancaina (the Peruvian classic of cold boiled potatoes drenched in spicy cheese sauce) luxuriate in a rich, slightly chunky yellow sauce, not chalky or bland as elsewhere; papa rellena is an ungreasy fried ball of subtly spiced mashed potatoes stuffed with tender ground meat; aji de gallina is a casserole with chunks of tender chicken and potato (along with ground walnuts, Parmesan cheese, and mirasol peppers) afloat in a sweetish sauce that's beautifully unified of flavor. Splendid fish ceviche (raw fish cooked through acidic limey marination) is quite spicy, the flesh so rich it's almost buttery; tacu tacu is a smooth, irresistible soupy rice with white beans (also available with meat). For dessert, helado de lucuma is a smooth and deep-flavored ice cream made from a popular (but untranslatable) South American fruit. Another dessert, choclo peruano, confronts you with

250

a small ear of huge-kerneled corn and a small brick of extremely mild cheese. At first you're not quite sure what to do, but nature quickly takes its course.

Other recommendations: The dynamite hot sauce contains some avocado; it's great for dunking bread in.

Summary & comments: Manhattan's been sadly lacking good South American food for years, but Rinconcito Peruano has upped the ante, serving Peruvian dishes worlds tastier than you'll find in even the best places in Queens and New Jersey (the food can't possibly be much better in Peru!). The well-meaning staff is decidedly not ready for prime time, however, and the kitchen gets especially overwhelmed when crowds peak (so go at off hours). But *gawd*, is it ever worth it. To find most of the menu actually available, go for lunch on a Saturday or Sunday.

Rocco's

CAUTION

Zone 14   S Brooklyn
6408 Fort Hamilton Parkway,
    Bay Ridge, Brooklyn
(718) 833-2109

Italian/Seafood
★★½
Inexpensive

Quality 83   Value A

Reservations:	Not accepted
When to go:	Anytime
Kind of service:	Cafeteria self-service and waiter service
Entree range:	$4–9
Payment:	Cash only
Service rating:	★★★
Friendliness rating:	★★★½
Transit:	N to Fort Hamilton Parkway
Bar:	Beer and wine only
Wine selection:	House
Dress:	Casual
Disabled access:	Good but cramped
Clientele:	Locals (mostly families)
Open:	Tuesday–Saturday, 7 A.M.–7 P.M.; Sunday and Monday, closed

Atmosphere/setting: A loud, lively Brooklyn clam-eteria, the kind of summery Italian family fish joint so poorly imitated all over the country. A huge cafeteria counter displays most of the food (heavy on the shellfish) over which regulars kibbitz boisterously with servers who look like they were born and raised in the place. There are tables with umbrellas outside, a labyrinth of crammed seating inside, and kids are practically encouraged—there's little they can do to harm the hard, shiny surfaces. If the beach weren't so far away, you'd call this the ideal summer lunch restaurant.

House specialties: Not everything's good; locals know to stick with things like calamari (as with everything else here, cooked so simply that it's easy to miss its deliciousness), baked clams, grilled (not fried!) shrimp, and tender seafood salad (forgive the fake crab meat). Stuffed artichokes and all of the vegetable dishes (escarole, zucchini) and salads (tortellini, string bean, and potato) are uncommonly fresh and delicious, probably due to all the wonderful produce markets in the neighborhood.

Summary & comments: It's always difficult to bring people to restaurants that serve the food they grew up with; they're never satisfied. The amazing thing about Rocco's is that the pickiest Italian eaters like the place, while non-Italians sometimes go away disappointed. This is because Rocco does not cook luxurious, broad-flavored, garlicky, cheesy, lusty Italian, nor does he cook olive oil, basil, and sun-dried tomato refined Italian. Rather, he cooks in the same extremely simple style that Italian American grandmas serve on Sundays. This kind of honest family food is very hard to find in a restaurant, and if you stick with the recommended dishes (see above), you may notice that your heart and stomach get a lot happier than your brain does. That's what soul food is all about; like your grandmother, Rocco cares more about how his food makes you feel than how you feel about his food.

Rosario's

Zone 1 Lower Manhattan	Italian
38 Pearl Street, Manhattan	★★★
(212) 514-5763	Inexpensive
	Quality 86 Value A

Reservations:	Not accepted
When to go:	Anytime
Kind of service:	Self-service
Entree range:	$4–8
Payment:	VISA, MC, AMEX, D
Service rating:	★★★½
Friendliness rating:	★★★
Transit:	N/R to Whitehall Street/South Ferry
Bar:	None
Wine selection:	None
Dress:	Casual
Disabled access:	Good; use stepless entrance but try to arrive before noon (very crowded after that)
Clientele:	Suits
Breakfast/Lunch:	Monday–Friday, 8 A.M.–3 P.M.; Saturday and Sunday, closed

Atmosphere/setting: This bustling no-nonsense cafeteria is surprisingly comfortable, extremely clean, and astonishingly well run.

House specialties: The extensive menu changes daily, but expect familiar dishes like lasagna, veal/chicken/eggplant parmigiana (plates or heroes), escarole, penne à la vodka, and minestrone.

Summary & comments: Rosario's makes their own mozzarella and their own pasta, and the food is remarkably tasty if not very elegant. Prices are almost insanely low; they make their profit from volume, processing dozens of tray-clutching businesspeople per minute with miraculous efficiency. Steam table service doesn't permit al dente pasta; if that bothers you, stick with soups, heros, and entrees. Why can't every neighborhood have a place like this?

Ruben Lunch ⬦CAUTION⬦

Zone 13   N Brooklyn
229 Havemire Street (near Broadway),
    Williamsburg, Brooklyn
(No phone)

Diner	
★★½	
Inexpensive	
Quality 90	Value A

Reservations:	None
When to go:	Anytime (but remember, they close early!)
Kind of service:	Waiter service at counter
Entree range:	$3.50–5.50
Payment:	VISA, MC, AMEX, D, DC, JCB
Service rating:	★★
Friendliness rating:	★★
Transit:	J/M/Z to Marcy Avenue
Bar:	None
Wine selection:	None
Dress:	Casual
Disabled access:	Step up (but there's a takeout window outside)
Clientele:	Local workers
Open:	Every day, 6 A.M.–4 P.M.

Atmosphere/setting: No tables, just a long counter in this narrow old-fashioned luncheonette. Sit near the door and watch the counter guys frantically whip up glass after glass of their trademark drink (and try to guess what's in the secret bottle).

House specialties: Morir Soñando ("to die while dreaming") is a Cuban shake made from orange juice (here squeezed fresh), carrot juice (likewise), and milk. This place also squirts nearly homeopathic quantities of a secret syrup, which I suspect to be mora (or blackberry), into the mix, and the result can be described as a postdoctorate Orange Julius. The older, shorter man with the round face and sly smile makes them best; in his masterful hands, flavors combine with laser-like focus and the result is cosmic: a drink with the balance and length of a fine wine. Alas, the matador often mans the grill, leaving others to mix merely superb drinks. In any case, you'll be offered a small preliminary taste for your approval—the sign outside says *You don't like? You don't pay!* You'll like. You'll pay.

Other recommendations: Standard luncheonette fare with few Latino twists. Sandwiches include ham and egg, bologna, liverwurst, egg salad, tuna salad, corned beef, and pastrami. Also available are burgers, eggs, and omelets, all decently prepared. Don't miss the home fries, nearly as orange (from achiote) as the morir soñando.

Summary & comments: You'll find Morir Soñando in many Latino places, but Ruben's version will spoil you for all others. Get there before their early closing time so that you won't have to die while weeping.

Sahara East

~~~~~~ ◆ CAUTION

Zone 5   East Village
184 1st Avenue, Manhattan
(212) 353-9000

Middle Eastern
★★½
Moderate
Quality 83   Value B

Reservations:	Accepted
When to go:	Warm weather
Kind of service:	Waiter service at tables
Entree range:	$8.95–14.95
Payment:	Cash only
Service rating:	★½
Friendliness rating:	★★★★
Transit:	L to 1st Avenue
Bar:	Beer and wine
Wine selection:	Limited
Dress:	Casual
Disabled access:	Poor; big step at front door
Clientele:	Locals, ethnic
Lunch:	Every day, 10 A.M.–5 P.M.
Dinner:	Every day, 5 P.M.–2 A.M.

Atmosphere / setting: A narrow little cafe with a surprisingly large outdoor garden in back, festooned with lights and hanging knickknacks.

House specialties: Falafel, grape leaves, fattoush (salad with pita croutons), lamb or chicken shish kebab, lamb or chicken couscous.

Other recommendations: Shisha (aromatic tobacco, optionally flavored with apple), smoked through ornate water pipes fueled by glowing coals; bargain lunch specials.

Entertainment & amenities: Live music Friday and Saturday, 9–11:30 P.M.

Summary & comments: Sahara can turn out some fine quality food, but the tiny kitchen gets overwhelmed when things are busy. The dilemma is that it's most fun when crowded, so one must weigh food against ambience (busy nights are Thursday through Sunday). On nice clear evenings, the garden fills up and the perfumed shisha smoke wafts as snakily as the music. Older Middle Eastern guys and East Village hipsters blend effortlessly into the scene, and it's transportive to be a part of it all. On these busy nights, stick with the above recommendations and you'll eat decently. For better food and less scene, go on off nights and ask the chef about the day's specials. In any case, service is earnest but maddeningly slack. Put yourself on the same slow track, puff on a hookah (try it—it's much mellower than cigarettes; this is the place that made shisha chic), and relax into the Egyptian groove.

Saigon Grill

CAUTION

Zone 10   Upper West Side
2381 Broadway (at 87th Street),
   Manhattan
(212) 875-9072

Vietnamese
★★★3
Moderate

Quality 87   Value B

Reservations:	Only for 5 or more; not accepted on weekends
When to go:	Peak mealtimes and weekends are very crowded
Kind of service:	Waiter service at tables
Entree range:	$6.50–14 (much less at lunch)
Payment:	VISA, MC, AMEX, D, DC, JCB
Service rating:	★★½
Friendliness rating:	★★
Transit:	1/9 to 86th Street
Bar:	Beer only
Wine selection:	None
Dress:	Casual
Disabled access:	Not accessible
Clientele:	Locals
Open:	Every day, 11 A.M.–midnight

Atmosphere/setting: Clean, bright, and plain, with tables packed much too closely together. Good for families.

House specialties: Barbecued spare ribs, pork chops, or chicken and grilled boneless chicken; summer rolls, coconut sticky rice (strewn with ground peanuts), and pickled vegetable salad.

Other recommendations: Perhaps the best dish of all isn't grilled: the crispy whole sea bass comes with a wonderful sweet-and-subtle sauce, and the fish is ultraflaky and fresh.

Summary & comments: "Grill" is right. This place turns out some of the best grilled dishes around. As with most Vietnamese restaurants, management is Chinese, but here the influence is overt—for example, wonderful barbecued spare ribs with peanut-plum sauce taste totally Chinese. But . . . whatever. In a neighborhood where good Asian food is rare, this hybrid is a godsend.

SAKA GURA

Japanese
★★★★
Moderate

Zone 9   Midtown East
211 East 43rd Street (between 2nd and
    3rd Avenues), Manhattan
(212) 953-SAKE

Quality 91   Value B+

Reservations:	Accepted
When to go:	Late nights
Kind of service:	Waiter service at bar and tables
Entree range:	$4–18
Payment:	VISA, MC, AMEX, DC
Service rating:	★★★★
Friendliness rating:	★★★
Transit:	S/4/5/6/7 to 42nd Street/Grand Central
Bar:	Full service
Wine selection:	None
Dress:	Casual chic
Disabled access:	Good (elevator); rest rooms not accessible
Clientele:	Middle-aged Japanese businessmen and younger Japanese chicsters
Dinner:	Monday, Wednesday, Saturday, 5 P.M.–2 A.M.; Thursday and Friday, 5 P.M.–3 A.M.; Sunday, 5 P.M.–12:30 A.M.; Tuesday, closed

Atmosphere/setting: Enter through a glary office building lobby, walk back toward the elevators, descend a dank staircase, and open the secret basement door to enter this supremely inviting inner sanctum that's all sleek lines and open space. There are some secluded tables (including an intimate parlor in the back that carries a steep minimum consumption charge), but the handsome oversize bar is where all the action is. Rest rooms are hidden inside huge round wooden fermenting barrels.

House specialties: Excellent simple dishes like udon (noodle soup) and cikuzen-ni (a spicy tangle of marinated earthy vegetables like burdock, carrots, bamboo shoots, lotus roots, and konyaku). Deep fried chicken is the work of real frymeisters; they achieve a remarkable stasis of crunchy skin and tender meat, but the chunks are a tad underseasoned (a dip in hot or soy sauce helps). Tori tsukuni (chicken meatballs) come dressed with a dab of sweetish sauce; they're very moist and intensely chickeny. Exotically delicious, Saka Gura–original, stewed, diced pork comes in a semigelatinous sweet sauce; slabs of fat pull away easily from the succulent meat. A very fresh sashimi plate comes with shrimp, mackerel, tuna, and bass (the sashimi deluxe plate adds yellowtail, sea urchin, and baby clams).

258

Other recommendations: This is first and foremost a sake bar, so as long as you're here you may as well enjoy the rice wine treasure trove. The drier varieties (e.g., Harushika, Otoko-yama) are the most interesting, and those who find sake an overly subtle drink should try one of the nama zakes, a variety with an especially broad flavor of considerable complexity. If you can afford them, aged koshu sakes (the cheapest—and it's very good—is kamo izumi koshu, at $15) have the length and complexity of great wine. Don't make the faux pas of ordering your rice wine hot; the good stuff is drunk cold or at room temperature (very dry ones can be warmed a little).

Summary & comments: The great food is a wonderful surprise in this swanky basement oasis, even though ambience and good sake alone would be a powerful draw. Management has an unerring sense of style, from the room's striking design to the unique glassware and beautiful sparkling ceramic serving bowls. Suave, helpful (if slightly aloof) servers offer hot towels as you arrive and a delicious green tea with the check.

Sal and Carmine's Pizza

Pizza
★★★
Inexpensive

Quality 90   Value A

Zone 10   Upper West Side
2671 Broadway (between 101st and
102nd Streets), Manhattan
(212) 663-7651

Reservations:	Not accepted
When to go:	Anytime
Kind of service:	Self-service
Entree range:	Slices, $1.75; pies, $14
Payment:	Cash only
Service rating:	★★
Friendliness rating:	★★
Transit:	1/9 to 103rd Street
Bar:	None
Wine selection:	None
Dress:	Casual
Disabled access:	Poor; step at door and narrow design
Clientele:	Local
Open:	Every day, 11 A.M.–11 P.M.

Atmosphere/setting: Classic Manhattan pizzeria: counter up front manned by cranky pizza technicians and functional seating in the back (or chomp your slice at the narrow ledge opposite the pizza counter).

House specialties: Uncommonly toothsome pizza by the slice.

Summary & comments: Ninety-nine percent of area pizzerias use the same ingredients. Sal and Carmine's is a rare exception, and people who remember how good pizza was twenty years ago will have tears streaming down their cheeks upon scarfing their first slice here. The cheese is several steps up from the usual gloppy, tasteless gunk, and while sauce and crust at first seem merely adequate (though dough is proofed the old-fashioned way in wooden drawers), they are in fact exactingly crafted to superbly support the cheese. Crust doesn't distract; it simply provides the canvas for this artistic study in mozzarella. Sauce binds and activates entirely behind the scenes, providing a subliminal catalyst for the slice as a whole. When at Sal and Carmine's, one must remember to eat (conceptually) from the cheese down, not from the crust up.

SAPPORO

Zone 8 Midtown West and Theater District	Japanese
	★★
152 West 49th Street (between 6th and 7th Avenues), Manhattan	Inexpensive
	Quality 78 Value A
(212) 869-8972	

Reservations:	Not accepted
When to go:	Anytime
Kind of service:	Waiter service at tables
Entree range:	$4–9
Payment:	Cash only
Service rating:	★★
Friendliness rating:	★★
Transit:	N/R to 49th Street or 1/9 to 50th Street
Bar:	Beer and wine only
Wine selection:	Very limited
Dress:	Casual
Disabled access:	Good
Clientele:	Japanese businessmen and tourists
Open:	Every day, 11 A.M.–12:30 A.M.

Atmosphere/setting: A plainly functional Japanese diner tucked conveniently on a prime Midtown side street. Brightly lit with well-worn tiled floors and sturdy coffee shop–style booths.

House specialties: All soups, yakisoba (slightly sweet, clove-scented, pan-fried noodles with diced pork or chicken), satisfying heaping bowls of ramen soup, hiya yakko (an ultrasimple dish of cold tofu topped with bonito flakes, scallions, and ground ginger; I like to dip it in dumpling sauce, though that's heresy), gyoza (fried dumplings), off-menu steamed crab dumplings (tiny, very delicate, frilly skinned things for dipping in mustard and soy sauce), and soulful katsus (cutlets of pork or chicken with or without scrambled egg).

Other recommendations: Real Japanese restaurants specialize; accordingly, this lowbrow diner doesn't even pretend to serve sushi, sashimi, teriyaki, or shabu-shabu.

Summary & comments: Sapporo is neither a fast-food noodle joint nor an elegant Asian Cuisine Experience. Rather, imagine a beloved Japanese truck stop serving good, honest, unpretentious chow slung (if indeed Japanese food can be slung) fast and cheap. Westerners expecting the standard sleek decor and prissy presentation will be disappointed, but those who crave unaffectedly plebian Japanese flavors will return again and again, as do multitudes of homesick Japanese.

261

Sapporo East

	Japanese
	★★½
	Moderate
	Quality 83 Value A−

Zone 5   East Village
245 East 10th Street (at 1st Avenue),
   Manhattan
(212) 260-1330

Reservations:	Not accepted
When to go:	Anytime
Kind of service:	Waiter service at counter and tables
Entree range:	$5.40–11
Payment:	MC, VISA, AMEX
Service rating:	★★½
Friendliness rating:	★★½
Transit:	L to 1st Avenue
Bar:	Beer and sake only
Wine selection:	None
Dress:	Casual
Disabled access:	Poor; accessible with assistance
Clientele:	Japanese bohemian kids and artsy young locals
Open:	Every day, 5 P.M.–12:45 A.M.

Atmosphere / setting: This warmly inviting but perpetually crowded corner spot sports a sparkling clean open kitchen, too-cool young Japanese servers, and colorful trippy signs announcing special dishes. Clever layout provides some relatively private nooks and crannies, but there's nowhere to wait for your table (and no reservations).

House specialties: Various ramen and udon soups are all very good, especially the interesting yasai udon, a mountain vegetable soup with carrot, burdock root, spinach, and excellent wide starchy udon noodles (it's even better if you spoon in some rice). Other than that, stick with comfort dishes such as seafood itame (a stir fry of squid, shrimp, octopus, and zucchini that's wonderfully elemental and permeated with good grilled onions), amazingly light, well-fried katsus (breaded pork or chicken cutlets—be sure to dunk in the accompanying sauce), and well-seared yakitori (grilled skewers of chicken and sweet onions). Vegetarians will be pleased to find brown rice plus a plethora of meatless dishes, both simple (oshitashi—an elemental pile of boiled spinach—and hiya yakko—cold bean curd served with ginger) and more involved (shigiyaki—deep-fried eggplant with sweet bean paste—and vegetable tempura).

Other recommendations: Sushi is fine, though you'll do a lot better at a specialist like Tomoe or Taka. The good house sake is served with some cucumber; the two flavors marry perfectly.

Summary & comments: The restaurant spectrum in Japan is far broader than is reflected by Japanese restaurants in this country, where you mostly see sushi bars, noodle shops, and places with overpriced, hyperextended menus that attempt to do it all. In Japan you also find down-home, family-style places where cooking is lusty, portions larger, and atmosphere convivial. Sapporo East (a different-flavored branch of Midtown's even more downscale Sapporo—see review) is a rare outpost for that kind of dining experience in New York.

Seamorhen II

Seafood/Southern

★★★½

Inexpensive

Quality 91   Value A

Zone 17   Southern Queens
118-29 Guy R. Brewer Boulevard,
    Jamaica, Queens
(718) 723-9181

Reservations:	Not accepted
When to go:	Tuesdays, Thurdays, and Saturdays when jerk chicken is made fresh
Kind of service:	Self-service
Entree range:	$6–8.50
Payment:	Cash only
Service rating:	★★
Friendliness rating:	★★★
Transit:	E/J/Z to Jamaica Center, Q111 bus down Guy R. Brewer Boulevard
Bar:	None
Wine selection:	None
Dress:	Casual
Disabled access:	Good, no bathrooms
Clientele:	Locals
Breakfast:	Every day, 7 A.M.–noon
Lunch/Dinner:	Monday–Saturday, noon–11 P.M.; Sunday, noon–7 P.M.

Atmosphere/setting: Bare-bones, mostly takeout fry shack, with just a couple of small tables for quick self-service on-premise eating. There are no bathrooms, and the operation seems somewhat ramshackle . . . until you take your first bite. Dishes are announced on zillions of paper plates taped to the wall, but you can view much of it on display in steam tables by the window and fry baskets across the long counter.

House specialties: Stellar fried fish has no secret ingredients or tricks; it's just flawlessly prepared with perfect batter, perfectly fresh fish, perfect frying temperature, and perfectly fresh oil. There's whiting, porgie, shrimp, and scallops, as well as fried and barbecued chicken (all available as sandwiches, plates with fries, or dinners with two side dishes). Jerk chicken is cooked out on the sidewalk in an oil can on four rickety legs; real smoked jerk is a holy grail (nearly everyone fakes it in an oven), and this is the real deal. For breakfast, there's fish and grits, or combos of eggs, sausage, and grits.

Other recommendations: Wonderful moist, flavorful yellow rice (studded with fried onions and peppers), candied yams (dosed with molasses as well as brown sugar), and all the other usual soul food sides like collard greens, potato salad, macaroni and cheese. French fries are superior, and even the bread is good (ask for potato bread).

Summary & comments: Don't be intimidated by this divey place; despite the dingy appearance, everything's super fresh and servers are quite courteous. Their name may be Seamorhen II (Seamorhen I doesn't seem to exist), but a promotion is certainly in order, given their terrific cooking. Jerk chicken is made fresh only three days a week—see When to go, above—but leftover birds—surprisingly good—are available reheated on other days.

Soul Fixins'

Southern
★ ★ ★
Inexpensive

Quality 88   Value A

Reservations:	None
When to go:	Anytime
Kind of service:	Self-service
Entree range:	$5–8
Payment:	Cash
Service rating:	★★½
Friendliness rating:	★★★
Transit:	A/C/E to 34th Street/Penn Station
Bar:	None
Wine selection:	None
Dress:	Casual
Disabled access:	Good
Clientele:	Local workers
Lunch:	Monday–Friday, 11 A.M.–5 P.M.
Dinner:	Monday–Friday, 5–10 P.M.

Atmosphere/setting: This was once a no-frills takeout lunch joint with a couple of tables. While there's still no waiter service, the place has been spruced up considerably. Lunches can still be crowded, utilitarian feeds, but hours have been extended and dinnertimes now offer a bit of mood. With the track-lit tables, new snazzy red-and-black color scheme, and a friendly, diverse clientele, this is now a happening enough scene to bring a date and the food is seductive enough to more than compensate for the bus-your-tray policy.

House specialties: Barbecued spareribs or chicken (not smoked, but they've found an awfully smart way to do them in the oven), well-seasoned candied yams, smoky, slightly chewy collard greens, and crusty macaroni and cheese. To drink, there's exemplary—and not oversweet—lemonade and smooth southern-style iced tea. There are fine desserts like excellent sweet potato pie (a great crust must have lard). Everything comes with good corn bread.

Other recommendations: Surprisingly, fried chicken is merely adequate.

Summary & comments: This very underrated place rivals the better soul food kitchens in Harlem, and its low prices are more uptown than midtown. While this can by no means be labeled health food, the chef does hold back on grease, salt, and pork by-products as much as he can and still have stuff taste good . . . which it reliably does. And the friendly staff, accustomed to serving impatient, harried Midtown workers, can be counted on to get you out in a flash.

Soul Food Kitchen

	Southern
Zone 13 Northern Brooklyn	★★★
84 Kingston Avenue (between Dean and Pacific Streets), Crown Heights, Brooklyn	Inexpensive
(718) 363-8844	Quality 90 Value A

Reservations:	Not accepted
When to go:	During daylight; the neighborhood (Bed-Stuy) gets rough at night
Kind of service:	Self-service
Entree range:	$5.50–7.50
Payment:	Cash only
Service rating:	★★½
Friendliness rating:	★½
Transit:	A/C to Kingston-Throop Avenues
Bar:	None
Wine selection:	None
Dress:	Casual
Disabled access:	Good; no rest rooms
Clientele:	Locals
Lunch/Dinner:	Monday–Thursday, 9 A.M.–11 P.M.; Friday and Saturday, 9 A.M.–1 A.M.; Sunday, 9 A.M.–10 P.M.

Atmosphere/setting: A small, bustling takeout vestibule where you're literally surrounded by great-looking food (and you get to watch the cooks whipping it up in back). There's some fast food–style seating next door if you just can't wait until you get home (they also promise to deliver "anywhere in Brooklyn," but that's got to be an overstatement). Crowds of hungry customers angle for position at the counter, stirred into a ravenous frenzy by the awesome sights and aromas.

House specialties: Any North Carolina barbecue fan will tell you that the state specialty, chopped pork barbecue, must be smoke-cooked with wood. This place—staffed by North Carolina expats—cheats, but they make an oven-baked 'cue that comes impressively close. Eaten in a sandwich with coleslaw and the slamming sauce (with just the right late-onset spicy bite), it's excruciatingly good. Also memorable: soupy, rich black-eyed peas, nearly blackened (but miraculously juicy) fried pork chops, luscious collard greens, great crusty-topped macaroni and cheese. The sauce used to smother chicken or pork chops is dead-on southern, flavored with only pan drippings, browned flour, and (lots of) salt and pepper.

Summary & comments: While nearby Gaither's (see review) does more "proper" southern boardinghouse-type cuisine, Soul Food Kitchen—as befits its ultradirect name—is more down-home; cooks distractedly nibble bits of barbe-cued pork with their fingers while they wait for chicken to fry, and lard—anath-ema elsewhere—is no stranger to these pans. The food is similar to what you'd eat at Sunday dinner in the neighborhood: full of soulful flavor and resolutely undi-luted for outsiders.

Soup Kitchen International

Zone 8   Midtown West and
    Theater District
259A West 55th Street, Manhattan
(212) 757-7730

Soup	
★★★½	
Inexpensive	
Quality 91	Value A

Reservations: None
When to go: Late in the day to avoid the worst lines
Kind of service: Takeout
Entree range: $6–10
Payment: Cash only
Service rating: ★★★½
Friendliness rating: ★
Transit: A/B/C/D/1/9 to 59th Street/Columbus Circle
Bar: None
Wine selection: None
Dress: Casual
Disabled access: Good
Clientele: Local workers and foodies
Lunch: Monday–Friday, noon–6 P.M. (sometimes later);
                      closed Friday, Saturday, and all summer

Atmosphere/setting: You wait in line, inching ever so slowly toward the venerable takeout window. Once at the head of the line, you peer in and glimpse a nervous, high-pitched buzz like a Broadway backstage; assistants go about their souply tasks at full tilt, braced for the inevitable calamitous repercussions should they err in even the most trifling detail. A number of signs—including an LED zipper—clearly state The Rules. At the center of this hurricane, a model of calm, haughty efficiency, stands The Soup Man.

House specialties: There's always a chicken-based soup (either chicken vegetable or chicken broccoli), comparatively light and simple, with plenty of meat and carefully cut vegetables. The chef's personal favorites are his bisques—seafood, lobster, or crab. These are the richest and most expensive choices, of an almost diabolical complexity. You'll find a not very spicy, medium-thick chili (turkey, vegetable, chicken, or beef), and often Indian mulligatawny (extremely complex and mildly sweet). The remainder are seafood chowders, various peasant soups, and delicious oddballs like mussels and spinach or bacon, lettuce, and tomato.

Other recommendations: In hot weather, there are cold soups like vichyssoise and gazpacho.

Entertainment & amenities: Watching newcomers fret and rehearse their order while in line.

Summary & comments: In spite of Jerry Seinfeld's famous sobriquet, owner-chef Al Yeganeh is *not* a Nazi. He's a very conscientious man who has a few irrefutably logical rules: know what you want by the time you reach the window after your 45-minute wait (duh), have your money ready, and move to the left so the next person can step forward and order. Al—regulars refer to him as Al, though none would dare call him that to his face—feels sorry for those waiting (he keeps raising prices to discourage crowds to no avail), so those who ignore his prominently posted rules and delay service receive no bread. Soup comes in small, large, or extra-large containers. If you order an extra-large, you'll be interrogated as to your intentions; food shouldn't go unrefrigerated for long periods, so if you order a big one you'd best be prepared to convince Al that you and several friends intend to ingest forthwith. Don't think of this as the most expensive soup in town; these ultranourishing concoctions (which come with bread, fruit, and a chocolate), are actually the cheapest four-star lunch in town. What's more, the price allows use of choicest ingredients: real saffron, fresh lobster, etc. The hallmark of Al's soups is the incredible spectrum of textures: from huge chunks down to microscopic, in-suspension particles and dozens of ingredients collaborating in a soupy symphony, each arranged in perfect balance. Eat on benches one block north at the northeast corner of 56th Street and 8th Avenue. In wintertime you won't notice even the coldest winds while huddled with your takeout container of steaming soupy magnificence.

Speengar Shish
Kebab House

Afghan
★★★½
Inexpensive

Quality 90   Value A

Zone 15   Northwestern Queens
40-09 69th Street (near Roosevelt
   Avenue), Woodside, Queens
(718) 426-8850

Reservations:	Not accepted
When to go:	Anytime
Kind of service:	Waiter service at tables
Entree range:	$5–8.50
Payment:	VISA, MC, AMEX, D
Service rating:	★★★
Friendliness rating:	★★★½
Transit:	7 to 69th Street
Bar:	None
Wine selection:	None
Dress:	Casual (shorts and short dresses out of place)
Disabled access:	Good; rest rooms not accessible
Clientele:	Local Afghans
Open:	Every day, noon–midnight

Atmosphere/setting: Up front, meats sizzle on the big charcoal grill. Go through a beaded curtain to enter the rear dining room (past a handwritten sign reading "Do not bring alcohol drinks") and you are in Afghanistan—not a plushly fancified, Disneyesque recreation of a fantasy Afghanistan, but a cafe that unself-consciously evokes Kabul in Queens. Large framed photos of scenes from back home dot the walls.

House specialties: Appetizers include two varieties of fried dumplings (bolani or samosa) that are reminiscent of Indian samosa but much more delicate. A duo of noodly steamed dumplings (manto or ashack), topped with minty yogurt and/or tomato sauce are also available. For entrees, it's kebabs or stews. Lamb, chicken, and keema (ground beef) kebabs are rich and smoky from the grill and astonishing bargains at $5 (an extra few bucks brings salad and/or rice). Stewy palows and chalows (Persian-influenced pilaf-like dishes, featuring curries that are, again, more delicate than the Indian version) are wailingly delicious. Kabli palow is a mountain of rice studded with raisins, shreds of carrot, and very slow cooked hunks of lamb; it comes with a side dish of still more lamb in a succulent curry sauce. Bandanjan burani consists of thick slices of fried eggplant done just to that borderline of firm and tender, doused with homemade yogurt and tomato sauce.

271

Other recommendations: Dough, a yogurt drink similar to Indian lassi, dosed with herbs and spices, is exotically delicious. A whole pitcher costs $3. Also for $3, try some meaty lobya (large red beans); this "side order" is enough to feed six.

Summary & comments: A stone's throw from the ethnic food wonderland of Jackson Heights and in the middle of a Filipino microneighborhood (see reviews of Ihawan and BJ's), Speengar is proudly, defiantly authentic. Their yogurty dough, acidic and spicy, isn't tamed for outsiders; kebabs are spiced for Afghan palates, and the stews (palows and chalows) can almost intimidate Westerners with their outrageous mountains of rice. Nonetheless, these victuals are easily enjoyed by newcomers; with its simpler flavors and more familiar ingredients, Afghan cuisine is more accessible than Indian.

Sripraphai Thai Bakery

Zone 15 Northwestern Queens	Thai
64-13 39th Avenue, Woodside, Queens	★★★½
(718) 899-9599	Inexpensive
	Quality 90 Value A

Reservations:	None
When to go:	Anytime
Kind of service:	Waiter service at tables
Entree range:	$4.50–10.50
Payment:	Cash only
Service rating:	★★½
Friendliness rating:	★★
Transit:	7 to 61st Street
Bar:	None
Wine selection:	None
Dress:	Casual
Disabled access:	Good
Clientele:	Local Thais and questing chowhounds
Open:	Every day, 11 A.M.–10 P.M.

Atmosphere / setting: A clean, well-lit white box. The ambience, like their name, is more bakery than restaurant, though there is table service.

House specialties: Chinese broccoli with crispy pork; sautéed noodles with meat, chili, and basil leaves; pan-fried egg with ground pork; sticky rice; Thai spaghetti with curry sauce; rice with mixed vegetables; banana sticky rice. All taste much more authentic than elsewhere in New York (if you can even *find* such dishes on other menus), though the kitchen is certainly not first class by Thai standards (many things are reheated, for example).

Other recommendations: Don't miss the impressive collection of freshly prepared cookies, crackers, and little Thai munchies near the cash register, available for in-store or takeout consumption.

Summary & comments: This is much more than a bakery, though it's by no means an elegant restaurant. Sripraphai is nothing less than the best—and only—authentic Thai eatery in New York. The people who run this place are very serious; they must be to steadfastly remain the city's sole bastion of genuine Thai cooking. If you want gringo-friendly Thai, eat anywhere else; if you want the uncompromisingly real thing, raw and unadorned, eat here. As a single concession to novices, there's a photo album with snapshots of most dishes. One caution: beware of the catfish: this ain't crunchy, fluffy, corn bread–battered catfish à la New Orleans; it's quite different and not recommended for beginners. Cookies and such are great, but don't miss the best dessert of all (maybe in all of New York): luscious banana sticky rice steamed inside a banana leaf.

STAMATIS

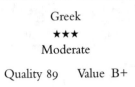

Zone 15   Northwestern Queens
29-12 23rd Avenue (between 29th and
    30th Streets), Astoria, Queens
(718) 721-4507; (718) 932-8596

Reservations:	Not accepted
When to go:	Anytime
Kind of service:	Waiter service at tables
Entree range:	$7–15
Payment:	MC, VISA, AMEX
Service rating:	★★★
Friendliness rating:	★★★
Transit:	N to Astoria/Ditmars Boulevard
Bar:	Limited; wine and beer only
Wine selection:	Good Greeks (particularly nice house red)
Dress:	Nice casual
Disabled access:	Good; rest rooms narrow
Clientele:	Local
Open:	Every day, 11 A.M.–1:30 A.M.

Atmosphere / setting: A much saner atmosphere than other local Greek restaurants in this price range; tables are well-spaced, carpet reduces sound levels, and seating is in comfortable wood-frame cane chairs. It's traditional to banter with the chef on your way into Greek places; peer into his open kitchen for a view of the day's specials.

House specialties: They're famous for soup, especially avgolemono, a superb thick lemony potage of tender chicken and plump rice. Grilled octopus is nicely meaty and charry, and while saganaki (battered fried cheese) tastes like the height of simplicity, it's really quite an accomplishment—batter, oil, and pan are optimized with a sure hand (it's greasy, yes, but good greasy). Don't miss perfect skordalia (cold mashed potatoes with garlic) or—often a special—fricassee of tender, long-cooked lamb (on the bone) doused with creamy lemon dill sauce and draped in escarole. Many dishes come with lemony oven-roasted potatoes (they've soaked up lots of olive oil; the downside of such old-fashioned cooking is heavy, rich preparations). Fry mix is an off-menu mélange of razor thin zucchini slices and thicker eggplant cuts, both lightly battered and fried crisp.

Other recommendations: The bread basket comes loaded with terrific, hot, thick-cut, fresh Italian bread toasted and lightly drizzled with olive oil and oregano.

Summary & comments: Real Greek food in this famously Greek neighborhood has gotten harder and harder to find; great old places keep closing and are replaced by glittery cafes favored by the more assimilated second generation. Famous spots like Uncle George's, Telly's, and Elias have been ruined by "me-too" food critics, but Stamatis remains a bastion, its kitchen turning out unadulterated Greek soul food that elsewhere tastes faded or gussied up. The service is old school, too; waitresses cut up the octopus for you, offer to apportion shared soups, and give reliable ordering advice. Whatever you do, don't miss the skordalia (neither snowy-smooth nor chunky, with a strong dose of garlic that never quite peaks into heat); this dish tests a kitchen's sense of balance, and Stamatis alone among Astoria's current Greeks passes the test.

Sucelt Coffee Shop

	Puerto Rican/Cuban
Zone 4 Greenwich Village	★★
200 West 14th Street (just west of 7th Avenue), Manhattan	Inexpensive
(212) 242-0593	Quality 82 Value A

Reservations:	Not accepted
When to go:	Everything's freshest at lunchtime
Kind of service:	Waiter service at counter
Entree range:	$5.25–7
Payment:	Cash only
Service rating:	★★★
Friendliness rating:	★★★
Transit:	1/2/3/9/A/C/E to 14th Street
Bar:	None
Wine selection:	None
Dress:	Casual
Disabled access:	Small step up; rest rooms not accessible
Clientele:	Local workers of every class and ethnicity
Breakfast:	Every day, 7–11:30 A.M.
Lunch:	Every day, 11:30 A.M.–2 P.M.
Dinner:	Monday–Saturday, 2–9:30 P.M.; Sunday, 2–9 P.M.

Atmosphere/setting: It's counter seating/service only in this vintage hole-in-the-wall much loved by a cast of regulars. Ask around to find out who's got the plastic tub of hot sauce.

House specialties: Sucelt claims to offer tamales from different countries, but they're pretty similar; the Venezuelan version—overstuffed with pork, chicken, and beef, dotted with raisins, capers, and chunks of green pepper—is best, but all are moister and softer than the more common Mexican type. Puerto Rican pasteles are akin to tamales but made with green plantains rather than corn. The fried snacks such as patties filled with cheese, meat, or chicken and the alcapurrias (green plantain croquettes stuffed with spicy ground beef) are outstanding and even better when dunked in the fragrant homemade hot sauce. Plantains and rice and beans are fine, but entrees (roast pork, codfish stew, and the like) are hit-or-miss.

Other recommendations: Nice, not-too-sweet milk shakes made from banana, mamey, pineapple, papaya, mango, guanabana, passion fruit, or trigo (malty wheat). Most are from commercial frozen fruit; banana is an exception.

Summary & comments: For serious eating, you'll do better at El Papasito, Casa Adela, and perhaps even Margon Restaurant (see reviews). But for snackier eats, this is a formidable choice—and those others don't have Sucelt's transportive old-time rice and beans luncheonette vibe.

SWEET-N-TART CAFE

Zone 16   NE Queens
136-11 38th Avenue, Flushing, Queens
(718) 661-3380

	Chinese
	★★★
	Inexpensive
	Quality 91 Value B−

Reservations:	Accepted
When to go:	Anytime
Kind of service:	Waiter service at tables
Entree range:	$3–10
Payment:	Cash only
Service rating:	★★½
Friendliness rating:	★★
Transit:	7 to Flushing/Main Street
Bar:	None
Wine selection:	None
Dress:	Casual
Disabled access:	Good
Clientele:	Chinese teenyboppers
Open:	Every day, 9 A.M.–midnight

Atmosphere/setting: This colorful, sleek space attracts Chinese youths (in leather and designer duds) mostly for desserts; meanwhile, a sprinkling of chowhound oldsters dive into main course offerings merely picked at by the comely young scenesters.

House specialties: House special baked chicken with ginger and scallion (immensely fragrant, delicate morsels of tender chicken nestled inside fried paper), hot pots (things like Chinese sausage, pork, taro, or eel with rice steamed in bamboo pots or baked in ceramic pots), Shanghai-style steamed dumplings (filled with soup and served with a great pungent dipping sauce), hearty congee (rice gruel), wonderful fresh juices (with floating orbs of tapioca for textural counterpoint), shakes and teas (like melon, coconut milk tea, black sesame paste drink, etc.), awesome ginger ice cream.

Summary & comments: A splendid meal can be built by ordering from myriad small plate offerings that include—in addition to occidental-friendly items such as those listed above—hard-to-find Taiwanese and Hong Kong treats, including pig's blood, pork intestine, and duck tongue. But it's not all viscera by any means; even the most skittish eater can find a lot to love here. Desserts are unmissable (mmm . . . that ginger ice cream) as are flavored teas (almond, taro, cinnamon, etc). Kids will go nuts over banana fruit shakes or colorful juices. There's another quite different Sweet-n-Tart Cafe in Manhattan (76 Mott, (212) 334-8088) that's also worth a stop for snacks.

Tadjikstan

	Central Asian
	★★★★
Zone 17 Southern Queens	Inexpensive
102-03A Queens Boulevard (near 67th	
Drive), Rego Park, Queens	Quality 93 Value A
(718) 830-0744	

Reservations:	Not accepted
When to go:	Anytime
Kind of service:	Waiter service at tables
Entree range:	$4–6
Payment:	Cash only
Service rating:	★½
Friendliness rating:	★★★
Transit:	G/R to 67th Avenue
Bar:	None
Wine selection:	None
Dress:	Casual (shorts and short dresses out of place)
Disabled access:	Good, rest rooms not accessible
Clientele:	What clientele?
Open:	Noon–midnight; closed Friday night through Saturday afternoon

Atmosphere/setting: A dank, dark storefront that's usually empty (unless, as is frequently the case, it's filled with a private party). Mom's cooking away in the back kitchen, and Dad hovers. Suspicion is in the air ("Who are these people and why have they come here?" seems to be the thought on their minds), but once you've torn into the food and experienced sublime revelation, your eyes turn bright, the ice melts all around, smiles come easily, and this drab room becomes a gaily colored paradise.

House specialties: You're highly unlikely to find most menu items in actual supply, but here goes (it's all kosher, by the way): various salads, like red bean (beans cooked to the instant of textural perfection, balanced perfectly with coriander and strips of marinated peppers) or cucumber (with lots of dill and onion). Mantoo (herby lamb dumplings shaped like ravioli), samsa (wonderfully flaky pastry stuffed with chunks of marinated lamb, onions, and spices), a pasta and lamb soup called lagman, and hearty, puffy lavash bread. Also, there are kebabs of marinated chicken, lamb, beef, or sweetbreads, and—if you're lucky, or have ordered ahead of time—heavenly pluv, the local variant of pilaf, a mound of broth-soaked short-grain rice flecked with sweet carrot shreds and chickpeas, scented with fenugreek and cumin, and topped with chunks of lamb (a condiment, really; rice is the thing) that will make you take boiling much more seriously as a culinary technique.

278

Tadjikstan *(continued)*

Other recommendations: If they're closed for a party, you can try for a take-out dish of whatever's being served at the affair (cry "Takeout??? Takeout???" beseechingly and hope they take pity). Since the party food is often their best stuff, it's worth the effort. Often you'll get party pluv, a fresher, richer version of the dish (you can special order it a day in advance, but bear in mind that all Central Asian restaurants—even if otherwise inexpensive—will soak you badly on this dish, so be sure to negotiate price carefully).

Summary & comments: This kitchen's food is magnificent, and if you can relax into the rhythm, the ambience and "service" (sic) become perfectly agreeable. But this is definitely a not-ready-for-prime-time eat. English skills are minimal, and as at many little Russian and Central Asian restaurants, the people who run this place think that they're doing you a favor by serving you. But here, they're at least *glad* to do you the favor (once you've worn through their preliminary suspicions). If you come twice, you become family.

Teddy's Bar and Grill

	Pub	
	★★½	
	Moderate	

Zone 13   N Brooklyn
96 Berry Street (at North 8th
    Street),
    Williamsburg, Brooklyn
(718) 384-9787

Quality 86   Value A−

Reservations:	Only for large parties
When to go:	Anytime
Kind of service:	Waiter service at bar and tables
Entree range:	$5–14
Payment:	VISA, MC
Service rating:	★★½
Friendliness rating:	★★½
Transit:	L to Bedford Avenue
Bar:	Full service
Wine selection:	Limited
Dress:	Casual
Disabled access:	Good; rest rooms not accessible
Clientele:	Local artsy, older regulars
Lunch:	Every day, 11 A.M.–5 P.M.
Dinner:	Monday–Thursday, and Sunday: 6 P.M.–midnight; Friday and Saturday, 5 P.M.–2 A.M.

Atmosphere/setting: One of Brooklyn's biggest secrets is its treasure trove of atmospheric bars. One of the oldest and most beautiful is Teddy's, which sports the high tin ceilings, antique tiled floor, stained glass window trim, mammoth upright piano, and column-framed bandstand of a classic nineteenth-century watering hole. To walk into Teddy's is to enter another century, yet the place remains warmly vital and utterly unself-conscious; grungy Gen-Xers discussing web page design fit the picture as easily as do the old Scandinavian longshoremen. Management has recently added an incongruous back room with brooding recessed lighting, brick, and candles, but it's wisely hidden out of sight.

House specialties: Great steak sandwiches made with fresh London broil, a touch of sharp jack cheese and browned sweet onions; very good burgers (best with some of those grilled onions), calamari (greaseless and crispy, though batter dominates); Caesar salad (exceptional croutons); delicate quesadillas with spinach and sun-dried tomatoes; and, believe it or not, a delicious BLT with salmon and homemade shallot-dill mayonnaise on toasted challah bread (sounds impossible, if

Teddy's Bar & Grill (continued)

not downright dangerous, but it works). Just as unlikely, Teddy's also makes one of the best hot fudge sundaes in town (certainly one of the best ever served up in a gin mill).

Other recommendations: This is one of only a handful of local sources for wonderful, spicy Zapp's potato chips from New Orleans, and the beer selection is broad and unusually fresh.

Entertainment & amenities: Teddy's frequently presents live music and poetry readings, which rarely draw much attention from drinking, eating, and chatting patrons.

Summary & comments: Area residents go to Teddy's to drink and to nearby Oznot's Dish to eat. The latter has grown pricey and variable, but Teddy's food gets better and better, though specials can be iffy (stick with the recommended dishes, above).

TERESA'S

Zone 5   East Village
103 1st Avenue (between 6th and 7th
    Streets), Manhattan
(212) 228-0604

Polish	
★★	
Inexpensive	
Quality 83	Value A

Reservations:	Not accepted
When to go:	Anytime
Kind of service:	Waiter service at tables and counter
Entree range:	$7–13
Payment:	Cash only
Service rating:	★★★
Friendliness rating:	★★½
Transit:	L to 1st Avenue, F to 2nd Avenue
Bar:	Full service
Wine selection:	Limited
Dress:	Casual
Disabled access:	Good; rest rooms not accessible
Clientele:	Cheapskates and anarchists
Breakfast:	Every day, 7–11 A.M.
Lunch:	Every day, 11 A.M.–4 P.M.
Dinner:	Every day, 4–11 P.M.

Atmosphere / setting: This formerly homely coffee shop was recently jazzed up to look downright chic with yellow mottled walls, modern mesh halogen light fixtures, expensive chrome ceiling fans, hip Asian paper-paneled room dividers, and framed eastern European deco prints.

House specialties: Catcher mitt–sized chicken or veal cutlets, pedestrian but satisfying beef goulash, skillfully boiled potatoes, and not-mushy steamed carrots. Roast duck, a perennial special, is better than you'd expect from such a simple kitchen (not to mention the $9 price tag), and soups are all memorable—especially white borscht (weekends only) and potato (Saturdays only). Very good rice pudding, too.

Other recommendations: Wonderful baked-from-scratch muffins.

Summary & comments: The East Village was, until recently, a working-class Polish/Ukrainian neighborhood. Most of the old bargain-priced Eastern European coffee shops are still in business, serving both the remaining old-timers and the young bohemian set that's made the neighborhood their own. Many locals tout nearby Veselka's, but Teresa's is tops. A few small touches here are extra pleasing, like real maple syrup for an extra charge (why don't more places offer this?), fresh-squeezed orange or carrot juice, and some of the city's only honest muffins.

Thai Cafe

Zone 13   Northern Brooklyn
925 Manhattan Avenue (near Kent
    Avenue), Greenpoint, Brooklyn
(718) 383-3562

Thai
★★½
Moderate
Quality 84   Value B−

Reservations:	Parties of 4 or more
When to go:	Peak mealtimes and weekends are very crowded
Kind of service:	Waiter service at tables
Entree range:	$4.95–11
Payment:	Cash only
Service rating:	★★½
Friendliness rating:	★★½
Transit:	G to Greenpoint Avenue
Bar:	Full service
Wine selection:	Very limited
Dress:	Casual
Disabled access:	Good
Clientele:	Local bohemians
Lunch/Dinner:	Monday–Wednesday, 11 A.M.–10:30 P.M.;
	Thursday–Saturday, 11 A.M.–11 P.M.;
	Sunday, 1–11 P.M.

Atmosphere/setting: Airy and sunny by day, romantically bohemian at night, this is a haven in a gray part of Polish Greenpoint that otherwise looks straight out of Warsaw. There's no waiting space, so avoid popular Friday and Saturday nights.

House specialties: All the usual Thai dishes, from satays to curries and salads and lemon grass dishes. One of the best is also one of the humblest: fried rice, made Thai style with very short grain rice. Avoid elaborate seafood dishes; at these low prices, the kitchen can't always offer the best quality.

Summary & comments: New York City has almost no truly authentic Thai food (Sripraphai—see review—is an exception), so diners must choose between different shades of inauthenticity. This kitchen may not please serious aficionados, but the food, however watered-down, tastes very good. Thai Cafe has a popular spin-off, Plan-eat Thailand (184 Bedford Street, Brooklyn, (718) 599-5758), which cooks similarly in slightly hipper, more colorful surroundings (to match its hipper Williamsburg locale).

TiEMANN OASIS

Zone 12   Harlem, Morningside
  Heights, and Washington Heights
52 Tiemannn Place (near Broadway and
  123rd Street), Manhattan
(212) 280-7832

Eclectic
★★★
Inexpensive
Quality 88   Value A

Reservations:	Only necessary if there's live music (call ahead)
When to go:	Anytime
Kind of service:	Waiter service at tables
Entree range:	$4.50–8.95
Payment:	Cash only
Service rating:	★★★
Friendliness rating:	★★★★
Transit:	1/9 to 125th Street
Bar:	None
Wine selection:	None
Dress:	Casual
Disabled access:	Good
Clientele:	Locals, students
Breakfast:	Monday–Friday, 10–11:30 A.M.
Brunch:	Saturday and Sunday, 10 A.M.–4 P.M.
Lunch:	Monday–Friday, 11:30 A.M.–3:30 P.M.
Dinner:	Every day, 6–10 P.M.

Atmosphere / setting: An award proudly hung on the wall says it all: "West
Harlem Coalition Anti-Gentrification Ass-Kicking Award: for waging an uncom-
promising, persistent, and imaginative battle against gentrification." This is a warm,
cranky, steadfastly unglitzy place where eccentrics, locals, students, and radicals of
all races gather to eat in a crashpad ambience so spare that you'll wonder whether
the entire enterprise has simply squatted in an abandoned storefront (they haven't;
this has been a neighborhood fixture for many years).

House specialties: Roti (potato and chickpea curry spiked with your
choice of chicken, beef, shrimp, conch, vegetables, or goat tucked into a spongy
thin dough wrapper), grilled falafel, hearty Middle Eastern rice dishes like makluba, hummus, and grape leaves, anything with black beans.

Entertainment & amenities: If bantering with the servers or chef (characters all) isn't sufficiently entertaining, call to find out whether they're still pre-
senting their Bohemia Unlimited live music series on Sunday nights.

Summary & comments: Chef-owner Saad Kadhim, a hip and laid-back fellow, is well versed in all sorts of Middle Eastern cooking, and even his Mexican

and Caribbean dishes betray a Middle Eastern touch (the picadillo—full of black pepper, not red—tastes almost Persian). His roti is wonderful but as coarse as the ambience (the ruggedly spiced meat is served bones and all—order shrimp, conch, or veg if this might bug you). He makes stellar makluba, a rare Iraqi soul food dish consisting of a huge portion of rice strewn with stewed vegetables, almonds, raisins, yogurt, and, optionally, chicken. Kadhim has an original touch, seen especially in his nutty grilled falafel, a version that makes you wonder why anyone would ever fry the stuff. Only about half the menu items are dependably on hand at any one time (weekends more stuff is cooked), but it's best anyway to just turn Kadhim loose to improvise your supper; he'll figure out what you need and whip up something uniquely satisfying.

Tindo

Zone 3   Chinatown, Little
   Italy, and Lower East Side
1 Eldridge Street, Manhattan
(212) 966-5684; (212) 966-9241

Chinese
★★★★
Moderate

Quality 92   Value A

Reservations:	Policy varies; call ahead
When to go:	Anytime
Kind of service:	Waiter service at tables
Entree range:	$9.95–17.95
Payment:	Cash only
Service rating:	★★½
Friendliness rating:	★★½
Transit:	F to East Broadway
Bar:	Beer only
Wine selection:	None
Dress:	Nice casual
Disabled access:	Poor; rest rooms and upstairs not accessible
Clientele:	Local Chinese chowhounds
Lunch/Dinner:	Thursday–Tuesday, 11–3 A.M.; Wednesday, closed

Atmosphere/setting: This warm, cheerful little triangular space is a bright beacon on a drab block. The upstairs auxiliary dining room (accessible through an unmarked entrance around the corner) seats larger groups but has considerably less charm—though it does sport a picturesque view of subways ascending the Manhattan Bridge.

House specialties: Anything on the little green specials menu, especially boiling-at-your-table hotpots like baby beef and black pepper, baby eggplant with squid and ground pork, and clams in Thailand sauce. Also, salt and pepper squid, steamed oyster in shell in cognac sauce, scrambled egg and shrimp (served atop velvety chow fun noodles), scallops with black pepper sauce, fried prawns topped with homemade mayonnaise and honey walnuts.

Other recommendations: Less to the Western palate: salted thousand-year-old egg with dried octopus and minced pork (a real homestyle Hong Kong dish that's not on the English menu; a dead ringer for corned beef hash with fried egg), chives with salt fish, ground pork with salt fish, stuffed goose intestine.

Summary & comments: Tindo is the top choice in Chinatown for home-style Cantonese. Shrimp with scrambled egg—dotted with scallions and served atop tender rice noodles—is the very essence of Cantonese comfort food, and the chef imbues it with love as well as scrumptiousness. The salt and pepper squid is among the best fried calamari in Manhattan, and fried prawns with mayo and honey walnuts (one of the few banquet-style offerings) are simply awesome. Some dishes (especially noodles and soups) on the regular menu are merely fair; stick with the specials menu or ask the owner (a bespectacled woman who's usually downstairs) for advice. Beware, however, of tips from the upstairs waiters, who may coax you toward the more expensive dishes—though nothing's *that* expensive here. The chef co-owns this place, so there's no danger of the usual Chinatown phenomenon of chef juggling, but the kitchen does have infrequent off nights when quality dips way down to merely very good.

Tokyo

Zone 9   Midtown East
342 Lexington Avenue (between
    39th and 40th Streets), Manhattan
(212) 697-8330

Japanese	
★★★½	
Expensive	
Quality 92	Value C

Reservations:	Accepted
When to go:	Anytime
Kind of service:	Waiter service at tables
Entree range:	$10.75–15.75 (English menu)
Payment:	AMEX, VISA, MC, DC
Service rating:	★★½
Friendliness rating:	★★½
Transit:	S/4/5/6/7 to 42nd Street/Grand Central
Bar:	Full service
Wine selection:	House
Dress:	Nice casual
Disabled access:	Good; rest rooms not accessible
Clientele:	Japanese businessmen
Lunch:	Monday–Friday, noon–2:30 P.M.
Dinner:	Monday–Saturday, 5:30–10:30 P.M.; Sunday, closed

Atmosphere/setting: A small, serene dining room with low-key elegance and soft lighting. The bar up front is cozy and very busy.

House specialties: There's a standard English menu of familiar favorites. Skip it entirely and go instead for the secret insider stuff (see Summary & comments for tips on how to go about this). Highlights: sake kasu (cod fillets marinated in rice lees—the dregs from sake making), harusame (an engrossing tangle of clear mung bean noodles, bamboo shoot, mushroom, watercress, and sautéed nuggets of pork), tako yaki (like okonomayaki pancakes, but baked in small balls), kyo fu (kyoto-style fried tofu), ganmodoki and daikon (tofu and the most delectable daikon floating in a slightly sweet sauce), stellar chunks of fried chicken (fermented starch in the batter functions like beer or seltzer, producing a fabulously crispy crust), and ebi shinjo (delicately fried shrimp mousse). One of the best and most original dishes is scallops and mushrooms marinated in mayonnaise, baked with flying fish roe, and served in a large scallop shell (the mayo and cream constrain the fishiness of the roe; the result is a revelation).

Other recommendations: Tokyo's English menu is far less exciting than their hidden offerings, but two of its more interesting selections are salmon meuniere Tokyo style (a very fresh fillet sautéed in butter; simple but nice) and beef katsu (a tasty battered and fried rib-eye steak).

288

Tokyo *(continued)*

Summary & comments: Tokyo—like the city itself—presents one face to tourists and another to insiders. The choicest things here are untranslated, and you must work a bit to get at them. Cram with Berlitz for a few months, bring along a Japanese friend, or else try the following strategy: call over the manager, and gesture broadly across the English menu while shaking your head emphatically, NO! You don't want *any* of that. You want only the Japanese specials, and you'll obediently eat *anything* you're fed. If he seems dubious, try to reassure him by dropping the names of some of the above-mentioned secret dishes (pronounce Japanese like Spanish and you'll rarely go wrong). Be prepared to spend freely; you may be able to set an overall price limit, but those needing advance description and price itemization of each plate may find themselves exiled to the English menu where such information is clearly presented. Be careful about drinks here; it's the kind of place where friendly waiters offer to top off your half-full glass, so it's very easy to lose track as your bar tab climbs to screamingly high levels. On the other hand, the food is so outstanding (the kitchen turns out an astonishingly wide range of dishes, each remarkably individual and fully developed) that you may want to throw caution to the wind and drink freely (expect to pay $60 or more per person if you do . . . $30–45 if you're more cautious). Parties of five or six work best for trying a broad assortment of the smallish portions.

TOM'S LUNCHEONETTE

Zone 13 Northern Brooklyn	American
782 Washington Avenue (corner of	★★★
Sterling Place), Prospect Heights,	Inexpensive
Brooklyn	Quality 85 Value B
(718) 783–8576	

Reservations:	Not accepted
When to go:	Anytime
Kind of service:	Waiter service at counter and tables
Entree range:	$2.75–6.50
Payment:	Cash only
Service rating:	★★★★★
Friendliness rating:	★★★★★
Transit:	2/3 Eastern Parkway/Brooklyn Museum
Bar:	None
Wine selection:	None
Dress:	Casual
Disabled access:	Good; rest rooms not accessible
Clientele:	Locals (mostly long-time regulars)
Breakfast/Lunch:	Monday–Saturday, 5 A.M.–4 P.M.; Sunday, closed

Atmosphere/setting: This is the ur-coffee shop, lovingly maintained in 1940s style (it's been in biz since 1936); lime rickeys and such are expertly crafted at the soda fountain up front, and woody booths are always full of eager patrons—most of them regulars. There's a screened-in veranda, and, over a radio somewhere, Tommy Dorsey is getting sentimental over you.

House specialties: Old-fashioned breakfasts (with fab crunchy, starchy home fries or excellent grits), good burgers and french fries, classic coffee-shop sandwiches (especially good: turkey melt with sage-scented stuffing tucked between slices of fresh-tasting turkey on grilled rye bread), cherry lime rickeys, and excellent lemonade.

Other recommendations: One flaw: egg creams here have been unjustifiably lauded. A real egg cream has the chocolate added last so that a pure white foamy head builds, untainted by brown syrup. But Tom's adds chocolate before the soda, and—blasphemy!—squirts whipped cream and sprinkles cinnamon (cinnamon!) on top.

Summary & comments: The food here is good, not great, but the incredible ambience, earnest friendly service, and palpable warmth elevate Tom's to the pantheon of old-fashioned New York restaurants. The kitchen plays it straight; carefully prepared old-time coffee-shop fare, but there are nice touches like flavored butters with the toast, cookies offered to those waiting for seating, and butterscotch candies alongside the check.

Tony and Tina's Pizzeria

Zone 18   The Bronx
24-79 Arthur Avenue at East 189th
   Street, the Bronx
(718) 733-8094

Albanian

★★★

Inexpensive

Quality 86   Value A

Reservations:	Not accepted
When to go:	Anytime
Kind of service:	Self-service
Entree range:	Bourek slices, $2.50; whole boureks, $10
Payment:	Cash only
Service rating:	★★½
Friendliness rating:	★★½
Transit:	C/D to Fordham Road, BX 12 bus to Arthur Avenue
Bar:	None
Wine selection:	None
Dress:	Casual
Disabled access:	Poor; high steps
Clientele:	Locals, Albanians from all over
Open:	Every day, 7 A.M.–midnight

Atmosphere/setting: Just a regular, ordinary-looking pizza shop, plain and simple. The sole indication that this is Albanian bourek ground zero is the photo of Famous Albanian Mother Teresa taped to the wall by the cash register, just beneath the shot of the original Star Trek cast.

House specialties: Boureks! Unbelievably wonderful pastry pies, stuffed with either peppery ground beef (very kreplach-like, if that means anything to you), herby spinach or rich pot cheese. The zillion-layered, glutenous dough is crispy on the outside, noodley soft inside, texturally dovetailing with the soft-cooked, soulful fillings with a grace that could only come from long tradition. Buy slices or an entire pie (leftovers reheat well).

Summary & comments: Turks make a similar dish (see Cafe Istanbul review), as do several Balkan cultures, but Albanians have a special knack. And while Albanians cook in many of New York's Italian restaurants, their own food is ultra-rare, almost entirely hidden in private clubs. Boureks are the pride of Albanian home cooking, and Tony and Tina's is a godsend, serving splendid ones every day to all comers—you don't even have to know a secret password (by contrast, just try to get admitted to private Gurra Cafe, down the block at 2325 Arthur Avenue). If you're lucky enough to arrive at the right time, you can watch the cook go through the rigorous process of making the many-layered dough; he's proud to demonstrate this most uncommon art. Important: Ask to have your bourek slices reheated in the pizza oven, not the microwave (which turns the pastry soggy).

Tre Pomodori

Zone 9   Midtown East
210 East 34th Street, Manhattan
(212) 545-7266

CAUTION

Italian
★★½
Moderate

Quality 85   Value A

Reservations: Recommended for large parties or at peak hours
When to go: Anytime
Kind of service: Waiter service at tables
Entree range: $6.95–15.95
Payment: Cash only
Service rating: ★★★
Friendliness rating: ★★★½
Transit: 6 to 33rd Street
Bar: Beer and wine
Wine selection: Small; South Americans best
Dress: Casual
Disabled access: Fair; very narrow and tight
Clientele: Older local businessmen and youthful bargain
                       hunters
Dinner: Monday–Friday, 5–11 P.M.; Saturday and Sunday,
                       5 P.M.–midnight

Atmosphere/setting: A very narrow, cozily romantic, softly lit parlor with
tiled floor, walls dotted with framed pictures, and tables with flickering candles.

House specialties: All pastas, especially linguine vongole (baby clams, oil,
garlic), agnolotti al porcini (super-mushroomy pasta pockets), linguine fra diavolo
(black linguine with calamari and spicy tomato sauce), and an angel hair pasta dish
with mushrooms and onions in a pink sauce, confusingly named cappellini campagnola at lunch and capellini boscaiolo at dinner. Also risotto, salads, and apple tart.

Summary & comments: This is *not* a great restaurant . . . but it is a very useful one. If you're looking for a low-key place to get surprisingly tasty plates of pasta
at bargain prices without getting gussied up, this is a top choice, particularly in east
Midtown where good informal restaurants are few and far between. The waiters
will serve fast for those rushing back to work (or out to shows), but lingering is
never discouraged. Avoid spotty appetizers (specials are often better, and salads are
always OK) and pricier entrees, and cut straight to what they do best: pasta. The linguine with baby clams is a splendid, classic version, very satisfying, and there's a
broad range of other choices—eighteen in all. Risotto, often a special, is also very
good, as are the gratis crunchy toasts with tomato and basil. Desserts are only fair
(best: apple tart). Service can be slightly confused but is always good-natured.

Umberto's

Zone 21   Nassau County,
    Long Island
633 Jericho Turnpike (just west of
    Lakeville Road), New Hyde Park,
    Long Island
(516) 437-7698

Italian/Pizza
★★★½
Moderate

Quality 91   Value A

Reservations:	Parties of 3 or more
When to go:	Peak mealtimes and weekends are very crowded
Kind of service:	Self-service for pizza, etc.; waiter service for full dinner
Entree range:	$10.75–22.50 (heroes, $5.25–6)
Payment:	Cash only
Service rating:	★★★★
Friendliness rating:	★★★
Transit:	Taxi from Long Island Railroad New Hyde Park
Bar:	Full service
Wine selection:	Italian
Dress:	Casual
Disabled access:	Good
Clientele:	Locals
Lunch/Dinner:	Monday–Thursday, 11 A.M.–11 P.M.; Friday and Saturday, 11–12:30 A.M.; Sunday, 11 A.M.–11 P.M.

Atmosphere/setting: Umberto's started out long ago as a simple neighbor-hood pizzeria. As people flocked in over the years for mind-bogglingly good pizza, they expanded, adding dining rooms, an annex, and finally a sea of swanky-looking tables up front (with recessed lighting and fancy brick and tile work). Lowbrow stuff like pizza and heroes remain available as a sort of restaurant-in-a-restaurant, though you'd never guess it from the swanky look. But they haven't forgotten their roots; self-service seating's still provided for slice-munching regulars, just a few feet away from diners paying $30 a person for "gormay" eats. Kind of cool.

House specialties: Sicilian (square-sliced) pizza (flavored with basil, not vulgar oregano) sports fresh tomato sauce, good cheese, and an awesome crunchy, chewy crust. The round, neapolitan pies are good, too (I like to order what I call a "mixed grill": one slice of each). Also top-notch: heroes (especially meatball parmigiana), calzones, garlic knots, and pasta fagioli.

Other recommendations: Just as Umberto's has constantly upgraded its look, it's also upgraded its menu, adding all sorts of fancy dishes and, recently, a brick oven. But while some of the cooking is quite good and the brick-oven pizza is excellent, only the Sicilian pies (from the conventional oven) are reliably worth a ride all the way out to Nassau County.

Summary & comments: When great places expand, it's usually the kiss of death. Well-honed routines must be replaced with new procedures, and new faces in the kitchen lack the experience of the old hands. But Umberto's has managed a double whammy: their new, fancified offerings are surprisingly good, and their old standbys haven't suffered a bit. This is still the best New York Sicilian pizza ever (with the exception of the late, long-lamented Eddie's of Fort Salonga), and locals know it; frenzied crowds angle for takeout slices with the frantic urgency of commodities traders (Umberto's staff, capable of incredible grace under pressure, never misses a beat).

Note: As this book goes to press, Umberto's has begun opening tons of branches. None are as good as the original, though two older spin-offs in Huntington (737 West Jericho Turnpike, (516) 423-2999) and Hicksville (420 Newbridge Road, (516) 433-7575) come close.

Uncle Vanya Cafe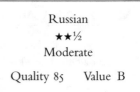

Zone 8   Midtown West and
   Theater District
315 West 54th Street (between 8th and
   9th Avenues), Manhattan
(212) 262-0542

Russian
★★½
Moderate

Quality 85   Value B

Reservations:	Accepted; recommended weekends
When to go:	Anytime
Kind of service:	Waiter service at tables
Entree range:	$7.50–12.50
Payment:	VISA, MC
Service rating:	★★½
Friendliness rating:	★★★
Transit:	A/B/C/D/1/9 to 59th Street/Columbus Circle
Bar:	Wine and beer only
Wine selection:	Very limited
Dress:	Casual
Disabled access:	Poor
Clientele:	Homesick Russians and neighborhood regulars
Lunch/Dinner:	Monday–Saturday, 10 A.M.–11:30 P.M.; Sunday, 2–11 P.M.

Atmosphere/setting: It's Christmas in the dacha; whitewashed walls are festooned with holiday lights and tinsel, hand-carved marionettes, decorative plates, and various other Russian tchotchkes. Traditional carved wood benches provide some of the seating in this informal, comfortable cafe.

House specialties: Zakuska (appetizers) are particularly recommended: well-marinated beet salad with currants and lots of dill, carrot salad, ribez (smoked white fish), spinach pancakes with sour cream (reheated but tasty nonetheless), varenike (potato dumplings with mushrooms, caramelized onion, and sour cream), village appetizer (chunks of fried potatoes with, again, mushrooms, caramelized onion, and sour cream). Winning entrees include stuffed cabbage that's well-nigh elegant in a clear, clean-flavored sauce, and unusual, startlingly delicious chicken pojharski, something like a chicken pancake. Entrees come with with kasha, fried or mashed potatoes (get the latter: they are awesome, uncommonly stiff, and texturally perfect, chunky to just the right point), and great chewy brown bread. Russian tea with cherry jam is a traditional closer.

Other recommendations: Skip the blah cherry blini dessert.

Entertainment & amenities: Guitar-strumming Russian balladeers croon for tips.

UNClE VANyA CAfE *(continued)*

Summary & comments: Order carefully; you don't want to slog through more than one dish topped with the kitchen's trinity of mushrooms, caramelized onion, and sour cream (it's delectable . . . once). This isn't refined czarist feast cooking; the sour cream is store-bought and not everything's made to order. But too many people overlook the comfort food satisfactions of this Midtown Muscovite.

Uzbekistan Restaurant

Zone 17 Southern Queens	Central Asian
91-02 63rd Drive (corner of Alderdon),	★★★
Rego Park, Queens	Inexpensive
(718) 997-7067	Quality 88 Value A

Reservations:	Accepted (but not necessary)
When to go:	Anytime
Kind of service:	Waiter service at tables
Entree range:	$4 and under
Payment:	Cash only
Service rating:	★★½
Friendliness rating:	★★
Transit:	N/R to 63rd Drive/Rego Park
Bar:	None
Wine selection:	None
Dress:	Nice casual
Disabled access:	Very poor; narrow front door, rest rooms difficult
Clientele:	Observant Jews from Central Asia
Open:	Every day, 11 A.M. to 11 P.M., except Friday night through Saturday afternoon

Atmosphere/setting: Not as tacky and Iron Curtain-ish as other local Central Asian restaurants, this place is comparatively sleek and modern with attractive floor-to-ceiling vertical venetian blinds and wall-to-wall carpeting. A few Brighton Beach touches—TV playing Russian music videos, glittery disco ball, plastic flowers—don't intrude much on the overall low-key ambience.

House specialties: The menu's similar to that of Tadjikstan Restaurant (see review): lamb soup, served with either vegetables (shourpa) or pasta (lagman), pelmeny (tortellini soup), well-marinated succulent kebabs such as chicken on bone, lula (ground beef), lamb, and sweetbreads. Mantey are black-peppery steamed meat dumplings with either olive oil or tomato sauce. The breads are particularly interesting; check out non-toki, a bowl-shaped, matzo-like flatbread dosed with sesame seeds and a touch of cumin, hot paprika, and perhaps onion. Lepiousha is the Uzbek version of round, pillowy lavash bread.

Other recommendations: There are various salty, pickled, marinated salads.

Entertainment & amenities: That disco ball makes you wonder whether this place has a secret nocturnal life as an after-hours dance club.

Summary & comments: Food here—though quite delicious—is not as inspired as at Tadjikstan (both are kosher), but Uzbekistan's ambience is less oppressive and marginally better English is spoken. Central Asian places are becoming almost common here in Rego Parkistan, but these two are the standouts.

Wangah Hut

Zone 17   Southern Queens
172-05 Baisley Boulevard (between
   Merrick and 172nd Streets), Jamaica,
   Queens
(718) 276-4857

Reservations:	Not accepted
When to go:	Anytime
Kind of service:	Waiter service at tables
Entree range:	$5–8
Payment:	Cash only
Service rating:	★★
Friendliness rating:	★★★
Transit:	E/J/Z to Jamaica Center, Q5 or Q85 bus down Merrick Boulevard
Bar:	None
Wine selection:	None
Dress:	Casual
Disabled access:	Fair; a few steps to the seating, but friendly staff will help; rest rooms not accessible
Clientele:	Local island expats
Lunch/Dinner:	Monday–Wednesday, 11:30 A.M.–8 P.M.; Thursday–Sunday, 11:30 A.M.–10 P.M.

Atmosphere/setting: A tiny, sparklingly clean parlor on an otherwise residential block. There are just a few tables, but they're quite comfortable.

House specialties: The highlight is oven-fried wangah chicken, bright yellow from spices, with succulent crust and wonderful sweet sauce sauce. Jerk chicken, quite spicy, is served with lots more sauce (heavy on the anise) than usual, and there are eight more chicken preparations as well. Pan-fried snapper is expertly fried in a batter similar to the wangah—you can almost taste the well-seasoned cast-iron pan. Curried goat features chunks of on-the-bone tender meat in a warm, broad, unpungent curry. Unusually greaseless fried plantains are really good, and coconutty rice and peas makes a fine counterpoint to the chef's intense sauces (none richer than that accompanying extremely tender oxtail). Fruit punch is delicious but sweet—cut it with water—and hard-to-find Ting brand grapefruit soda is available.

Other recommendations: As in many Jamaican restaurants, some Chinese dishes, like chop suey and fried rice, are offered—legacies from the many Chinese laborers who earlier in the century greatly influenced the cuisine.

WANGAH HUT *(continued)*

Summary & comments: There's a ton of Jamaican food available in New York, much of it decently made. It's very hard, though, to find the cuisine cooked with a personal touch. Wangah—which seems anything but personal from its stark exterior—has this touch in ample abundance. The staff is friendly, but in spite of an astonishingly high employee-to-customer ratio, you may wait a good long while for your food. Cooking this skilled is well worth waiting for, though.

WEE KEE

Zone 14   Southern Brooklyn
5414 8th Avenue (between 54th and
  55th Streets), Sunset Park, Brooklyn
(718) 438-9348

	Chinese/Amer./Norwegian
	★★★
	Inexpensive
	Quality 86 Value A

Reservations:	Not accepted
When to go:	Anytime
Kind of service:	Waiter service at tables and counter
Entree range:	$4–10
Payment:	Cash only
Service rating:	★★½
Friendliness rating:	★★★
Transit:	N to 8th Avenue
Bar:	None
Wine selection:	None
Dress:	Casual
Disabled access:	Good; tight turn into rest room
Clientele:	Mostly Chinese plus a few older Scandinavians
Open:	Wednesday–Monday, 10 A.M.–10 P.M.; Tuesday, closed

Atmosphere/setting: A shiny old Brooklyn luncheonette, with booths, spinning counter stools, and formica everything. It was once a Norwegian-American restaurant and still looks much the same, aside from the woks.

House specialties: Norwegian and American touches have been slowly morphing back into Chinese here since the Norwegian chef left (see below), though heavenly, gossamer-thin, multilayered Norwegian pancakes are still served for breakfast. In some cases, blurred boundaries have led to inspired cooking; meaty chicken wings, for example, are great simply battered and pan fried (soul food style) or else deep fried and finished in the wok with a light coating of oyster sauce. Pork chop parmigiana over rice is a top seller, and they also do a mean salt-and-pepper corned beef. Blah pot roast is served with canned peas and carrots, just like in the old days, but while the thick brown gravy looks straight out of Any Diner, USA, there are some foxy Asian spices and smoky wok flavor way back in the mix. You're no killjoy to order straight Cantonese fare; it's quite good and far more subtle than you'd expect from such a setting. Good luck ordering, though: the Chinese menu is entirely untranslated (servers will help up to a certain point, but they quickly grow impatient with too much questioning). The following suggestions will get you started (you can also point at others' plates): very fresh bok choy with lots of ginger and garlic, homey beef with tomatoes, lightly sautéed asparagus with flaky nuggets of greaselessly fried fish, beef chow fun (made with quality meat), pig knuckles in ultrasticky brown sauce, and thin-skinned Hong Kong–style shrimp and pork wontons in a refined, sweet soup.

Other recommendations: Horlick's malted milk powder, once a staple in soda fountains across the country (and one of the most delicious mass-produced foodstuffs ever), has been adopted by Asians. It's sadly no longer produced in the United States, but it has returned to this lunch counter after a 16,000 mile round-trip voyage. Sip a malted milk drink—the staff considers it one of the most purely Asian delicacies—and try not to get woozy from all the . . . er . . . dis-orientation.

Summary & comments: OK, here's the story: This was once a Norwegian neighborhood, but a decade ago New York's fast-growing Sunset Park Chinatown swallowed much-loved Atlantic Restaurant, Brooklyn's last Norwegian kitchen. Wee Kee opened in its place, but old Norwegians kept coming around and asking for cod and pancakes. The new owner, an enterprising Cantonese, hired back one of the old cooks to teach the staff how to make some of that stuff, and thus was born New York's most unusual hybrid. I haven't spotted that Norwegian cook in recent years, and you don't find *fiske* (cod) pudding on the menu much (Sundays are the most Norwegian), but deconstructed elements from the old Atlantic Restaurant keep cropping up where you least expect them. This is not without precedent; flexible Cantonese cooking has often shown its ability to incorporate foreign ingredients and techniques. But it all makes for a wildly perplexing meal; at this point, Norwegian American touches have been so completely integrated that it's impossible to guess the chef's intentions in serving, for instance, gingery steamed tripe atop a bed of elbow macaroni. Is tripe also Norwegian? Is elbow macaroni Cantonese? Are the herbacious chunks of boiled potatoes in the oxtail noodle soup Cantonese or Scandinavian? One wonders whether to use chopsticks or a fork—or to keep switching between the two. You glance at the clientele—mostly immigrant Chinese—for guidance, and they're mostly using the latter, even for wholly Chinese dishes. "Forks are just easier," explains the kind but harried manager. You don't really understand, but you nod as if you do. There's a lot here you'll *never* understand.

White Bear Ice Cream and Wonton Shop Cuisine

Chinese
★★½
Inexpensive

Quality 85   Value A

Zone 16   Northeastern Queens
135-02 Roosevelt Avenue (corner of
    Prince Street), Flushing, Queens
(718) 961-2322

Reservations:	Not accepted
When to go:	Anytime
Kind of service:	Self-service
Entree range:	$2.50–4.75
Payment:	Cash only
Service rating:	★★½
Friendliness rating:	★★★★
Transit:	7 to Flushing/Main Street
Bar:	None
Wine selection:	None
Dress:	Casual
Disabled access:	Good; rest rooms not accessible
Clientele:	Placid older Chinese and hurried younger workers
Open:	Every day, 10 A.M.–7 P.M.

Atmosphere / setting: This is one of the tiniest, most overlookable holes-in-the-wall in Flushing Chinatown. You order at the counter directly from the cook, and as plates materialize—one at a time, as your order is completed—you tote them back to one of the tiny tables for consumption amid a constant tumult of harried customers darting in and out for takeout. Only elderly Chinese seem to have time to sit down and eat here; do as they do and settle in to peacefully enjoy your dumplings and noodles, unperturbed by the commotion.

House specialties: Dumplings with pork, shrimp, or sea cucumber are all good; dumplings with leek (and pork) are better still. Also try rice cakes with Chinese cabbage and pork, rugged, cold, spicy sesame noodles, various soups and bean thread dishes. It's not easy to find a kitchen that really understands its culinary mission, but White Bear's is unequivocally painted right onto the facade: "wonton soup, dumpling, rice cake, bean thread, sweet food, cold drink, hot dishes, steamed rice noodles."

Other recommendations: One of the best sweets in Flushing: amber pecans (or walnuts) sold in plastic takeout containers. They're not too sweet, mildly crunchy, with just a trace of spice. The ice creams (standard Asian varieties like green tea and red bean) are true-flavored but not too rich; like everything else here, they're unsophisticatedly delicious.

Summary & comments: This is not the pinnacle of Chinese cuisine; those searching for the most ethereal dumplings, exotic stir-fries, and refined flavors will do far better elsewhere. White Bear serves very tasty, charmingly simple snacks that are similar to what you'd imagine being served after school by your grandma in Taiwan. This mom-and-pop spot cooks guilelessly, and their homey touch pervades each soothing bite. The check is as unaffected as the cooking; it's easy to just keep on ordering things—at these prices there's no reason not to.

Woo Chon

CAUTION

Zone 8   Midtown West and
  Theater District
8 West 36th Street (near 5th Avenue),
  Manhattan
(212) 695-0676

Korean
★★★
Expensive
Quality 88   Value C

Reservations: Accepted
When to go: Anytime
Kind of service: Waiter service at tables
Entree range: $10–20
Payment: VISA, MC, AMEX
Service rating: ★★½
Friendliness rating: ★
Transit: B/D/F/N/Q/R to 34th Street/Herald Square
                       or 6 to 33rd Street
Bar: Beer and wine only
Wine selection: Very limited
Dress: Nice casual or better
Disabled access: Good
Clientele: Korean businessmen, aficionados
Open: Every day, 24 hours

Atmosphere/setting: Two levels: a rather intense downstairs space (spotlit and dramatically appointed with lacquered calligraphy, dark wood, and Asian ink prints) and a slightly more laid-back upstairs room.

House specialties: Attention centers on the great bulgogi—sweetish garlic-marinated rib-eye prepared on the grill set into each table (wrap the beefy chunks in lettuce leaves with a little rice and dab on sweet red-bean paste). Unfortunately, the tableside grills are outfitted for gas flame rather than glowing coals, but Woo Chon's awesome marinade—so delicious that they bottle the stuff for sale—and top-quality meat easily compensate. Kalbi (beef short ribs) are equally recommended. Panchan, the traditional gratis assortment of little vegetable and fish starter plates, are unparalleled in their freshness, all flavors clearly focused and balanced (feel free to ask for extra helpings of your favorites). Yookgaejang (a restorative spicy beef soup) and dduk (a hearty dumpling soup) are both good choices, as are rice and noodle dishes that come with toppings for mixing in (look for "bibim" as a prefix), but be aware that the cold buckwheat noodle items serve more as palate-cleansers than as main courses. Woo Chon elevates lowly pajun (crunchy-spongy pancakes available with extras like seafood or kimchee) to an almost highbrow level, evoking subtle flavors from this snacky favorite. Also try gooksoo, a lot like shabu-shabu.

Other recommendations: A special $40, twelve-course feast must be ordered in advance (bring a group and reserve a private room for the full effect).

Summary & comments: While Woo Chon is the most respected name in New York Korean food, it's important to be aware of where its strengths lie. As in many Korean restaurants, the menu stretches well beyond those strengths in an effort to please a broad audience, so stick with the recommended dishes and avoid stews (jigae), intricate seafood or vegetable preparations, and homier items (this is no grandma kitchen; for down-home Korean, try Bo or Kang Suh—see reviews). Management's haughty manner has unfortunately been adopted by many of the waiters. Woo Chon has a branch in Flushing at 41-19 Kissena Boulevard (718) 463-0803.

XUNTA

Zone 5   East Village
174 1st Avenue (between 10th and 11th
    Streets), Manhattan
(212) 614-0620

Spanish/Tapas
★★★
Inexpensive

Quality 88   Value B

Reservations:	Only for 4 or more
When to go:	Before 7 P.M. to avoid crowds; Tuesdays are also light
Kind of service:	Waiter service at tables and bar
Entree range:	$5.25–16.25
Payment:	VISA, MC, AMEX, D, DC
Service rating :	★★½
Friendliness rating:	★★½
Transit:	L to 1st Avenue
Bar:	Full service
Wine selection:	Good Spanish wines
Dress:	Nice casual
Disabled access:	Very poor; three steps
Clientele:	Young locals
Dinner:	Sunday–Thursday, 4 P.M.–midnight; Friday and Saturday, 4 P.M.–2 A.M.

Atmosphere/setting: Funky basement with Iberian touches and a young clientele; this seems more like a hangout than a restaurant.

House specialties: Pulpo a feira (octopus with paprika), tortilla española con cebolla (Spanish potato omelet with onion), lulas recheas (stuffed calamari), gazpacho, sardines, gambas a la plancha (grilled shrimp), interesting regional cheeses, hard-to-find Galician white wines (Albariños).

Entertainment & amenities: Live flamenco musicians and dancers Mondays and Thursdays at 8:30 P.M. (call to confirm).

Summary & comments: The tapas craze has hit New York in a big way, but this Galician bar is the only venue for the real stuff. Serious tapas like octopus and potato omelet taste much like those served in Spain, and tart young Albariño wines can be sipped the authentic way, out of white ceramic bowls (ask for a tazón). Items can be ordered either as small tapas-sized portions or in larger raciones. Bear in mind that genuine tapas are unpretentious lusty accompaniments to drink, not haute cuisine . . . so the rollicking bar scene and crude seating are part and parcel of the experience.

Yakitori Taisho

<CAUTION>

Zone 5   East Village
5 St. Marks Place (between 2nd and 3rd
  Avenues), Manhattan
(212) 228-5086

Japanese	
★★★	
Inexpensive	
Quality 83	Value B+

Reservations:	Not accepted
When to go:	Late
Kind of service:	Waiter service at counters and tables
Entree range:	$6.95–9.50
Payment:	VISA, MC, AMEX
Service rating:	★★★
Friendliness rating:	★★★★
Transit:	6 to Astor Place or N/R to 8th Street/NYU
Bar:	Beer, sake, and scotch
Wine selection:	None
Dress:	Wear black
Disabled access:	None
Clientele:	Young East Village Japanese hipsters
Dinner:	Sunday–Wednesday, 6 P.M.–1:30 A.M.;
	Thursday–Saturday, 6 P.M.–3:30 A.M.

Atmosphere/setting: As you enter, chef-owner Kenji Mizogami—rotund, bearded, and sporting a blond mohawk—lets forth his customary guttural Japanese scream of welcome. He's stationed, as always, at his sizzling coal grill, expert pudgy fingers maniacally turning skewers. All the young East Village Japanese hipsters working here don way-cool black t-shirts emblazoned with a cartoon of Kenji's smiling face encircled by flames. There's outdoor seating in front of the basement entrance (enclosed with plastic sheeting in foul weather); inside it's a warm, groovy subterranean lair, all rough-cut wood and hanging lanterns, with tables in back and a long bar with squat stools under the low ceiling—a claustrophile's delight.

House specialties: Yakitori (chicken skewers) themselves are pretty enjoyable (sweet roasted onions work well with the sweetish marinade). Better skewers include kawa (chicken skin, a decadent treat), niku (garlic cloves), bara (plump chunks of pork), and tsukune (moist chicken meatballs). Best nonskewered specialties: sautéed bacon and garlic sprouts (pure Japanese soul food) and grilled sardine stuffed with spicy cod roe. Yaki onigiri (grilled rice balls) make a bland but good counterpoint.

Other recommendations: Okonomayaki is a seafood-laden pancake squirted with ketchup and mayonnaise and sprinkled with bonito flakes that wave to and

Yakitori Taisho *(continued)*

fro from the heat. It's gloppily filling bar food, the Japanese analog of nachos. (Warning: Acquired Taste Alert.)

Summary & comments: This is half Shinjuku subway station tent village yakitori joint and half bohemian East Village Japanese late-night hangout. It's the most evocative scene imagineable, with taped music ranging from cacophonous avant garde jazz to bouncy Japanese sugar pop. Anyone over twenty-four will feel very, very old (hide out at a back corner table and breathe in more hipness than you've experienced in ages).

YEMEN CAFE

Zone 13   Northern Brooklyn
176 Atlantic Avenue (between Court
    and Clinton), Cobble Hill, Brooklyn
(718) 834-9533

	Yemeni
	★★★½
	Inexpensive
	Quality 90 Value A−

Reservations:	Accepted, but not necessary
When to go:	Anytime
Kind of service:	Waiter service at tables
Entree range:	$6–10
Payment:	Cash only
Service rating:	★★★★
Friendliness rating:	★★★★
Transit:	2/3/4/5 to Borough Hall or F to Bergen
Bar:	None (and BYO is not permitted)
Wine selection:	None
Dress:	Casual (shorts and short dresses out of place)
Disabled access:	None
Clientele:	Local Yemen expats
Open:	Every day, 10:30 A.M.–10 P.M.

Atmosphere / setting: Once a forbidding basement Yemeni social club, the cafe has moved upstairs to a much more inviting space with peach-colored walls hung with Yemen travel posters. A new spirit of openness (Yemenperestroika?) is proclaimed to outsiders by a sign reading "Welcome, come try our original yemenite dishes!"

House specialties: Don't miss off-menu, slow-roasted lamb in a crust of spices (they'll hack a piece off of a whole critter; glistening, fibrous, gamey meat hanging off of big, crude bones; eat with your fingers). Other dishes combine Indian and Arab influences, none more so than the enormous blistery bread prepared in a tandoori-ish oven. Also, there are curries (more delicate, less pungent than Indian versions), basmati rice, fatta (strips of buttery bread served with butter, honey, and red pepper as an appetizer or with meat as an entree), unbelievably satisfying lamb soup served in metal bowls (ask for and spoon in the superb hot sauce); smooth, thick chicken soup, glaba and loubyia (two versions of chewy lamb chunks in an oniony sauce over rice), and ambrosial "Special Yemeni Tea," spiced with a mesmerizing blend of cinnamon, cloves, nutmeg, and honey.

Other recommendations: The national dish of assid takes some getting used to, but this huge quivering boob of semigelatinous wheat paste—half submerged in gloppy brown gravy (you also spoon in hilbeh—fenugreek sauce—and hot sauce) is worth a try for the adventurous.

Summary & comments: We're not talking Israeli Yemenites here; this place cooks the cuisine of Yemen, an Islamic country on the southwest corner of the Arabian peninsula. The food will transport you there, and when in this particular Rome, gobble solids with fingers and the wet stuff with pinches of bread. Don't worry, the eyes that peer as you enter are merely curious, not suspicious; staff and customers are friendly and open almost to a fault.

Political note: It takes good people to cook truly profound food, and the management here is not afraid to stand up for what's right. The restaurant is named "United Yemen" in Arabic, and the menu features photos of both the northern and southern capitals—rare conciliatory gestures considering that the country's embroiled in nasty regional strife.

ZLATA PRAHA

Zone 15   Northwestern Queens
28-48 31st Street (between 30th
    and Newtown Avenues),
    Astoria, Queens
(718) 721-6422

Czech/Slovak
★★
Moderate

Quality 82   Value B−

Reservations:	Accepted
When to go:	Catch the great $5.95 lunch special or come later to drink beer with the old guys
Kind of service:	Waiter service at tables and bar
Entree range:	$6.75−19.25
Payment:	VISA, MC ($25 minimum)
Service rating:	★★½
Friendliness rating:	★★★
Transit:	N to 30th Avenue
Bar:	Full service
Wine selection:	Decent
Dress:	Nice casual
Disabled access:	Poor; small step up; rest rooms not accessible
Clientele:	Czech and other locals
Lunch:	Tuesday−Sunday, 11:30 A.M.−3 P.M.
Dinner:	Tuesday−Sunday, 6−11 P.M.; Monday, closed

Atmosphere/setting: You *are* in Prague. Up front is a most inviting bar where Czech old men argue at 8 P.M., sing at 10 P.M., and weep at midnight and comely young women pour tall glasses of Czech pilsners. Segregated from all this boisterous fun in an adjoining space, an evocative, primly pretty dining room looks as though it was shipped piece by piece from the Czech Republic. Nice tablecloths and knickknacks galore (native costumes, dolls, paintings), and there's also garden dining in warm weather.

House specialties: Smoked pork loin with dumplings (whole slices of steamed bread) and cabbage, goulash, boiled beef in dill sauce, veal cutlet cordon bleu, roast chicken in garlic sauce, beef in cream sauce with dumplings. You get the idea. For vegetarians, there's a lean cuisine alternative: fried cheese and cauliflower.

Other recommendations: A terrific lunch deal: soup, main course, dessert, and wine or soda for $5.95 (Tuesday−Friday, 11:30 A.M.−3 P.M.). Several times a year, the restaurant hosts huge celebrations: pay-one-price blowouts with special delicacies like boar or venison.

Entertainment & amenities: Sometimes there's a live accordian player, but it's never clear whether he's hired entertainment or just a customer moved to song.

ZLATA PRAHA (continued)

Summary & comments: The food is sturdy fare, cooked honestly and without much subtlety. But the eating is as evocative as the restaurant itself, so this makes for a great change-of-pace meal, a mini-European vacation right in Queens. If you make friends with the old Czech guys at the bar (you must stop there for at least one drink), they may offer you tastes of off-menu dishes like skvarky (pork fat and garlic) or teach you Czech drinking songs.